THE GOVERNOR

MY LIFE INSIDE BRITAIN'S MOST NOTORIOUS PRISONS

VANESSA FRAKE

WITH RUTH KELLY

HARPER
element

HarperElement
An imprint of HarperCollins*Publishers*
1 London Bridge Street
London SE1 9GF

www.harpercollins.co.uk

HarperCollins*Publishers*
1st Floor, Watermarque Building, Ringsend Road
Dublin 4, Ireland

First published by HarperElement 2021

3 5 7 9 10 8 6 4 2

© Vanessa Frake and Ruth Kelly 2021

Vanessa Frake asserts the moral right to
be identified as the author of this work

A catalogue record of this book is
available from the British Library

ISBN 978-0-00-839005-1

Printed and bound in Great Britain by
CPI Group (UK) Ltd, Croydon

MIX
Paper from
responsible sources
FSC™ C007454

This book is produced from independently certified FSC™ paper
to ensure responsible forest management.

For more information visit: www.harpercollins.co.uk/green

For my wife Ju and our daughter Annie-Mae.
Always.

CONTENTS

PROLOGUE

Now

The salty sweet smell of warm pastry rushes up my nose. I quickly pull the scalding-hot tray of scones from the oven and slide them onto the rack to cool off just as the phone rings.

'Yep!' I answer, hooking the receiver between my ear and shoulder while gently prodding the pastry to check it's cooked through.

It's Paul, he manages the Angela Reed café, which is just off the main square in the picturesque town of Saffron Walden in Essex. Nice guy. He has a way about him that keeps the customers happy. Bites his tongue, unlike me, who can't help saying what I think. That's probably why I'm never front of house but spend my time downstairs in the basement, cooking. That, and the fact I love baking.

'We've just had a woman come in who's bought your entire batch of fruit scones,' he exclaims. 'How long until the next batch is ready?'

THE GOVERNOR

It was a bigger shock to me than anyone when I heard my culinary creations had become legendary in the town. Me, who has spent the best part of my life living off microwave meals, who wouldn't have been seen dead attempting to make a gluten-free lemon and almond sponge. Just one of many on my repertoire these days.

'I'm on it,' I say, scooping the scones into a bowl and placing them in the dumb waiter. Door shut. Button pressed. Hey presto and then, all of a sudden, it strikes. Blood – everywhere, spraying across the kitchen surfaces, pooling on the floor. I scrunch my eyes shut, trying to push the memory away.

'Alrighty, what next.' I chat to myself, hoping that will keep me in the present. I grab a Pyrex bowl and get to work on making my signature cherry almond Bakewell cake.

Butter and sugar – I start beating it together. I'm looking for a light and fluffy texture. The mixture clumps, sticking to the spoon like mud. I prise it off with my forefinger and thumb and begin again. Round and round I beat it, giving it some welly.

I've been downstairs baking away since I began my shift at 8 a.m. My face is powdered with a dusting of flour. Dough is crusted into the corners of my fingernails. Upstairs it'll be getting busy. Locals coming and going, picking up a slice of their favourite cake. Dropping in for their morning cup of coffee and a catch-up. Saffron Walden is a bustling market country town where gossip is rife.

I'm the one secret no one knows about though.

PROLOGUE

The pressure is on to get my almond and cherry creation into the oven. Four eggs – I crack them one by one on the side of the bowl and mix them in. There it is again, hitting me like a tidal wave. All of a sudden, I'm back *inside*. Thrust into the industrial-sized kitchen in the bowels of the prison …

The long chrome work surfaces were laden with platefuls of the day's lunch. White stodgy baguette filled with coronation chicken with a sprig of lettuce and cucumber on the side and something very dodgy moving through the lettuce. The yellow strip light above was flickering; it was enough to drive anyone around the twist. It would be next year before anyone got around to fixing that. I caught a glimpse of my reflection in the hotplate – the silver trolley we were loading up with lunches to take through to the wings. I looked exhausted, my under-eyes a bruised purple thanks to many a long shift.

'Ready, ladies?' I said. I had a woman who'd been done for arson and attempted murder on my left and a child sex abuser on my right. Today's kitchen helpers.

It happened in the blink of an eye. Quite literally. One minute I was giving Jane Finch orders, the next her cheek opened up. It was like watching something move in slow motion. There was no blood at first, the skin simply parted to reveal pinky-white flesh and thread veins.

Jane touched her face. 'What's that?'

Before I had time to answer, the blood rose to the surface – gushing. There was claret everywhere.

She stared at her red fingers, her body began to tremble, her eyes were bulging with fear and shock. I thought she was going to pass out.

'What's happening?' It came out as more of a whisper. The unharmed side of her face had turned as white as ash. Blood was spraying across the hot plate, splattering the baguettes.

'Oh my God!' She found her voice. 'Arrrrrrgh.' She erupted into an ear-piercing scream.

One of the officers punched the alarm on the wall while me and another prison officer jumped on Carrie Webber.

Carrie Webber – one of the most violent female prisoners I'd ever encountered. Prisoners, officers, she wasn't fussed who she attacked. She spent her days making weapons out of whatever she could get her hands on. Every night we'd search her cell and without fail we'd find something deadly she'd made or adapted out of prison materials. Shanks. Knives welded together from plastic and razor blades. Every morning we'd go in again and there'd be the garrotte woven from toilet paper, as strong as any rope. She slept with it all night long hidden under her pillow, plotting who to hurt next.

The officer held Carrie down while I removed today's weapon of choice. A toothbrush with two razor blades melted into the plastic. Deadly, deliberately so. Carrie had designed it to cause maximum damage. She'd known full well that two slices across the skin, close together, would be much harder for the nurse to stitch back up than a single gash. Jane's face would be disfigured for ever.

PROLOGUE

We'd warned Jane not to tell anyone what she was in for, but she clearly chose to ignore our advice. Anyone who hurts children is seen as the lowest of the low in prison and Jane's crime was particularly sickening. She held down her own children while her husband raped them. Carrie must have found out and thought Jane deserved her special kind of punishment.

The alarm rang like a drill through my ears while Jane continued to scream. The noise was unbearable.

'Get her out of here!' I ordered. Carrie stared daggers at me with those dark piercing eyes of hers. She was a big woman, thickset, and she looked mean – you know the way some people can? There was no expression in her eyes, they were cold and penetrating.

She wriggled and raged as they carted her off to the segregation unit for solitary confinement punishment, furious at me for cutting her vigilantism short. Meanwhile, Jane was sobbing her eyes out as she was taken off by the nurses to get stitched up, leaving a trail of blood in her wake.

I feel my stomach make an unpleasant somersault as I remember the gruesome sight. The smell. Everything about that horrific memory hitting me hard. I'm a nightmare around blood; just the smallest drop makes me feel queasy. I put down my spoon and grip the edge of the counter, taking a deep breath in and a long exhale out, blowing away the past.

Most days it feels like a lifetime ago. But sometimes, often in the most innocuous of moments, my past creeps up on me. Dragging me back behind those twelve-foot-high walls. It's inevitable really, considering I spent twenty-seven years in the prison service. Most of the time I'm Vanessa, but occasionally I'm Frake again. Or Frakey, or simply gov.

Today, I bake cakes and pastries to rival Mary Berry's, if I do say so myself. I say that with a twinkle in my eye of course. Back in the day, I was Governor of Security and Operations for HMP Wormwood Scrubs. Ahead of you lies the story of my journey from A to B. If you're easily shocked or offended, you best look away now.

Chapter 1

NEW KID ON THE BLOCK

HMP Wormwood Scrubs:
March 2002

I guess it would be fair to say I started my first day at one of Britain's most notorious men's prisons feeling bitter.

There was a staff shortage, so me and another female senior officer had been transferred. That's the way things went in the prison service and there was nothing I could do about it. We'd had just the weekend to prepare after someone from HMP Holloway turned up on my doorstep with a letter. A bit like what you see in the movies, when someone gets 'served' with their court papers.

The woman thrust the envelope at me with an outstretched hand and I just glared at her, knowing full well it was bad news. I have a sixth sense for knowing what's coming. You'll get to know that about me the more you hear of my story.

'Just tell me what it says,' I said, not wanting to bother with the ceremony of opening it.

'You're moving to Wormwood Scrubs.'

1

My stomach clenched. 'Alright. Fine.' I drew on all my strength to hide my emotions. 'When?'

'Monday.'

Monday?! You're having a giraffe!

'Great, thanks,' I replied, tight-lipped. I closed the door, my heart sinking, my resolve melting to form pure undiluted anger.

I never did open the letter. I binned it. Like I say, bitter. I'd given that women's prison sixteen years of my life and, just like that, they wrenched me from everything I'd known and shoved me into a world I'd deliberately avoided. A men's prison.

I barely said a word to Sarah as she drove us through London rush-hour traffic to our new life. My thoughts were churning, mainly with dread.

HMP Wormwood Scrubs' reputation preceded it. Built in the Victoria era it was one of the oldest prisons in the UK. Dirty, rat-infested, rundown, with a serious drug problem. You get to hear all the stories working in the industry. 'A prison that continues to fall short of expected standards,' if you prefer the more diplomatic description used by the chief inspector of prisons. On the tier system, it was ranked three, teetering on two. Four being the best. One being the worst. You get the idea.

Aside from being grubby, it was also one of the largest prisons in the UK, locking up 1,237 prisoners compared to the 400 to 500 we had at Holloway. 'The Scrubs', as it was better known, was just as famous for its list of well-known convicts. From Moors murderer Ian Brady to the Yorkshire Ripper Peter Sutcliffe; Leslie Grantham, better known as Dirty Den off *EastEnders*, Rolling Stones' Keith Richards, 'Britain's most violent prisoner' Charles Bronson; George Blake, the British spy who betrayed M16 agents to the KGB. They'd all done time there. Rather fittingly, Wormwood Scrubs meant 'snake-infested woodland' in Old English.

Being in central London, right next to Wormwood Scrubs Common in Shepherd's Bush, it was situated in spitting distance of the city's magistrates and crown courts, which is why it was mainly used as a remand prison. In fact, as many as 80 per cent of the prisoners in the Scrubs were awaiting sentencing. Remand prisoners bring a whole set of problems on their own compared to convicted criminals, but more of that later.

In a nutshell, I'd been sent to an absolute hole full of lairy men who'd been accused of everything from murder to rape to plotting to blow up our country. It was a category B prison, so some of the most serious of crimes.

What they'd done didn't bother me though – I'd met all sorts working at Holloway, from serial killers to child murderers to IRA members. I'd had the Angel of Death, Beverley Allitt, on my wing. She'd murdered four babies and attempted to kill nine more through insulin or potassium overdoses while working as a hospital nurse in Lincolnshire. Doesn't get more grim that that. So no, I wasn't intimidated by their crimes. It was more about what they were – men.

Even though I was what you might call a sturdy woman at five foot nine inches tall, I wouldn't stand a bleedin' chance against some six-foot-six bloke built like a brick shithouse, who had the added strength of ten men thanks to a drugs rush he'd just got from contraband smuggled into the prison. What if things kicked off, which they inevitably would being a prison, and I got attacked? Would I be able to put them in their place? No doubt I was going to be in a minority among the staff. Would I enjoy working alongside male colleagues? Would they respect me? I was stepping into a man's world and I was panicking whether I had the balls to handle it.

Giving up wasn't an option, though. This was my career, I'd chosen to do it, and I wasn't quitting for anyone.

I wound down the window so I could have another fag. That made four already. I'd been puffing away like a trooper, and on an empty stomach. My insides were digesting themselves.

Sarah slammed on the breaks as yet another plonker stepped out in front of us. It had been stop-start the whole way so far. That was something I'd also have to get used to – the commute. I'd been lucky enough to avoid London traffic up until now thanks to my flat being a five-minute walk from Holloway. The two-bed had been given to me as part of my training scheme when I joined the prison service. I wasn't giving that up, why should I? Anger, that's what I was feeling now as I inhaled deeply on my cigarette. I was angry *and* bitter.

We were on the final stretch. Du Cane Road, Hammersmith Hospital on our right. Less than a hundred yards more and there it was – the gatehouse. The main entrance to the Scrubs. I don't think there is anyone in the country who wouldn't recognise those iconic towers. Formidable. Steeped in history. Used in countless films and TV shows. The gateway to our future. I felt queasy.

We pulled up in the staff car park and made our way along the gravelly track. Still barely saying a word to each other. The crunch of the stones underneath our black shoes filled the silence.

I was wearing my uniform. Black trousers and a white shirt, but no epaulettes. I'd refused point-blank to put them on that morning. I didn't want any more association with Holloway; I'd cut all ties the moment that letter arrived.

The staff entrance was a far less glamorous side door. I wasn't expecting the welcome committee but a bit of acknowledgement would have been nice.

'It's senior officer Frake reporting for duty,' I announced as we rocked up at the gate. I handed them my ID.

The bloke behind the glass checked his paperwork and looked up. 'We don't have anything to say you're coming in.' Off to a good start then. I looked around me. Less than impressed. *Bite your tongue, Vanessa.*

'Wait here a minute.' He picked up the phone. I was hardly going to go anywhere. My sarcasm was running rife. I slid my gaze across to Sarah who looked equally hacked off. I didn't believe in omens but was this someone's way of trying to tell us it was all downhill from here? *Seriously, Vanessa, just calm yourself down.*

I don't know how long it took, but eventually the head of HR came down to get us. I'd spent that time chewing the fat, working myself up. Notching up my levels of dread ten rungs higher, if that was even possible. So when the woman from HR greeted us with a huge welcoming smile, I was taken aback.

'Right, you two,' she said, pointing. 'Come up to my office, I'm going to make you a cup of tea.'

That was music to my ears. Tea and fags. My two favourite things.

We were escorted to a 1960s prefab building on the other side of the entrance, so nothing like the historic buildings we were yet to encounter. Sarah and I took a seat opposite the HR lady on the other side of the desk; she chatted away while I nursed my cuppa. The woman was lovely and welcoming but I just wasn't in the right frame of mind for banter.

'How do you feel about being here?' she finally asked.

I shrugged. Speaking for the both of us I replied: 'How do you think we feel!'

'This is a fresh start for you here. The Scrubs will be what you make of it.'

I made a small shrug. 'Okay.'

She smiled kindly.

Draining my mug, I placed it down on the edge of the desk. 'So where are we going then?' I said. Despite her hospitality, I really wasn't in the mood for small talk. I just wanted to get on with my job, do what I'd been paid to do. No more dilly-dallying.

Sarah was sent to work at the security office. I was allocated D wing. That's where the 'lifers' were locked up.

Lifers, i.e. criminals who were serving a life sentence because their crime was that heinous. The worst of the worst.

I'd never worked with lifers before. Of course I'd come into contact with them at Holloway, but I'd not been responsible for them on a day-to-day basis. As the senior officer on the wing, I'd be in charge of 244 of them.

'Someone will take you there,' the HR woman reassured me.

'No.' I shook my head defiantly, or some might say stubbornly. 'Just point me to where the wing is and I'll make my own way there.'

She looked at me closely, trying to read my eyes, and then nodded. 'Okay, as you prefer. We'll get your keys sorted and let you make you make your own way there.'

'Thanks,' I replied, standing up. Preparing to slip out of the office and to my new posting without any more fuss or bother.

My footsteps echoed as I made my way along the bleak corridors. The brand new Scrubs epaulettes sparkling on my shoulders were going to scream 'fresh fish' to the prisoners. Apart from the duty staff walking to and fro, the place was desolate. The only time prisoners walk between wings is on 'free flow' when they're escorted to their jobs or education. Clearly neither was happening right now.

First impressions? It was huge, three times the size of Holloway. Dirty. Rundown. And it stank of men. Of stale

BO, musty unwashed clothes and urine, to be specific. It was so pungent it made me want to gag.

But despite the stench there was something unusual about this prison. You could really feel the history as you walked through it. It's hard to put into words what it felt like; it was a kind of vibration. As if the walls were alive, humming with the ghosts of prisoners past.

I reckon, back in the day before it was torn down and rebuilt in the 1970s, Holloway would have given off the same sort of vibe. But when I worked there it felt more like a hospital with giant communal wings that resembled wards in a mental asylum.

The Scrubs couldn't have been more different in layout. Five wings, marked A to E, five imposing red-brick buildings, huge long wings with three or four landings, joined together by a canal of corridors. They were all separate entities. I wondered what delightful character traits my wing would have. Miraculously, I'd managed to navigate my way without stopping to ask for directions. I'd been handed my own set of keys and all that now stood in the way of me and those serving life imprisonment were a double set of iron-clad doors.

The key turning in a lock in a prison, that's a sound and a half. Metal on metal. A dragging, scraping noise that can send a chill right through you. It becomes part of you when you work in the nick though. That and the sound of keys in your pocket, jangling with every step. When I worked in Holloway I could tell who was about to appear around the corner just by the clink of their walk. It would only be a matter of time until I knew who was who here. It's not for nothing jails are nicknamed 'the clink'.

As the first set of gates slammed behind me, I gave myself a talking-to. Whatever I was feeling inside – nerves, trepidation – under no circumstances could I let that show. As senior officer on the wing, I needed to project an image of being in charge. To the other officers and, most importantly, to the prisoners.

Prisoners can smell fear a mile off. I once heard from a psychologist that a woman who has been raped walks differently. She takes quicker steps and has a less confident stride. They're such slight differences you or I wouldn't detect them. Prisoners are looking out for these weaknesses though; they search for chips in your armour, for ways to get under your skin so they can dominate. I learnt a long time ago that in order to survive working in a prison you had to wear a 'game face'. A neutral expression no matter what. I could never let on what I was really thinking, because if they know they've got to you, with the insults they hurl or the violence they threaten you with, they've won.

The second and final door clanged shut, juddering at my heels.

My breath escaped me. *Bloody hell*, this place was enormous. It was the stuff of movies. Four storeys high with metal staircases taking you up the landings. Netting was strung up between the floors to stop prisoners jumping to their death. Suicides, a big part of prison life.

Because the ceiling was so high, the noise was deafening. BANG! BANG! BANG! The sound of fists on doors rung in my ears. It was almost noon, their lunch break, or association hour as we call it, and the inmates wanted letting out.

A friendly older officer approached me. He was what I would call 'old school', impeccable manners, no-nonsense, probably ex-army. 'And who are you, ma'am?' he asked politely.

I took in a deep breath. 'I'm your new SO.'

'Ah, right.' He looked a little taken aback. 'Would you like a cup of tea?'

'Yes, thank you. And then I'll have a tour of the wing and you can show me what's what.'

I was right about the epaulettes. They attracted the prisoners like bees to a honeypot. Amazing really considering how small they were, a single diamond with the crown HMP on either shoulder to show I was a senior officer. But the prisoners' beady eyes don't miss a trick. Because the epaulettes were shiny, because they hadn't seen me before – all of them assumed I was new to the job. Wet behind the ears. Someone they could take the piss out of, which is exactly what they did, or at least tried to do.

The conversations that lunchtime were much of a muchness and all went something a little like this: Prisoner would sidle up to me, look shifty, glancing left to right, and then when he was confident he was out of earshot from the other officers working on the wing, he'd say: 'You're the new SO then?'

'Yeah, that's right,' I'd reply. Playing along.

'So here's the thing, miss, the old SO who worked here always used to give me an extra visit.'

Lifers were allowed one visit from friends and family a month and if they were an Enhanced prisoner, i.e. if they behaved well, they would get an extra visit, making two visits per month. This particular prisoner was angling for me to bend the rules and give him one extra. Little did he know who he was dealing with. But I played along. Not just because it was mildly amusing to see what lies they spun, but because you can glean a lot from small conversations like that. Namely, who I should be keeping an eye on. It allowed me to work out who was who and who the biggest players were. If they were brazen enough to try it on with me, they were likely to be the ones dealing in contraband. And I don't just mean drugs. Phones, weapons, cigarettes, home-brewed – or, rather, cell-brewed – alcohol. So I smiled and played along, but took note.

The questions kept coming.

'So where have you worked before? Do you smoke?' Checking to see if they can blag any fags off you. 'How long have you been in the job?' That was their favourite.

'Oh, one or two years,' I replied, a wry smile growing. A twinkle in my eye.

Finally, they caught on.

'Eugh, you're not new at all, are you?'

'Nope.' I grinned.

Three things I gleaned on my first day. Number one – all that dread I'd worked up had been for nothing. These men didn't seem half as bad as I'd imagined they'd be. In fact, I'd go as far to say I felt incredibly comfortable with them. There was a 'what you see is what you get' sort of attitude about them. These were guys, banged up for serious crimes, yet they appeared a lot more straightforward than the women I'd dealt with.

Second thing I learnt. Both male staff and male prisoners have potty mouths. I think I possibly heard more bad language on my first day in the Scrubs than I'd ever heard. Which included homophobic and racist references. I have no idea why. Without meaning to sound sexist I think it's just what men do – banter – they don't see it as inappropriate. I was not impressed, but I was hopeful my presence as a female would make a difference to how the majority of staff and prisoners spoke.

Lastly, I couldn't believe how dirty the wing was. The floor was absolutely minging and in need of a good polish. The place stunk to high heaven. D wing was crying out for a woman's touch. Luckily for them, I'd arrived.

Chapter 2

GAME FACE

HMP Holloway: 1986

'Fresh fish! Fresh fish! Fresh fish!'

Anyone who has watched the film *The Shawshank Redemption* will remember the scene where the prisoners have their hands threaded through the bars, clapping while they chant 'Fresh fish' at the newcomer. Intimidating him. Testing him. Trying to break him down. The banging and the clapping bellowing out across the wing.

Fresh fish, that's what I felt like on my very first day inside a prison wearing nylon blue overalls with a big sticker saying 'NEPO – New Entrant Prison Officer'. Talk about drawing attention to yourself. All nine of us from the training course stuck out like sore thumbs.

'NEPO! NEPO! NEPO!' There was no clapping, but there may as well have been. The chanting rang through my ears.

Twelve weeks later, I'd passed my training and exams and

THE GOVERNOR

I was back at HMP Holloway, this time in my official uniform, ready to report for my first day at work.

Understandably, I was slightly wary after my initial welcome into the prison, but I thought things would be different now I was a fully fledged staff member.

My uniform consisted of an air-force blue A-line skirt that flared out almost as far as my arms could stretch, a white shirt, a jacket and a blue felt hat. The hat could scrunch up and fit it in your pocket, which was just as well as it was hideous and any chance not to wear it, staff would take.

The thought of working and living in London excited me though. I'd grown up in the countryside near Bedford, Bedfordshire, since I was eleven years old and this was my first venture into the Big Smoke. Holloway, which was located in north London, was a Cat B prison, the largest in western Europe run by women for women. So no male officers though we did have male AGs (assistant governors). It was also massively understaffed. They were at least sixty to seventy staff short when I rocked up and those that were working often called in sick. I had a feeling I was going to be kept busy.

I'd barely been through the gates five minutes when a female officer stopped me and without so much as a hello, said: 'So which way do you bat then?'

That got my goat.

'None of your business!' I fired back, protectively. Followed by a sudden rush of fear that I'd overstepped the mark as I carried on with the other new recruits down the hallway.

14

As it happens, I am gay. None of her business though. Or anyone's for that matter. Does it hinder me from doing my job properly? No, absolutely not, so why discuss it? Sadly, there was more talk of my sexuality to come though and in a way that would make my run-in sound positively polite.

D3 wing, that's where I was starting out, where all the new prisoners were. I was a little nervous; it was my first day after all. I was also young at twenty-three, and somewhat naive despite my robust character.

One last iron of my ridiculous skirt with my hand and I stepped though the barred gates onto D3 wing. Turns out, a change of clothes didn't stop me being fresh fish.

'Oi oi, who's this?'

The prisoners milling about on association pressed their backs to the landing rail to let me pass. Their eyes locked on me, with such intent it was like they were drilling a hole right through me.

'Fucking dyke,' another cried out.

'Dyke, bitch.' The insults kept coming thick and fast.

No matter what they teach you in those twelve weeks of training to be an officer, nothing could have prepared me for the reality. Catcalling. Insults. Derogatory comments. You name it, it was slung at me.

How did they even know I was gay? Because I had short hair? That's hardly a prerequisite. They couldn't have any idea, which was how I twigged what their game was. Winding me up. Trying to provoke a reaction. Testing me to see how easily I broke. It was a game, and in those opening minutes I knew I had to develop a game face or I'd be lamb to the slaughter.

A lot of those women in Holloway were huge butch ladies, shaved undercuts, covered in tattoos, with big gobs. I quite simply, with want of a better phrase, had no choice but to 'butch up myself'. So I threw my shoulders back. I took larger, more assertive strides along the landing and if anyone tried to stare me down, I wouldn't look away or at the ground: I'd stare right back at them. It's like playing a game of chicken. Who's the first to pull away? It wasn't going to be me.

It was like running the gauntlet and when I got to the other end, I felt a tremble inside. A slight shake of my hands with adrenaline. I shoved them into my jacket pockets as I took a few deep calming breaths. *You got this, Vanessa, don't let them rattle your cage.* I'd put all those months of work into making this my career; it was teething problems, I was sure of it.

It was nice to be able to share stories with the other nine recruits at lunchtime. As we left the prison in search of the local pub I discovered I wasn't alone; pretty much everyone had endured similar experiences that morning, if not worse. At least I hadn't had anything thrown at me or been attacked.

The local was a bit of a dive, but it was nearby and served hearty pub grub. Pie and mash, fish in batter with chips and peas, that kind of thing. We were wearing our uniforms when we came in but had our civvy jackets over the top and our hats in our pockets. It wasn't obvious where we worked, but I guess to any local you could tell straight away.

The landlord was perfectly friendly, happy to have a big group of girls in his otherwise fairly empty pub I'd say. I could feel the morning's tension evaporating as I worked my way steadily though my pint of Diet Coke. We were waiting for our food to arrive when the door swung open. *Bang.* It smacked hard against the wall. Everyone looked up as the rowdy group of lads piled inside. They were gobby twenty-something-year-olds with a mouthful of expletives. I noticed the landlord roll his eyes.

Our table was on the way to the bar. We carried on talking among ourselves above the rabble, trying not to give them any of our attention. Suddenly, what I would guess to be the leader of the group stopped in his tracks, halting his mates with an outstretched arm. He was glaring at us, his eyes narrowing.

What the bloody hell did he want? Some of the girls hadn't noticed yet, but I had. I was watching him closely because there was something very off in his demeanour.

He started walking towards us, his friends in tow. I had no idea what his beef with us was. I'd have guessed we were about to witness a poor attempt to crack onto us if it weren't for the flash of anger rising in his expression. I clocked how the landlord had moved to the near side of the bar so he could keep an eye on them.

He was wearing jeans with paint stains, trainers, his hands shoved deeply into the pockets of his grey hoodie. His face was thin and weather-beaten making him seem a

17

lot older than his age. His lips thin and twisting into a sneer.

Playing up to the gallery, he rocked back on his heels and exclaimed: 'Oh look! A load of fucking screws!'

Oh bloody hell. Here's trouble.

He then proceeded to wind his neck in, purse his lips and, to our horror, hurled a giant mouthful of spit at us.

It rained down on us. Narrowly missing my face but landing on Katie who was sat next to me. She got it in her hair and it splattered across her cheek.

A stunned silence fell across our group while he gleefully wiped his mouth with the back of his hand. His mates behind him were laughing away. 'Nice one, mate,' they sniggered.

'Oi,' the landlord bellowed. 'None of that in *my* pub!'

The thug held up his hands in fake apology as he swaggered back over to the bar. 'Give us a pint of Carlsberg will you, mate.'

The landlord flashed him a disapproving look and then got on with pouring the drinks for him and his mates, preferring to keep the peace than cause a scene by chucking them out.

I felt deeply sorry for Katie and the others as they wiped their faces with the table serviettes while everyone else in the pub stared on. It was humiliating and degrading for them and I hated he had made them feel that way. It was worse than anything we'd been subjected to in the prison that morning.

Why had he done it? Where had his hatred come from? I couldn't understand it. Coming from the countryside, I'd lived a fairly sheltered life and hadn't witnessed any aggressive behaviour in public before. There was the occasional debate down the local in Bedford but that was as heated as it got. I knew some people liked to call coppers 'pigs'. Perhaps this tosser's attitude was one of the same? A despising authority mentality – they are locking us up, they are stopping us having fun. An us versus them kind of attitude. Who knows.

The longer I worked in the prison service the more I came to understand how prison officers are seen as the lowest of the low by the public. Mostly referred to as warders, screws and turnkeys, spoken about as if we enjoy locking people up. Never mind all the good we do, how we try to keep our country safe. Never mind that there is so much more to the job than just turning a key – we're a counsellor, a social worker, a mental health nurse, a peacemaker, all rolled into one. Most people couldn't cope with what we do once in a lifetime let alone on a daily basis. Oh, and never mind we get paid pittance to do it. You get more money flipping burgers at McDonald's. Okay, rant over.

These are thoughts I've formed along the way, of course. Back then, though, while I watched my friends wipe the spit from their faces, I simply felt angry. Furious, in fact. And also sad, because despite feeling immensely proud about my new career and all the hard work I'd put in to get the job, I knew, from that day on, I'd never wear my uniform out in public again. It wasn't worth the aggro after a hard day's work. Pick your battles and all that.

Not surprisingly, our appetites had been somewhat ruined by what happened and I for one didn't want to share my oxygen with those idiots for a second longer, so we headed back to work. It had been a crappy first day, but I was optimistic things would get better. Not for a moment did I entertain the idea of throwing in the towel. I'm not a quitter. If I start something, I finish it. There was no way I would have given up unless there was something medically wrong with me.

Anyway, I'd pretty much mastered my game face and it would be a crying shame to waste my new skill set. It wasn't long after starting at Holloway that I got to put it to the test on a very high-profile murderer. This particular prisoner wasn't threatening or wanting to get a rise out of me, but I knew that she was the sort that would get off on noticing any difference in my facial expression. I didn't want to give her the satisfaction. Especially not after what she'd done to children.

The encounter took me by surprise though.

It was mid-morning and a bunch of us had been asked to escort four prisoners to HMP Cookham Wood – which back then was a female-only jail in Kent – though now it's a young offenders' prison. Prison officers had to take it in turns doing escorts – transferring prisoners to other jails or taking them to court for their hearing – and my number was up.

I was excited about the prospect of getting a gander at another big estate. I was interested in how it might differ from Holloway. *It might be somewhere I'd like to work in the future*, you never know. It was also just nice to ride in the van and get out for a few hours.

It's a bit of a procedure transferring a prisoner from one estate to another though. As the most junior of the three officers going, I had to run around doing this, that and the other. Gather the prisoners' property up, make sure we had all the correct paperwork and, most importantly, that we had the warrants issued by the court, because without them a jail will not accept a prisoner, under any circumstances.

We loaded the prisoners into the van – which was effectively a raised minibus. They were nicknamed pixie vans. I have no idea why – maybe because pixies sit high off the ground on toadstools? The women were handcuffed to each other, done in such a way they would find it impossible to run if something was to happen like an ambush or a crash or anything that could lead to prisoners on the run.

Hierarchy is everything in the prison service and being the junior I had the pleasure of sitting right at the back of the van, above the wheels, the most bumpy seat in the house, where you could feel every lump and pothole in the road. Joy.

The principal officer saw us off at the gate. 'Hats on,' she tutted at the senior officer. I was feeling smug because mine was already in place. No sooner had we driven out of the gates and turned left onto the Holloway Road that we all whipped them off, stuffing them back into our pockets.

The long journey to Kent was pretty non-eventful. I stared out of the window, watching the city morph into countryside. Switching off from the background chatter from the prisoners. They were nattering about boys, make-up and saying how they hoped they would be sharing cells in Cookham.

We were met at the gate outside the reception wing by a senior officer. A big burly woman. Like you'd imagine a school matron to be.

Out of nowhere, she suddenly bellowed: 'My-ra!'

Cor blimey – we looked at each other – who's she shouting at like that?'

A woman appeared from around the corner of the building. She was wearing a baggy mottled jumper that had seen better days.

'Myra, make these officers a cup of tea,' the senior officer ordered.

'Yes, miss,' the woman nodded.

She went between us collecting our orders.

'Cup of tea, two sugars, that will be great thanks,' I told her.

She was very courteous and polite and then disappeared back inside to crack on with sorting out our refreshments. Meanwhile, the senior officer in charge turned to us with a raised eyebrow.

'You know who that is, don't you?'

I had no clue.

'Myra?' I shrugged.

'Yeah, Myra who?' she added, willing me to finish her sentence.

'Myra I don't know, Myra who makes tea?' Too cocky for my own good I was.

'That' – she paused, building suspense – 'was Myra Hindley.'

'Yeah right!' I scoffed.

'No, that was Myra Hindley.' Her eyes widened as if she wanted me to be awestruck.

Myra Hindley, the Moors Murderer, serving life for torturing and killing five children with her partner Ian Brady in the 1960s. Labelled by the press as one of the most evil women in Britain.

'Well let's hope she makes a good cup of tea then,' I replied in my typical dry manner.

I hadn't put two and two together because she didn't look anything like *that* photo. The infamous mugshot of her with platinum blonde hair and an intense stare. Her hair was still short and tapered into the neck but it was mousy brown. She had on some sort of old woolly jumper that made her look frumpy. She was average weight for her five foot five height. Put it this way: she wouldn't have stood out in a crowd, that's for sure.

I'd heard lots of stories about Hindley since I started in Holloway though, mostly related to how manipulative she was. She was legendary for getting staff wrapped around her finger and then there was the famous story of her affair with prison officer Pat Cairns, who had planned to break her out and escape with her to Australia.

These things were all racing through my mind as the serial killer returned with my cup of tea. As for the murders, I couldn't bring myself to think about them or her involvement in them. It was too horrific. Most of the detail of what she did to those kids was kept out of the papers it was so sadistic.

'Here you go.' She handed the mug to me.

Don't flinch, Vanessa. I flattened all my expression. My game face switched on.

I'd read the profiles: Myra Hindley was a narcissist of the purest kind. The sort of person who would get a kick out of seeing my shock-horror face. She craved notoriety. She wanted to be feared and revered. She would have loved nothing more than to watch my eyes grow wide upon her return, and I wasn't going to give her the satisfaction of thinking she had that effect on me.

'Thanks very much,' I said.

'Anything else I can get you?' she asked, as if butter wouldn't melt in her mouth. It was hard to imagine she'd committed such evil. The juxtaposition between the woman bringing me tea and the woman who'd tortured all those kids was almost disorientating.

'No thanks,' I replied with the same indifference I'd give a barista in my local coffee shop.

And that was it. Exchange over.

To be fair to the other officers, they acted the same. Their expressions were also unreadable. Nobody wanted to give Myra Hindley a kick.

It wasn't long after our encounter that Hindley was back in the press. In 1987 she returned to the Moors to help the police find the remains of missing victims Keith Bennett and Pauline Reade. A load of hoo-ha over nothing, they didn't find a thing. The families of the victims were subjected to yet another painful episode where their hopes were dashed. Not long after that, Myra pleaded with the public for forgiveness, saying she'd served her time in prison and deserved a second chance. It was hard to believe her admission of two additional murders were a genuine repentance. More a calculated measure to try and get herself released. She applied for parole countless times, but every attempt was thwarted by the government. Successive home secretaries knew there would be huge public outcry if it were granted.

I do find the way in which the public treat female killers in comparison to male ones interesting and surprising though. Myra's crimes were abominable, no question there, but there are many men who have done similar, if not worse, crimes and have not been given the same life sentence.

I think it comes down to how society views women. We are meant to be gentle, kind, nurturing, the caregivers, the ones who protect children, not kill them. Hindley became the embodiment of all that's unnatural in a woman – *a she-devil* – and her long sentence was in part a punishment for that – for being a freak of nature.

Back in the olden days she would have been burned at the stake just like witches were.

Chapter 3

ONE BAD APPLE SPOILS THE BUNCH

HMP Wormwood Scrubs:
May 2002

A woman's touch. That's what D wing needed. And that's what it got. Well, it got me, at any rate.

For starters, I persuaded the number one governor to invest in an industrial-sized buffer to clean the floors, the type that makes your whole body judder as you hold on.

I was still reeling about the move from Holloway, but throwing my energy into improving D wing shifted my focus. I'm not a moaner or a moper; I'm a – excuse the pun – dust myself off and get on with it sort of person, and making the best of a situation was my only option. I'd like to add a little side note now, while I can: at no point was I doing any of this with the intention of getting a promotion. Climbing the ladder was of zero interest to me. All I've ever cared about is doing my job to the best of my ability. Whether I was in the jail I wanted to be was by the by.

ONE BAD APPLE SPOILS THE BUNCH

The principal officer raised yet another eyebrow as I asked him if I could have another load of cleaning products ferried in, but he signed off the form anyway. After the landings were sparkling I moved on to the offices. There was one on every floor, on the ones, the twos, the threes and the fours, as they were referred to. The SO's office was on the ground floor – the ones – and it was a right old pigsty. I sorted it out with a proper filing system, steadily making my way through the backlog of paperwork piled high on the desk. It wasn't all about me, and improving my work environment. I wanted to make sure the officers – all thirty of them – were happy too. They were a nice bunch who had made me feel welcome. Happy officers equal a better and more efficient work environment. Logical thoughts like those came naturally to me. They always have done, ever since I was a little girl.

I can vividly remember being three years old, waking up in the middle of the night to damp sheets. I'd wet myself. I was devastated. Frightened. All the normal things a child feels when they don't understand what's happened but worries it's going to upset their parents. Mum was fast asleep, so I instinctively got on with fixing the problem. I knew where the clean laundry was kept because I used to sit with Mum while she ironed and folded it away. I crept out of my room, on tiptoes, and made my way across the landing to the linen cupboard. I piled my arms so high with new bedding I could barely see over the top. I wobbled my way back, stripped and made my bed. Good as new. Not even a corner left untucked; no exaggeration I promise. Three years old and I was already fiercely independent. You can only imagine what a force to be reckoned with I became the older I got.

I bartered some more with my superiors and had them agree to new furniture so the officers wouldn't have to endure sitting on lopsided chairs on their break time for a second longer. I left it a few days and then I was at it again, this time pushing for an actual staff room on the wing. The poor buggers who worked there didn't have anywhere to go at lunchtime; they had to sit alone in their cupboard of an office on the landing. I got to work creating a staff room for them on the twos, with comfy chairs.

You wouldn't have thought there were two other senior officers managing the wing would you? They just did what I said, to be honest. I took over. But nobody seemed to mind. I think they appreciated an assertive woman coming in and shaping the place up. The prisoners liked it too.

I was firm, but I was always fair. If I said I was going to do something, I did it. The guys in there appreciated my no-bullshit attitude because that way they knew where they stood.

It seems like such a small point, but routine, order and boundaries mean everything to prisoners. They'll try and see how much they can get away with but they appreciate knowing what's what. It helps them get through their day, cope with their time inside. They've already been stripped of everything, so they like knowing there will be no more nasty surprises.

Most importantly, I didn't treat the prisoners as if they were a lock-up behind a door. When I wasn't managing the detail, sorting through the mountains of paperwork, being an authoritative presence, an extra pair of hands on the wing, I talked to them. I'd have a cup of tea and a fag on the landing with them. I'd ask them about their families on the outside, show a professional interest. Never about their crimes though; it wasn't my job to ask and I didn't want to know. To work in a prison, to not allow your emotions to colour your judgement, it's best not knowing too much about what they're in for.

But if they broke the rules, then I'd punish them.

As I mentioned earlier, after all my fretting, it turned out I didn't have an issue with working with men. Quite the opposite, in fact. Unfortunately, I couldn't say the feeling was mutual. I think it would be fair to say there were some prisoners whose noses were put out of joint with my arrival on D wing.

We had this one guy who thought he was something a bit special because he'd killed three people. Shot them dead. It was all to do with drugs and gangs. The killings probably gave him some level of notoriety with his peers back home. He was used to being top dog and expected the same sort of ceremony in the nick. Nah, that wasn't how I liked to run a wing.

Not only did this guy have a huge chip on his shoulder, he also clearly had an issue with women being in charge. The tension had been mounting since I started. Derogatory mutterings under his breath like *fucking dyke* or *fucking bitch*. Glares. Looking me up and down like I was scum. A general bad attitude. He thought he ran that wing and could manipulate anybody he so chose. I couldn't stand him.

It was morning time and the day had started like any other. They'd just had breakfast. Some were exercising on the exercise yard just off the wing. Some were mooching about. Some had gone to work. When I say work, many of the prisoners had jobs to earn extra money, such as sorting through the laundry or helping prepare the meals. They were also financially rewarded for taking part in education courses, everything from learning to be a gym instructor to health and hygiene courses, to painting and decorating courses.

They would earn, on average, five or six pounds a week. If they didn't contribute, unemployment pay was £2.50 a week. The money would go into their personal account and they could choose to either send it out to family – as many of the foreign national prisoners did – or use it in the prison canteen, which was to all intents and purposes the prison shop. Once a week prisoners were allowed to spend their wages in the shop. They could buy cigarettes and matches (back in the day when prisoners could smoke), various chocolate bars, cereals, fruit, etc. It was all done electronically. No cash ever changed hands.

The door of my office on the ones was always open. I wanted the other officers to know they could approach me with anything. The prisoners used to come knocking too, on their association hour.

So this one morning, Dave, let's call him, appeared at my desk. He breezed in, knowing full well what my protocol was.

'KNOCK!' I sent him back out. It was one of the few rules I had. It was a rule and one that I used to enforce rigidly. He glared at me through narrowed eyes as he reluctantly struck the door.

'Come in.' I masked my true feelings with a flat smile.

Dave hovered in front of my desk. He was a big black guy. Shaved head. Huge arms. Dark, piercing eyes, lined with life experiences.

'So what can I do for you?' I sat back, crossing my arms.

Dave explained he wanted to change jobs to the laundry room. Laundry was sought after because it paid well. He hadn't been in his current post attending the education department for long, which wasn't ideal, but he was within his rights to ask for a transfer. So I did check: as I said, I was firm but fair. The guy deserved a fair crack at laundry, whether I liked him or not.

I made some enquiries while he waited there. It didn't take long to have an answer, and I knew he wouldn't like it.

I put down the phone and shook my head. 'Sorry, there's no room at the moment.'

He stood perfectly still, his eyes, staring me down. I could feel the rage building. The tension was palpable.

'They're not recruiting at the moment,' I reiterated. I wanted him out of my office.

All that hatred towards me which he'd bottled up in order to ask me a favour suddenly exploded out of him.

He turned on his heels and marched out, slamming my office door. And I mean he proper slammed it – the door rattled on its hinges.

I'd treated him fairly and this is what I get in return? His attitude inflamed me. I'd had enough. I leapt out of my chair and followed after him. Up onto the landing.

'You fucking bitch,' he yelled over his shoulder. His feet stamping on the metal like a tantrum-y child.

'Bitch. Dyke.' He launched into a tirade of abuse, the typical derogatory comments. His voice blasted and echoed across the entire D wing, which of course attracted the attention of all the other prisoners. Everyone stopped what they were doing and came to watch the show. Hanging over the landings.

Staff from upstairs were quick to peer over the railings to check if I needed help.

'I've got this!' I shouted back. I wasn't afraid of this tosser, I was furious – at the way he thought he could speak to me. How dare he talk down to me because I was a woman. And I didn't want the other prisoners getting any ideas. I stomped on, closing in on his heels. Despite my saying I could handle the situation, I was suddenly surrounded by staff who wanted to protect me.

He was a short man. Maybe he seemed that way because I'm tall for a woman. Who knows. He was on the stairs when he suddenly swung around to square up to me. Two or three steps up from me. Even though he was short, the steps gave him an added advantage and he towered over. His eyes were wild; he'd completely lost the plot. He wasn't far off spitting and snarling.

I steeled myself. Shoulders back, standing tall and firm as he lunged his neck forwards, thrusting his face inches from

32

mine. Trying to intimidate. Face to face, looking down on me. I could smell his stale fag breath.

Coolly and calmly I said: 'Don't speak to me like that, or you're going to find yourself in 'the Seg'.

The Seg, short for segregation unit, where prisoners are locked up in isolation for twenty-three out of twenty-four hours for punishment, for their own protection or to protect others from their violence. A hole where you don't want to be.

'I'm not messing here,' I added for good measure.

His eyes grew even wider. His voice even louder. He pointed his stubby finger at me and threatened: 'You should be fucking scared of me. I could have you shot outside this jail.' He clicked his fingers. 'Shot, just like that.'

I raised an unimpressed eyebrow.

'I've killed three people and you're nothing compared to that.'

I couldn't help chortle a little at his pathetic bravado. Still keeping my calm, I replied: 'I'm really not interested in what you think you can and can't do. I'm telling you, as the senior officer on this wing, you either go back to your room now or I'll have you taken to the Seg.'

He carried on with his abuse. Prisoners were crowding in on us, telling him to back off, saying, 'Dave, calm down, leave it, mate. Don't have a go at the SO.' One of the more junior officers pushed his way onto the stairs and launched himself between us.

'Gov, gov, he's not kidding,' he said, trying to protect me.

It wasn't his place to restrain Dave, not until I had given the order to do so.

'Move out of my way.' I pushed through, taking a step closer to Dave as I prepared to deliver the news. We locked eyes.

'Take him to the Seg.'

'Fucking bitch,' he spat as the officers grabbed hold of him.

I pulled my radio from my belt and immediately got hold of the Seg team, which was located next to B wing.

'Hello MJ from Delta 1, I have one on route under restraint to the Seg from D Delta wing. Can you inform the Seg staff and orderly officer to meet us there? Delta 1, over.'

'Hello Delta 1 from MJ that's all received, MJ standing by.'

Not long after his spell in the Seg, Dave was transferred to another prison. I'd had enough of him; I wasn't having any more of his shit. He disrupted the wing – one bad apple spoils the bunch and all that. And at the end of the day, he threatened my life, whether you take what he said seriously or not.

I personally didn't take it seriously, because I could just as easily walk out of the jail and fall under a bus than be killed by one of his minions. I simply couldn't allow myself to live in fear. How would I be able to go about a normal life if I spent my entire time looking over my shoulder for people trying to revenge someone I had locked up?

ONE BAD APPLE SPOILS THE BUNCH

After Dave was carted off, I calmly walked back down the stairs to my office, took a seat and picked up my mug of tea. My fingers weren't trembling. My heart wasn't racing. It was like nothing had happened. Well, I was annoyed my tea had turned stone cold in the interim, but that was it. It must sound strange reading this, I know that, but this 'water off a duck's back' mentality I'd acquired served me well. Having said that, my ability to turn my emotions off may explain what happened to me later on.

Chapter 4

CHIRPY CHAPPY

HMP Wormwood Scrubs:
July 2002

It didn't take me long to get to know all the characters on the wing. Being lifers, they weren't going anywhere anytime soon unless their conviction was overturned – which can happen but rarely does – so there was a much smaller turn-over of faces.

Phones 4u was someone I became well acquainted with. A young lad in his early twenties, white, British, who'd got himself mixed up in gangs and a murder. Wrong place at the wrong time kind of thing. He had a cell on the twos. Ricky was his real name, but we nicknamed him Phones 4u because, as the name might suggest, we were always finding mobiles on him which he'd had smuggled in, enough to start a shop.

Phones are like gold bullion in a prison. An old Nokia that wouldn't go for ten quid on the street would fetch £800 in the nick. Not to be underestimated, they're as deadly as a weapon because they can do just as much damage, if not more. Phones can be used to arrange for drugs to be brought inside the prison. They can be used to order a hit on someone on the outside. Threaten and intimidate a witness. Frighten a partner or wife into dropping charges. The list is endless. The damage caused limitless.

It was easy enough to catch him because he wasn't the sharpest tool in the box, bless him. He hid the phones in all the usual places – taped underneath his wardrobe, under his mattress. Beneath the toilet cistern lid. He used to lend them out for money, that was his game, so he had enough up top to work out the trade but not enough to stop people finding the phones. Anyway, when we caught him red handed, he would be punished. Down to the Seg, a couple of weeks there and then back to my wing. Apart from his sideline business, Phones 4u wasn't too bad a character. He was quite a chirpy chappy in fact, much like the budgie he shared his cell with.

Lifers were the only prisoners who were allowed to keep a budgie.

The pets were allowed under the Incentives and Earned Privileges scheme, which was designed to encourage responsible behaviour. This all stopped in 2007, but up until then, if a lifer wanted a bird, they could apply. As with all things in the prison service there was a procedure involved to see if a prisoner was deemed suitable to be an actual pet – bird – owner. It was fairly straightforward getting one, but if he had a history of bestiality or some other cruelty towards animals we obviously wouldn't let him have one. Badly behaved prisoners also didn't stand a chance.

They had to buy the birds out of their own pocket and they were responsible for feeding and cleaning them. The whole thing wasn't to be taken lightly as anyone who didn't take care of their budgie could be charged with an offence against prison discipline.

Why budgies? Because they make great companions. They're clever little things and the prisoners liked to teach them tricks. They would build them toys out of matchsticks. There were a fair few budgerigars on D wing, five or six, and all different colours, yellow, blue, green ... They'd have a cage in the cell but the inmates mostly let them out. You'd glance through the hatch to often find one sitting on a lifer's shoulder.

There'll be some of you reading this who are feeling outraged – questioning why murderers should have the right to have a companion in their cell. The families of the victims for one. I totally, totally get that if you've lost a loved one; all you'd want is for their killer to be shut in a room and the key to be thrown away. An eye for an eye.

Unfortunately, it doesn't work like that. All we'd be doing is creating a ticking time bomb. Treat people like animals and they'll act like animals. The prisoner will feel hate and grievance, and they'll want vengeance. At some point, that door has to be opened, whether it be to a chaplain, prison staff or when they're eventually allowed back onto the streets. If you've created more of a monster while they've been inside, then you've got an even bigger problem on your hands.

Dynamic security, that's what I believed in – encouraging everyday communication and interaction with prisoners with, of course, one of the major aims being to assist offenders in their rehabilitation. Budgies were a form of rehabilitation because they evoked positive emotions – caring for something, taking responsibility. Essential qualities a person needs in order to function successfully in society.

If prisons didn't have a privilege scheme and we fed everyone on bread and water you'd have riot after riot. It would cost millions to rebuild the prisons and there would be a massive public outcry. Why is our taxpayers' money being spent on these rebuilds? Why aren't our prisons safe? So a budgie might be a tiny little bird, but it carried a big meaning.

Anyway, back to the story ... This one day I was sat in my office, doing paperwork, door open as usual, and Phones 4u came knocking.

The only other time I sent people away apart from not having the manners to knock was if their trousers were hanging halfway down their arse showing off their boxer shorts. I'd tell them to come back when they were dressed properly. Anyway, I digress. Phones 4u knocked and said: 'Gov, can I see you for a minute.'

In the women's prison they called me Frake or Frakey or miss. But straight off the bat I was called gov or boss in the Scrubs, even though I wasn't a governor. Don't know why that was, it's just the name the men gave to anyone in authority.

'Yeah, come in,' I replied, my nose still deep in paperwork.

I sensed him shift from one foot to the other, slightly uncertain about whatever he wanted to ask. I looked up, and there, perched quietly on his shoulder, was his blue budgie.

'The thing is, gov, I've got a visit from my mum and dad now but my budgie needs exercising. Can I leave him with you?' He flashed me one of his cheeky grins. 'He'll sit on your shoulder, you won't even notice he's there.'

The thing about me is I've got a serious soft spot for animals. I'm a massive animal lover and I'd have adopted half of the animals at the RSPCA if it wasn't for the fact I was never home to look after them. So I didn't have any qualms with Phones 4u's request.

'Okay, go on then.'

Phones 4u leaned over my desk and gently coaxed his budgie to step from his shoulder onto mine. I felt his feet claw into my jumper as he moved about, making himself comfortable.

'Stay!' He pointed to his little friend, ordering him around like a dog.

It was a struggle to keep a straight face.

'So how long is your visit for?' I asked, looking sideways out of the corner of my eye at this blue budgie who was staring right back at me.

'An hour.'

'An hour!'

He smiled sheepishly.

'Well, what do I do if I need to leave the office?'

'You can take him with you. He'll go wherever you go.'

'Okay fine, that's sorted then.' I sighed.

Just as Phones 4u was leaving I asked: 'Has he got a name?'

'Fred.'

I think Fred may even have given Phones 4u a cheep as he left.

I sat there for a while carrying on with my work while Fred twitched and fidgeted around on my shoulder. It wasn't long before I was feeling parched. I'd held out for a cup of tea for as long as possible but I was close to breaking point.

I looked sideways. 'Do you mind if I get a cuppa?' I asked the bird. 'No? Okay let's go for a little walk then.'

I got up slowly, being extra careful not to knock Fred from his perch. I then made my way out of my office and onto the wing, keeping my body perfectly straight and taking small steps.

I was walking up the landing with this budgie on my lapel when I suddenly clocked the head of the entire prison, the number one governor, coming towards me.

Christ.

A look of bewilderment passed through the gov's eyes as they flitted between me and the bird. He stopped in front of me.

'Miss Frake.'

'Governor.'

'Are you budgie-sitting?'

Yeah,' I replied with a sigh and a roll of the eyes.

'Ah, bless.' A smile broke across his face. 'So how is he today?'

'Chirpy!'

'Good, good. Well, have a nice day.'

'And you, sir.'

We both walked on. I glanced sideways at Fred, giving him a 'Well, that was bloody awkward' look.

Fred sat on my shoulder for the entire time Phones 4u was with his family. I was slightly sad to see him go at the end of it. I enjoyed bird-sitting. I didn't let that on to the lifer though or he'd be knocking on my door with Fred every time he was sent down to the Seg.

Apart from budgie-sitting, my time on the lifer wing was also giving me an education in the psyche of men. Compared to women prisoners, they were a lot more selfish. Hear me out. When a woman gets sent to prison she spends her time worrying about the people she's left behind. If she has a family, nine times out of ten she's the carer of it, the one who runs it, so she's worrying about the children – who's feeding them? She's panicking about the husband or the boyfriend – who's looking after him? All these kind of domestic issues race through her mind, keeping her up all night fretting.

When a man gets sent to prison, all he wants to know is who's going to look after him. Who's going to bring him in money for his canteen treats or for his fags (this was back when prisoners could smoke) or whatever other privileges he's entitled to. I'm not saying this because I'm some sort of feminist who hates men. Far from it; I was bedding into D wing nicely. It was just an observation having spent time in both male and female jails and having had the pleasure of inmates bending my ear over their domestic problems.

When it comes to their love life, it's also all about him. He wants to know his bird isn't cheating and that she's waiting for him when he gets out. However, it's often one rule for him and another for his woman. I had one lifer who thought he could have the best of both worlds. Being the only female in charge of the wing, I somehow ended up becoming the resident agony aunt.

It was association hour, and I was in my office working away (you can see a pattern developing here, i.e. we were snowed under in a backlog of paperwork). *Knock knock.* The familiar tap at my door. It was very difficult for me to get the work done because for some reason everyone wanted to ask me something, all the time.

'Yep,' I said. Perhaps a little abruptly.

I glanced up. It was Craig, and he was looking a bit sheepish.

'Gov, can I have a word?'

I sighed deeply, casting my eyes back over the piles of papers to my right.

'It's, umm' – checking over his shoulder to make sure no one was listening in – 'it's women's issues.'

I raised an eyebrow. 'Go on then.'

'So umm …' He paused, shifting from one foot to the other.

'Yes.' Both my eyebrows now peaked with interest.

'So, I was just wondering, how do you, sort of, get yourself out of shit with your bird when she finds out you've been seeing someone else?'

I leaned back in my chair and chortled. 'Good luck with that one!'

He leaned in. 'No, gov, I really need some serious advice here. I'm in deep shit.'

It couldn't have been more of a departure from Craig's usual tough-man persona. He was a hardened crim, in the Scrubs for murdering his business partner. They had a scrapyard together and he bumped him off for money, A proper geezer, an East End Jack the Lad type. In his forties, bald, built like a Rottweiler because he used to work out. He had biceps and triceps as big as my thighs. Tattoos across his knuckles: love on one, hate on the other. Tattoos of nude women with massive breasts running down his arms. A big crucifix on the side of his head. Put it this way, I wouldn't like my daughter to bring him home.

'So what have you done?'

'I put the wrong letter in the wrong envelope and my wife's found out that I've been writing to someone else.'

'Let me just reiterate that. You sent a letter for a woman you've been seeing behind your wife's back to your wife?'

'Yeah.' His brows knitted. 'But … little does she know I've been writing to four others as well.'

'Four others?'

'Yeah.' He bowed his head.

'Seriously?'

'Yeah.'

'Well, how long have you been with your wife for?'

'A long time. She's the mother of my kids.'

'This just keeps getting better,' I scoffed. 'And the other woman?'

'I've got a kid by her too.'

I blew into my cheeks. 'Well, then, the biggest lesson you can learn is to keep it [nodding in *that* direction] in your pants.'

'Seriously, gov. What should I do? He was wringing his hands out nervously.

'I was being serious!'

'The problem is I see these women and I just can't help myself.' He stared at me, pleading with me to give him some 'female advice'.

I leaned on my desk, locking my hands together. 'I'm not sure I'm the Claire Rayner of Wormwood Scrubs, but all I can suggest is that you grovel like anything to your wife, and the mother of your …' I paused. '… several kids, and maybe cool things with the other one and stop writing to the others.

'Do you think, gov?'

'Yes I think. To be honest, you're in a situation where you're not going to win any which way. A very sticky place to get out of.'

'Yeah, you're right.' He nodded as if he'd only just seen the light. 'I just hope my missus doesn't come to the prison and wait outside for the other one.'

'Well, let's hope not, eh.'

The chances of that were very slim. Being a convicted lifer, Craig was only allowed one visitor at a time. He had to send a visiting order out to whoever he wanted to see. So for one of his women to randomly turn up was unlikely. All that guilt must have been making his imagination run wild.

He thanked me and left my office looking deep in thought. I have no idea how or *if* he resolved his massive cock-up, but what I do know is, after that, Craig was nice as pie and became one of the most polite prisoners on the wing. 'Morning, gov', 'Afternoon, gov', 'All right, boss', he'd say whenever he saw me. I think he was grateful I'd given him ten minutes of my time just to confirm 'You're in the shit, boy, and you need to do something about it. Pronto.'

Chapter 5

LORDING IT UP

HMP Wormwood Scrubs:
September 2002

Almost all the lifers were in for murdering somebody. Some had murdered their children. Quite a few had murdered their wives. We had a guy whose kid had watched him slaughter his wife, the poor boy's mum. The jury had had to listen to the 999 call the child made while he cowered in the corner of the room. Another guy killed his missus after he found out she was cheating on him. He proceeded to cut her up into twenty or so pieces, wrap them up in bags and stick the bits of her in bins all around Liverpool. You wouldn't have known it looking at him. He was a bit geeky looking, wore glasses, and now and then he liked to work out in the gym. That's the thing about murderers, they don't have a tattoo stamped with *killer* on their forehead. Most of them, you often wouldn't think they'd committed such an atrocity.

Most of the time, the atmosphere on D wing was calm, and I put that down to the fact that lifers have a completely different mindset to other prisoners. They'd come to terms with their conviction and wanted to get on with serving their sentences. As you probably know, life, in many cases, doesn't actually mean life imprisonment.

Prisoners are handed a 'life tariff', which, for example, might be twenty years. Before they're released, they have to prove to a parole board that they're no longer a threat to the public. If they can't, they might end up serving many more years than their original tariff. Lifers will always be on a 'life sentence', even after their release. They can be sent back to prison on a very minor charge such as drunk and disorderly. Remand prisoners on the other hand are a completely different kettle of fish. They are still waiting to be sentenced or awaiting trial by jury. This, understandably, makes them feel vulnerable and they can become volatile. I found remand prisoners much more bolshy and generally a pain in the arse to deal with.

Occasionally you did get a lifer who claimed, 'I didn't do it, gov'. 'I'm innocent, gov.' Two such individuals come to mind from during my time on D wing. The first one didn't cause me much bother other than having me run around honouring his rights. He knew exactly what he was and wasn't entitled to and made sure those rights were carried out. He demanded a laptop so he could work on his case. He wanted books sent to the library so he could read up on the law – he was planning to defend himself if his case went to appeal. He was determined to overturn his conviction come hell or high water.

It was a high-profile case, I knew that much. In 1996 Russell Causley became the first killer in British legal history to be found guilty of murder without his victim's body ever being found. He was convicted more than a decade after his wife Veronica Packman went missing never to be seen again. He swore blind that he didn't do it, and did so in a very articulate way. He was well spoken, well educated, well turned-out even in his prison clothes. We had an ironing board on every landing and he pressed his trousers and sweater each morning. He didn't give me much bother, so I didn't have much to do with him other than filing his requests.

The second one did cause me strife. A very wealthy man who'd been jailed for bumping off his wife for a younger model. Claimed he didn't do it and he had a serious attitude problem. The type that thought he was really smart, a cut above the rest, but he couldn't have been that clever or he wouldn't have been caught, surely?

Let's call this lifer James. Word on the wing was that James used to be a businessman, lived in north London, very wealthy, very well-to-do in the Jewish community. He was married but having an affair with a younger woman. From what I can remember, he stabbed his wife in the morning but turned up the heating in their house to full blast in an attempt to mask the time of death to later that day, to when he was at work. He thought he'd be able to keep his wife's body warm enough to create an alibi and blame the killing on a burglary gone wrong.

He overlooked some major details though – i.e. the heating trick didn't work, as you can't warm a dead body up with household radiators, and, even more incriminating, they found a speck of his wife's blood on the shirt he'd worn to work. He also didn't stop to think that the police might do some digging into his background. Nine times out of ten the murderer is known to the victim in one way or another. The coppers found out he was having an affair and that he'd changed his wife's life insurance. Classic case of how not to get away with murder!

James thought he was exceedingly clever, though, and would look down on all the other prisoners in the wing. Most murderers can be classified as narcissists, for a number of reasons – they lack empathy, they have a hugely inflated sense of their own importance, they are vain to the point they think they will never get caught. James would definitely have fallen into every category.

He was arrogant, rude, dismissive of me, and despite being allocated one of the most sought-after jobs – the laundry room – he refused point blank to work. All convicted criminals in the Scrubs *had* to work and attend workshops directed at their rehabilitation in order to eventually be released. James refused to work on the grounds that he was innocent. He wasn't innocent: he was bang to rights guilty!

He was constantly trying to override my authority by putting in requests to see the number one governor, insisting on putting his case across to him. The governor was fed up to the eyeballs of James asking to see him and for not pulling his weight, so he asked me to have him transferred. That happens a lot in the prison service, inmates being moved about anywhere from the Isle of Wight to the other end of England. Prisons call in favours from each other

– you scratch my back and I'll scratch yours kind of thing. I had to pull a few strings to get it done, but let's just say I wasn't shy about delivering the news.

I vividly remember him leaning over my desk, having what could only be described as a hissy fit, when I told him he had one last chance to pull his socks up or he was moving away from London.

'I don't know who you think you are,' he raged at me in his posh voice.

'Step back,' I warned.

He didn't move.

'Step. Back. Now.'

'Who are you to tell me what I can and can't do!'

He was a short man, maybe five foot six, and I couldn't help feeling he was trying to make up for his height. He eventually moved back; he knew he wasn't going to get any more out of me until he did.

'To answer your question, I'm the senior officer on the wing and I've already told you, you need to work. Failure to do so will lead to a transfer out of this prison. So,' I said, sighing, 'that's where we are at the moment.' The news was delivered coolly and calmly, of course.

He rolled his eyes. 'YOU can't move me.'

The threat of being moved on to another jail was often enough to get prisoners to toe the line. Why? Because a transfer would more often than not take them far away from their family, friends, legal team – anyone who might still be supporting them. Thus, isolating them even more than their life sentence had already done.

51

I knew for a fact James cared about seeing his kids because he'd made repeated attempts to contact them – which were rebuffed due to legal reasons. His dead wife's family were looking after them until they were eighteen and old enough to decide for themselves whether they wanted to visit their father.

'Unfortunately there's your first mistake. I can, and, if you're refusing to work, I will.' I sounded like a stuck record, we'd been here so many times before.

Meanwhile, he sounded like a five-year-old. 'I don't have to work. You can't make me.'

'I don't *need* to make you. If you don't contribute to this prison then you're moving out of it, buddy.'

James glared at me.

'I have nothing more to say to you. You have twenty-four hours. You can either get your head down and start working or you're out of here.'

I thought the idea of being far from his kids might have made him have a rethink but James's feelings of entitlement came first in the end. After twenty-four hours of sulking he told me he wasn't going to lift a finger, so I lifted the phone receiver instead and dialled him out of the Scrubs.

Lack of empathy on the scale at which James displayed wasn't uncommon among lifers. It's one of the reasons *why* people kill – because they don't feel anything when they do it. They are disconnected from the pain they inflict on others. That lack of empathy extends to all living creatures. How many times have you read a profile of a serial killer who, when they were a kid, liked to pluck off the legs of daddy longlegs or dissect dead birds or drop kittens from great heights? That kind of sick stuff. As you now know, I love animals, so to have to witness that level of cruelty broke my heart and filled me with rage.

Carl Johnson had not long been transferred to the Scrubs from HMP Brixton. He was in for raping and murdering his partner and was one of several sex offenders that had been moved over to D wing. He brought his pet budgie with him, which apparently he hadn't had for long. A sweet little green and yellow thing.

My first impressions of Carl were that I didn't have much of an impression. He wasn't gobby or obnoxious, he flew under the radar, more of a skulk around in the background type.

It was association hour and I'd been away from my desk for a short time, chatting to an officer on the fours. When I returned to my office I felt something crunch underfoot. I glanced down to see a crumpled piece of white, ruled paper. It wasn't uncommon to receive notes from prisoners. 'Gov, can you sort my visit out for me please.' A lifer might ask for me to speed up a request to see a family member. That kind of thing. Today's note was something quite different.

The handwriting was difficult to decipher but I got there in the end.

Gov, you need to check on Johnson's budgie.

That's odd. My brow furrowed.

Carl was never particularly into his budgie, and by that I mean making him toys, taking him out and about on the wing, doting on him the way some of the other prisoners would with their birds, so I wouldn't have immediately noticed its absence. It also wasn't my job to check over the cells every day.

Holding the piece of paper in my hands, I felt a sudden pang of unease. Something wasn't sitting right. Without further ado I got straight on the Tannoy.

'Can Carl Johnson please report to the SO's office.'

He was at my door within a matter of minutes.

'You wanted to see me?' He hung back by the entrance.

Carl was a mean-looking guy. Hard cold eyes. He'd clearly been in a fight or two. His cheek was scarred. His nose had at some point been broken. He had tattoo sleeves on both arms.

'I did. Come in, come in.'

He skulked up to my desk. His hands shoved deep into his pockets, his shoulders hunched forward.

'I haven't seen you with your budgie recently. Where's he gone?' I got straight down to business.

Prisoners weren't allowed to give their pet away if they'd had enough of them. It was their responsibility; those were the terms of agreement on which they were granted one.

'It's dead.' He coughed as he said it.

'It's dead?'

'Yeah.'

Not a flicker of emotion.

'Well, where is it now?' I asked.

'I flushed it down the toilet.'

All my hackles went up. 'Really! What a lovely gesture that was.' I was of course being somewhat sarcastic.

'Why on earth would you do that? Apart from it blocking up our sewage system, why would you do something so callous?'

He fired back: 'What's it got to do with you?'

I brushed away the confrontation.

'What happened to it?'

'It had an accident.'

Chills ran down my spine.

'What do you mean it had an accident?'

'I had some Blu Tack on the floor which he walked over and got stuck on.'

I raised my eyebrow sharply. 'Did it indeed.'

'Then he started losing his feathers.'

'Really.' The other eyebrow went up.

'And then it just died.'

'Is that so.' I felt sick to the stomach with his cock and bull story. 'You did that to that budgie, didn't you? Plucked out its feathers. You killed it?'

He looked at me and shrugged. No remorse. No feeling. There was nothing behind that cold stare.

I let my anger hang in the air for a moment. He didn't seem the slightest bit bothered.

'I can't believe how you thought doing that to a defence-less creature was acceptable. Especially one that already had enough punishment being stuck in a cell with you.'

'So what if I did?' he spat back.

My eyes narrowed. 'Get out of my sight!' My blood was curdling as I watched him slope off back to his cell. I felt sick to my stomach. Truly nauseous. I couldn't bear to think what that poor bird had been through. I just prayed he'd given it a quick death.

Not all lifers lacked empathy. Not all their crimes were cold-blooded murder. The prisoners we'd authorised to have budgies had all been carefully vetted first. You wouldn't catch Phones 4u flushing Fred down the toilet when he was done with him. Carl displayed the classic signs of a psychopath. Someone who I would never have granted a budgie to in the first place.

I needed to get to the bottom of what had happened. I did some sniffing around – asking the guys on his landing if they had seen or heard anything. I chatted to those that regularly interacted with Carl. He was the sort of bloke who would have gloated about what he'd done. I was sure there was someone on the wing he'd spoken to about his bird.

It didn't take long. I was right – he had mouthed off. The truth was even more grim than I'd imagined.

A lad two cells down from him told me how Carl had nicked some Blu Tack from the noticeboard in the education department. He had tried to stick the budgie's feet to the floor and when he couldn't manage it, Carl proceeded to pluck every single feather off it. Apparently he laughed when he described how it went into shock with the pain. He finished it off by drowning it in his sink. The fact he'd bragged about the torture made the whole thing even more sickening.

How had this fiend ever been granted a budgie in the first place? I couldn't rest until I knew the full story. I needed to know everything about him. What his backstory was. I was certain, thanks to my years of experience reading and understanding criminals, that this wasn't his first instance of cruelty beyond the poor woman he murdered. I returned to my office and pulled out his file.

Bloody hell. It was as thick as an encyclopaedia. There was my answer. I doubted anyone at HMP Brixton had taken the time to wade through all of this before they granted him his budgie.

The file made for a grim read. I didn't study the murder too closely, as I was interested in his behaviour leading up to it. Bingo. There, in the post-sentencing report, was my confirmation. Carl had previous – when he was twelve years old he'd strangled a cat and there were countless other incidents of him hurting animals. The news didn't surprise me one bit.

His current behaviour alarmed me greatly though. The sadistic way in which he killed his bird and the fact he showed no remorse, not a flicker of emotion over it, spelled trouble for D wing. If he could do that to a small defence-less animal while part of a rehabilitation programme, what else was he capable of? Prisons are delicate ecosystems. One badly behaved prisoner could rock the boat enough to make the whole wing capsize with similar violent and disruptive behaviour. Things can turn quickly in a volatile environment.

Not to mention the threat Carl now faced from other inmates. That's the funny thing with prisoners: they're quick to pass judgement over what they believe is right and wrong and quick to inflict their own kind of punishment. Paedophiles are always the ones at greatest risk of being lynched. Sex offenders are seen as the lowest of the low, so Carl already had his rape sentence weighted against him. If Phones 4u found out what Carl had done to his budgie, he'd be a dead man.

Carl Johnson's feet barely touched the ground after the full story came out. He was sent to the Seg for about a week and then I had him transferred to a higher security prison – HMP Full Sutton in Yorkshire.

Before he left I made sure he would absolutely, under no circumstances, ever be allowed to own another budgie. In the history report that was to be sent to the next prison I described what he'd done, in graphic detail, practically underlining my thoughts on the matter.

Chapter 6

WHAT DOESN'T KILL YOU MAKES YOU STRONGER

Bedford:
1975

The bright sunshine streamed through my bedroom window but I wasn't interested in what spring had to offer. I was lying on my bed, my hands clasped behind my head, staring at the ceiling, churning over feelings of anger and resentment. I was thirteen years old, hormonal and lost. I'd not long returned to England after spending nine years in the States. Mum had remarried and even though my new dad was a nice guy, I resented him because he wasn't my real father. I begrudged that my mum had taken his surname – Smith – and I was still called Frake. It made me feel like an outcast, and I already felt like one of those at school thanks to my American accent and how nobody else's parents seemed to be divorced. Blended families are all the rage now, but back then I was from the 'broken home'. I stuck out like a sore thumb! Early questions about my sexuality were also rippling through me, compounding my sense of being different.

I don't belong anywhere. Nobody really loves me. I'm all alone in the world. I stared at the cracks in the ceiling, my thoughts spiralling.

A knock at my door broke my fall into despair.

'Who is it?' I grunted.

My mum poked her head around.

'Fancy a drive, love?'

I looked at her suspiciously. It was Sunday. Going for a Sunday amble through the countryside was something I might do with my nan or granddad – who lived down the road – but not Mum.

'Ummm …' I hesitated.

'Come on, grab your things.' Her smile was a little too forced. Something was up.

She gave me little choice but to follow, so I slipped on my trainers and grabbed my jumper. Jeans, T-shirt and an unshapely pullover were what I lived in. I wasn't a trendy teenager – I wore what was comfortable. I'd had my hair chopped into a short 'Lady Di' do after a perm that went wrong. Again, it was practical, as it kept the hair out of my eyes.

We lived in a village not far from Bedford in a two-up two-down semi-detached house. Parked on the driveway was our Ford Capri with the longest bonnet I'd ever seen on a car in my life. It was a sickly mustard yellow colour.

'Well, get in,' Mum said briskly.

I yanked the car door open and slid inside. Still highly suspicious of 'our drive'. *I must have done something wrong.*

WHAT DOESN'T KILL YOU MAKES YOU STRONGER

The school's complained about me again and Mum's been waiting for the right moment to deliver the news. I was convinced I was in for it.

The drive through the twisty country lanes was filled with chitter-chatter, which was even more alarming. Mum didn't do light banter and something in the tone of her voice was off. Tense, I squinted into the glare of the sun, my cheeks burning as my anxiety rose. *Just spit it out* I wanted to yell.

There was a beautiful reservoir coming up, called Grafham Water, where Nan would take me for picnics. Nan spoilt me and my granddad rotten. She had the full picnic set – the woven basket with the compartments for the knives, forks and condiments, and it was always brimming with treats, including her perfectly triangular cut egg-and-cress sandwiches.

To my surprise, Mum turned off there. We pulled into the car park, the gravel crackling beneath the tyres. She switched off the engine and there was a pause. I reached for the door handle but Mum gently patted my leg to stop me.

Oh God, here it comes. Dread rose into my throat. I threw on my stroppy face in pre-defence for whatever telling-off I was going to receive.

But Mum still didn't say anything profound. She just carried on with her chit-chat, talking about everything from what a nice day it was to what she was planning on making for supper. She went around every house in Bedford before she finally got to the point.

Finally, there was a sharp inhale of breath. 'There's something I need to tell you,' she said.

'Oh-kay.' My heart fell through to my stomach.

'Your surname, Frake …'

'Yeah …'

'Well, it's about that.' Mum began nervously ironing the fabric of her trousers with her hands. She was always immaculately dressed. When she wasn't wearing her nurse's uniform – she was a nurse at Bedford hospital – she wore a skirt or slacks, blouse and a cardigan. Her shoulder-length hair was styled in big waves. She looked just like Deirdre from *Coronation Street* with her oversized blue-rimmed glasses.

'Go on.'

'Mr Frake, Gene Frake, he isn't your father.'

I was speechless.

'He adopted you when you were three, when I married him.'

What? Adoption? My face drained of colour. 'Oh my God, I'm adopted!'

'No, no, *he* adopted you. You're my child.'

None of this made any sense. My head suddenly exploded into a volley of questions, namely, if Gene wasn't my dad, who the hell was? Followed by: where is he? Is he English or American? What does he look like? How tall is he? Are we similar? Where does he live? And why, why didn't you tell me the truth?

I fired them out in such quick succession I barely gave Mum a chance to speak. She looked overwhelmed, like a rabbit caught in headlights.

She took in another deep breath. 'You real father is called Albert Schumach.'

'Is that German?' I exclaimed. 'That explains my blonde hair and why I'm so tall and …'

'No, he was American' – she paused – 'and I was in love with him.'

'Oh-kay, well, what happened?'

Tears filled her eyes as she went on to explain how my real father was a bit of a war hero. He was a test pilot in the US Air Force who performed many daredevil manoeuvres and then, one day, a stunt went very wrong.

Her gaze was fixed on the horizon as she said: 'He died in a crash. I was heartbroken.' She turned her head to face me. 'The good thing that came out of it was you.' She smiled through her tears.

'Have you got any photos of him?' I was off again, hunting for the truth.

That was the start of her shutting down.

'No.'

'Where did he come from?'

'Alabama.' One-word answers.

Have I got any relatives?

'Not many.'

'What does he look like?'

'Exactly like you, tall and blond. I don't want to talk about it any more.'

'But I've got lots of questions!' I pleaded.

'I knew you would and I can't answer them all. I just thought you ought to know.'

It was clearly extremely painful for Mum to relive the past. I could read that from her eyes. I was torn. I had all these unanswered questions which could finally put an end to my feeling lost, yet at the same time I didn't want to hurt my mum further by reopening wounds beyond what she could cope with. We rowed but I loved her deeply and I was fiercely protective of her. I was also only thirteen, and ill-equipped to deal with such an emotional blow. So, I did the only thing I thought I could do. I bottled up my feelings and left it.

There was no chitter-chatter on the drive home. The silence was deafening. My brain swimming. I concluded that Mum must have been married to my real father. After his death she married Gene Frake. When that went tits up she divorced him, returned to England where she then met my stepdad.

As soon as we got home, I leapt out of the car and ran up to my room. I felt like I was going to explode with emotion and I couldn't do it in front of Mum because she was already at breaking point. I lay on my bed, my heart ping-ponging between feelings of anger and heartbreak. I hated Mum for letting me believe Frake was my dad all of my life. He hadn't once written to me or tried to contact me since we left America and I thought he just didn't love me. That I was unlovable. I was also grieving for my dead father who I'd never get the chance to meet.

I grabbed Wendy, my panda teddy bear, and buried my face in her black-and-white fur. One of the last things Mum told me before she shut down was that it was my real dad's decision to call me Vanessa and he gave me Wendy on the day I was born.

Suddenly, the pain that had been building surged to the surface. The floodgates opened and I sobbed and sobbed. I lay there for what seemed like for ever, crying, clutching my beloved teddy bear, the only thing I had left of my father.

'How could she put herself through such abuse every single day?' I know you must be thinking. 'Why join the prison service?' I suppose it began when my mum told me about my father. When I say began, I mean that was when I learnt how to steel myself against pain. To block it out in order to protect myself. The thought of not knowing anything about my real dad hurt me like nothing else. It ate away at me like an insect gnawing from the inside out. I couldn't go on thinking about it, so instead I stamped it, him, out, obliterated every memory of the past from my mind. He simply didn't exist any more. Much like the prisoners I went on to deal with. If they were rude or abusive in anyway, I stamped out their comments in my head. Water off a duck's back as they say. Sounds cheesy, but I became like titanium. So that's why I told you a little about my childhood, so you could understand a little more about the *how*.

As for why I actually filled out the application form for the prison service when I was twenty-two years old? Honestly, I didn't know what else I was going to do. I'd been working with animals up until that point – milking cows to be specific.

I had a diploma in agriculture from Cannington College in Somerset and had been relief-milking on dairy farms in the countryside up until the milk quota crisis hit. The EU brought in new legislation whereby farmers who overproduced would be fined. As you can imagine, they had to make cutbacks, and the first people to go were the temp staff brought in to deal with the overflow, i.e. me. Work, excuse the pun, dried up, and I had to rethink my career.

I would have loved more than anything to carry on working with animals but there was no way I could be a vet. I'd seriously struggle with putting them to sleep; it would be heart-breaking. Most of the other animal-related jobs were charity ones or didn't pay enough and wouldn't bring me close to my dream of one day owning a farm out in the middle of the countryside. So, it was back home to Mum in Bedford and to the drawing board.

One thing I was certain of was that I wanted to make a difference to our country. The forces were out of the question. I'd applied and had been accepted into the navy – the Wrens – when I'd finished school at sixteen, but immediately turned it down when I found out that I wouldn't be sailing the world with the fleet. Women back then were strictly land based in mostly admin posts. I wanted to leave England, go to war and be in the front line. None of this desk-based nonsense, thank you.

The police force was next on my list. I could see myself patrolling the streets, being in the line of fire – in a different kind of way – and then I saw a poster in the London Underground that changed everything.

'You can make a difference.' It was a prison officer wearing a cap pointing his finger right at me. *I could make a difference*. The words called to me. The poster resembled General Kitchener's 'Your Country Needs You'. A nod to the forces. Maybe that's what caught my eye – the idea that I could serve for my county but in a different way, through the prison service.

I could do that job, I told myself. When I decide to do something, I always give it 110 per cent and that's what I felt about this. I hedged my bets and filled out both application forms, for the police and the prison service.

Mum didn't take the news well, and that's putting it mildly. It also didn't help it was around the time she found out I was gay. 'So that's why you want to go into the prison service then,' she snapped, feeding off the ridiculous stereotypes that only gay people want to be prison officers. Hurt people hurt people, I get that. I knew she was just upset and fearful. She was terrified I was going to get my head kicked in and she was right to worry. I tried to reassure her, but the conversation exploded into a row again when I asked her if she could dig up my birth certificate for the prison application.

I was sitting at kitchen table trying to make my way through a form that was as long as *War and Peace*. Who was my mother's mother's mother's gardener sort of level of detail. She came down the stairs clutching my birth certificate, her eyes red and brimming with tears and then, quite literally, she threw it across the table at me.

'Hey, what's going on?'

Crossing her arms defensively she said: 'Your father Albert Schumach is on there and I don't know if he's dead or alive.'

'What?' I was like a cartoon character shaking my head in disbelief. Surely this can't be happening again?

'I don't know if he's dead or alive. He didn't die in the plane crash but he might be dead now.'

I just stared at her. All the wind had been knocked out of my chest.

'Are you kidding me?'

'I want you to promise me you'll never try to find him.'

'But Mum ...'

'Please.' Tears were now running down her cheeks.

I was back between a rock and a hard place.

'Okay, but this time you've got to answer some of my questions. This is not fair on me. For nine years I thought my father was dead, and now you're telling me he could be alive.'

She nodded, and sat down opposite me at the table. Her hands were trembling. She clasped them together to steady herself.

'Firstly,' I said, 'was he a pilot?'

'No.' She dropped her head, shaking it.

'Okay. Was he even in the air force?'

'Yes.'

I tried so hard to ask open-ended questions, but it was hopeless. Mum's barriers had gone up again and she wouldn't let me in. My father must have hurt her so deeply, that's all I could think explained her behaviour. Mum has only ever wanted the best for me; I was mature enough to understand her defensive behaviour was all about her, not me.

That didn't make it any easier though. Everything I'd come to terms with, everything I'd believed since I was thirteen, shattered before me. My father, the war hero, was a lie. Yet again, I had no choice but to accept what little information my mum gave me and bottle up how it left me feeling. All her reveal served to do was add yet another ten layers of bricks onto the stronghold I'd built around me.

The prison service came back to me first, so I went with that. As it happens, the police force accepted my application two weeks later. I'd already made up my mind though and when I do that, I stick to it.

The time spent waiting had given me a chance to reflect on the two career paths. Although they were both in law and order, there was one very major difference between them. When a police officer arrests somebody, that's it, his job is done. He dusts his hands of the whole thing and moves on to his next case. A prison officer, however, has the job of looking after that somebody for however many years the judge has put him away for. They have the time and the chance to work with the prisoner and to hopefully rehabilitate them.

Not everyone sent to prison is beyond redemption. Many have made stupid mistakes, often through drug and alcohol dependency, and with a bit of help they could make a better, more useful life for themselves when they came out. I truly believed that.

THE GOVERNOR

I've got all the time in the world for genuine people who need help and want to better themselves. I wasn't naive: I read the papers and watched the six o'clock news. I knew our country had a problem rehabilitating prisoners, that various governments had tried it the hard way, the soft way, with not much luck. But I wanted to give it a shot. After everything I'd been through, I knew I had the strength to do the job.

Chapter 7

SHIT SHOW

HMP Wormwood Scrubs:
October 2002

I was having a week of it. Gobby prisoners giving me stick.

Lifers were in general okay to manage because, like I said, they had mostly accepted their sentence and were fairly settled. They were also much more tidy than those on remand because their cell was their home, for the foreseeable future. It isn't uncommon for lifers to develop OCD, obsessive-compulsive disorder, whereby they clean their cells repeatedly and have their belongings lined up in a certain order. Disorder is rooted in a feeling of a lack of control. Being locked up against your will is unnerving to even the most cold-hearted killer and I suppose many prisoners find if they can control their environment they can create a sense of inner calm.

One particular prisoner didn't manage this. Jayden Scott was near feral. He also had a mouth on him that was particularly foul whenever he came into contact with women. I had a couple of female staff on my wing and this vile individual would take every opportunity to spit lewd comments.

'I can see your bra through your shirt, miss,' he said to me once. Still on the subject of breasts: 'You don't get many of them to the pound do you, miss' was another corker he came out with.

He was in for aggravated burglary. When he broke into the couple's house he tied them up, beat them up and then ransacked the place. Nasty bit of work. He was twenty-five, white, shaved head. Skinny, the type that could be a lot stronger than his wiry frame let on.

Apart from being very rude, Jayden was generally provocative, causing me unnecessary grief. He was always the last to get locked up in his cell at night and always the first to challenge my orders. Clearly he had issues with discipline and female authority.

I'd already had him sent to the Seg for a tirade of threatening and abusive language. I didn't put everyone on report who insulted me, especially if they'd just had a 'Dear John' or something had happened to cause them to verbally lash out. I could be understanding. But this guy, as usual, had taken things too far.

It was fair to say my fuse was already short when Gemma, a prison officer, came up to me in near tears saying Jayden had been giving her hell. When she tried to put him in his place he'd said to her: 'What's wrong with you, have you got your period?'

My insides internally combusted with rage. For her and all the women he'd mouthed off to.

'That's it, I've had enough,' I snapped. 'We're putting him on basic.'

Basic – he'd have his TV removed, his association time reduced. He wouldn't be allowed out of his cell when the others were out. All privileged visits from family and friends were to be stopped. His canteen spending reduced. Limited fags and treats – that would hit him hard.

I rang up the twos, where he was, and told the officer up there what was what. Jayden went doolally. Kicking and screaming and throwing his stuff about the cell. I went up to see to his tantrum.

'What the hell do you think you're playing at?' I said, surveying the mess.

He called me every name under the sun. Think of the worst possible insult you can imagine. Got it? You're not even close to what he unleashed on me that day. It was the final straw. He could forget about being on basic; he was going back on report.

Report is what you do when someone is sent down to the Seg. It's what it says on the tin – a report on the incident, where the prisoner has to go before a Governor and plead guilty or not guilty to alleged breaking of prison rules, known as an adjudication – a mini court hearing. The Governor will decide after hearing the evidence whether the prisoner is guilty or not. If found guilty the prisoner could have a range of punishments given, from a caution to Cellular Confinement (known as CC). The prisoner is moved from his unit or wing to the segregation unit for a period no longer than 28 days. Other such awards could be loss of canteen (the ability to spend money in the prison shop), loss of TV, loss of association (mixing with other prisoners when unlocked in the evening), forfeiture of wages for a set number of days – basically, the loss of privileges in any combination the Governor saw fit. For serious breaches such as assaults on staff or other prisoners, the Governor could refer the matter to the police for investigation and possible prosecution. The prisoner will have two officers flanking him, the Seg senior officer and the officer who filed the report – i.e. me.

The grounds for proving an adjudication are 'beyond reasonable doubt'. This means that in order for a prisoner to be found guilty, the case presented by the officer who filed the report must be enough to remove any reasonable doubt in the mind of the governor in charge. Very often the prisoners held up their hands and admitted to their bad behaviour, knowing they didn't have a leg to stand on.

Jayden wasn't an immediate threat to staff or to other inmates, so his adjudication was put off until the following morning. He kicked his door for a while in protest but eventually settled down.

The governor found him guilty and he was given three days in solitary to think about his behaviour. That was a fair punishment I felt. I hoped it would be enough for him to clean up his act, although I wasn't holding my breath.

It was up to me to manage him when he returned. As always, I was firm but fair, treating him as I would any of the other lifers despite how much he'd pissed me off.

Two days later there were murmerings on the wing. That volatile atmosphere Jayden seemed to invoke returned. It was lunchtime, the prisoners were milling around, playing pool, dipping in and out of each other's cells, as they normally did, when a lifer called Miengo who was from Kuwait pulled me aside for a little tête-à-tête.

We were on the landing of the threes. I casually leaned on the railing so as not to draw any attention to us, while he did the same.

'What's up?' I said.

Miengo was a chubby guy, one of the few lifers who avoided the gym like the plague. He was in for a gangland murder, similar to Phones 4u. Wrong place at the wrong time. Friendly chap, had a good sense of humour. Rarely caused me any strife.

Flashing me a sideways glance, he said: 'Just wanted to give you a word of warning, gov. Watch your back.'

My eyebrow shot up. 'Okay, any particular reason I should?'

'I heard things. Be careful.' He lowered his voice.

I nodded. 'Thank you.'

That's what happens if you gain respect. Prisoners work with you rather than against you.

My antennae were up after our little conversation. I had eyes in the back of my head, on high alert waiting for something to kick off. Of course I had my suspicions – it didn't take a genius to figure out if someone had it in for me, who it might be: a certain foul-mouthed individual on the twos.

Sadly, it's not uncommon for prisoners to attack officers. Only the week before one of the staff had had an HP sauce bottle smashed over his head. He was rushed to hospital with a gash the width of my hand across his temple. Needed forty stitches. Officers having their jaw smashed to pieces by a prisoner welding a pool ball in a sock was another common assault on the wings.

I worried what was in store for me. I liked my face how it was.

It was my turn to be on duty that evening, which meant overseeing the wing while the prisoners were out on teatime association.

I was in my office, door open, my ears finely tuned in to the frequency outside. All of a sudden, the alarm went off. The noise was piercing, the walls of the huge wing almost juddered with its vibration. I could see from the flashing light in my office that someone on the threes had pressed the alarm. *This must be it.* This had to be what Miengo was on about, although I had no idea what to expect.

With the safety of my wing at the forefront of my mind, without a second thought I leapt out of my chair and sprinted onto the wing, heading straight for the stairs to the threes.

Two more paces and splash. It felt like I'd been rained on. Seconds later, I was hit with the stench – of faeces. I stopped dead in my tracks.

What the hell?

I glanced down. My arms, my chest, my entire body was covered in what I could only describe as watery brown

76

lumps. I was drenched in shit. It was even running down my face, dripping off my chin. I looked up to see who had thrown their faeces over me, but the balconies were clear, not a soul on them. Whoever had done it had stepped back into their cell.

This was one of those impossibly hard moments where I had to draw on all my strength not to show any emotion. Whoever had done the deed did so in order to humiliate me and get a reaction. Their second goal was still in my power to squash.

I wiped my face with the only clean fabric I had, the underarm of my sleeve, and calmly returned to my office to Tannoy for the wing to be locked up.

That would make whoever lobbed the shit over me very unpopular, as he was cutting everyone else's association time short.

Senior officers from other parts of the prison came rushing onto the wing having heard the alarm. As they filed through the door I greeted them with a calm and polite 'Evening!' Still dripping in shit.

'Potting' was what it was better known as in jail. A popular trick whereby a prisoner shovels their faeces into a plastic bottle. Pisses on it for a few days. Gives it a good old shake every now and then and chooses an opportune moment to hurtle their delightful cocktail on to some unsuspecting victim. In this case: moi.

The duty governor was next to race through the gates. There were seven governors in the Scrubs, each with their own specialism, but they all took it in turns to be on duty/

do the evening shift, everyone except for the number one that is.

He took one look at me and said: 'Come on, let's get you over to the uniform stores.'

I couldn't head there fast enough.

Once I'd collected my fresh trousers and shirt I went to the gym – which officers shared with the prisoners at alternate times – to use the showers.

Half an hour, at least, I must have stood underneath the hot water, scrubbing myself down with soap. Even then I thought I could still smell the stench on my skin. I ventured back to the wing with prune-like skin an hour and three fags later.

I clocked off at 11 p.m. and headed straight for the service station to console myself with a particularly unhealthy microwave meal and a bottle of vino. To hell with it. It was one of those days where I just didn't care.

The following morning, I was still fuming. Luckily I didn't have to go searching for an answer; Miengo met me on the landing. He began by telling me how pissed off all the lifers were for having their association ruined. I could tell a revolt was on the cards.

'You know I said to watch your back,' he went on.

'Yep.'

'What happened last night, that was the reason why.'

'I figured that.' I snorted. 'So who did it, Miengo?'

He glanced left to right, hesitantly. 'I can't really say, gov.'

'Miengo,' I pressed.

The big guy from Kuwait sighed out deeply. 'All right, gov …'

He proceeded to tell me who the perpetrator was. Two guesses who.

'Thanks very much.' I nodded. We went our separate ways. If it's possible to be furious and gleeful at the same time, that's what I was. Jayden may have tried to humiliate me but I was going to have the last laugh. I marched back to my office and picked up the phone.

'Could you please come and see me in D wing, sir.' I set my punishment in motion. And let me tell you, it was going to be far worse than three days solitary confinement.

The orderly officer arrived and this time I closed the door to my office so no prying ears could listen in.

An orderly officer is the same rank as a principal officer – so one above a senior officer – except they are also in charge of the day-to-day running of the prison. They are responsible for the timings of free flow, when the prisoners are escorted between wings, and they manage incidents alongside the duty governor. They would have the job of locking the wing up or moving the prisoner to the Seg. He or she was also responsible for sending prisoners out to hospital if required and also for the staffing of the jail.

'Right then, sir, about this potting,' I kicked off the conversation. 'A trusted source has informed me that Jayden was the culprit. I want him off the wing.' I made sure to list extensive abusive behaviour beyond his attack on me.

'I want him somewhere north of Watford,' I stipulated.

The orderly nodded. 'Let's get the bastard put down the Seg.'

We went up to the twos together, our shoes stomping across the metal grates. Anger powered through my every footstep. I couldn't wait to see him get his just deserts.

I stood back as the orderly cracked his door open. I had to be careful not to be seen to be driving the show because that might be read as vindictive. This wasn't revenge. This was justice.

Jayden was lying on his bed. His hands folded behind his head. He barely moved when the orderly entered his cell.

'You're coming with me!'

He didn't look the least bit surprised. He knew it was coming.

'You're going down the Seg. Get up and get moving.'

Jayden slowly rose to his feet. 'What about my stuff?' he said.

'Don't worry, we'll get it all bagged up and sent down to you.'

There were no tantrums this time. But as he walked past, he glared at me. I smiled back, cheerfully adding: 'Enjoy your stay.'

There was no question I'd got the wrong man. I trusted my source, plus Jayden didn't deny it at his adjudication. I'd just like to add, I wouldn't take the word of a prisoner every time, they could be lying too from vested interests, but I was pretty certain it was Jayden, even before Miengo grassed him up.

While Jayden was spending some quality time with himself, I spoke to my mate in OMU – Offender

Management Unit, the department responsible for transfers – and asked if there was a prisoner I could do a swap with, somewhere far far away from Shepherd's Bush.

She swiftly came back to me saying she had just the swap, with HMP Full Sutton in Yorkshire. So that was that. Bye-bye Jayden.

I got a bit of a surprise a week later. A member of the Prison Officers' Union rang me after hearing about my assault.

'Did you know you can get criminal compensation? Being potted is worth two grand,' he said enthusiastically.

Two thousand pounds for having shit showered on you.

'I'll get you the form if you want?'

That sounded like dirty money to me.

'Nah, you're all right, don't bother,' I replied.

Chapter 8

THE FIRST CUT IS THE DEEPEST

HMP Wormwood Scrubs: February 2003

I sat up bolt upright in bed, covered in sweat. The image of *her* planted in my mind. This poor woman, dying in pain, the bed sheets soaked with her blood. She was writhing around, her last breaths laboured as she died from what he did to her. What he did to her insides.

Vanessa, get a grip.

But my heart was still going. Pounding from my nightmare. Only, it wasn't make-believe. It was real. It did happen to her. She did die in excruciating pain.

It was the only time in my career that I couldn't shake the thought of what a prisoner had done. Hounding me, the images followed me everywhere. When I went to work, when I came home, at night – when I lay in bed. I'd thought nothing could get past my wall. I was wrong.

* * *

THE FIRST CUT IS THE DEEPEST

The day had begun the same as all the others. Arriving at the Scrubs at 7 a.m. Work didn't officially start until 8 a.m. but I always like to be early for things. It also gave me an hour to acclimatise. Have my cups of tea, smoke my fags, glance over the papers. Have a natter with staff on the nightshift who were about to clock off, find out how the lifers had been behaving since I last saw them. I didn't have to do it, but there was something in me that wanted to get ahead. Just in the small things, nothing particularly ambitious. I liked to know the lay of the land as it gave me an advantage, and having the upper hand on the prisoners was how you ran a wing successfully.

The day ticked along nicely, no major incidents, nothing noteworthy to report. And then Steve popped his head in my door come home time at 7 p.m.

'Fancy one down the pub?' he asked.

I glanced at the pile of manila files towering to my right. Reports: I hadn't had to write them when I was at Holloway; it was something you had to do every twelve months on the lifers here though. Bit like a school report, reviewing their behaviour, their interaction with prison staff and other lifers. Were they taking part in classes? Were they doing their jobs without too much whinging? Were they keeping their noses out of trouble? The better their report, the more likely they were to move through the system without any hiccups, i.e. earning privileges along the way and avoiding anything that might add to their already lengthy sentence. If they behaved themselves they didn't risk being moved on to a category A prison.

THE GOVERNOR

It was a lengthy old process, a bit of a chore and not something you could do with people knocking on your door every five minutes, so I saved it for after teatime when the wing had quietened down.

'Sorry, mate, love to, but I'm snowed under,' I replied.

I was staying late to get it done. But, if I'm honest, I would have turned down the offer of a drink anyway.

There is a massive drinking culture in prisons. Staff are generally big boozers. It's easy to understand why: it took us away from the brutality of the world in which we worked. Police officers see similar violence in their jobs and are equally as partial to a drink when their shift ends. It's not for nothing they are always characterised as troubled on TV dramas. Like us, their work–life balance is askew. I drank a lot when I worked in HMP Holloway. Too much, maybe three bottles of Bacardi a week. Never on my own, always down the pub with the girls when we clocked off. Something shifted when I moved to the Scrubs though. Initially, I think it was my bitterness at being forced to leave the place I loved to work in a men's prison. I wasn't interested in becoming mates with the staff after hours because I didn't want to invest my heart in the job. What was the point? I might be moved on again.

However, as time passed, and as I grew to love my job, I also stopped missing the taste of alcohol and the feeling it gave me. I'm not painting myself as a saint here – I still drank, the odd glass when I got home, but nothing like before. My head felt clearer, my brain felt sharper and I found the professional distance I now had with my colleagues beneficial.

Steve left for the local with the lads while I poured myself a cuppa and cracked on with the backlog of work. I had a slurp and picked up the next file to the right of me: Matthew Waldram. It was so thick it could have been a novel.

I sighed heavily before opening it. I didn't like the guy; there was something particularly unsavoury about him. Hard to put it into words, but he had a sinister way about him that left me feeling cold after our interactions. He was a big bloke in his thirties, worked out in the gym every day; put it this way, I wouldn't like to be caught down a dark alley with him. I knew he was in for murdering his partner, as so many of the lifers were, but I had no idea of the ins and outs of his case.

The court transcripts were included in his file, which I had to read to make my report. They contained everything – from what happened, to what they were charged with, the whole shebang. All the info I needed to draw a full picture of the prisoner's rehabilitation.

I said I was like titanium, and for the most part I was, but every so often, something slipped through my guard. This was one of those evenings. For that reason it remains one of the most memorable in my career.

The prosecution in Matthew's case told how he was watching porn at home with his girlfriend. This led to them having sex. No surprises there. It was thought they were both taking drugs.

So far, nothing too shocking. I took another sip of tea and turned the page.

As you might expect when a couple watched porn together, things started to get heated. He treated her more roughly. The sex turned increasingly violent.

Okay, this was more like the sort of behaviour I'd expect from a murderer. I turned the page.

What Waldram proceeded to do to her was so appalling, so violent, that he caused severe internal haemorrhaging.

I felt my stomach knot.

Instead of rushing her to a hospital, he let her bleed to death, and then dumped her body like she was a piece of rubbish.

A roll of nausea worked its way from my stomach to my throat. It was horrific. Truly sadistic. I couldn't quite believe one human could do that to another.

I'd heard and I'd seen a lot of gruesome things by this point in my career, but Matthew's case disturbed me more than anything I'd experienced. I don't know if it was because I suddenly felt my vulnerability as a woman. Because the violence was so extreme? I'm not sure what happened, but I just couldn't get the images from my head.

Part of the problem was that I'd never had any profes-sional training to deal with hearing such graphic abuse – none of us staff had. I was unsure how to deal with the overload of information.

I was conflicted. Part of me wanted to throw the file across the room, to get it as far away from me as possible. At the same time I wanted to read on. I needed to know how the story ended, even though I knew the ending. The judge always does a summing-up at the end of a case and I hoped he'd say something poignant, call Matthew a monster, beyond redemption, condemn him to the fate he deserved. I suppose, as strange as this might sound, I was searching for some sort of justice beyond knowing he was banged up 50 yards away from me on the twos.

The judge didn't let me down. He described the murder as a heinous crime. Matthew was branded nothing short of evil for showing no remorse.

I closed the file and slid it to the side. Breathing a deep sigh of relief that justice had been served.

Hang on a minute. Why was I still feeling anxious? Why couldn't I shake that icky feeling? I pulled out a fag from my top pocket. *That'll do it. That always calmed me down.* I inhaled deeply, taking the smoke into my lungs.

The cigarette did work, right up until I stubbed the end out in the ashtray. It was like she was there in the room with me. I could see her on the bed, her face as she lay dying in pain.

For fuck's sake. I stood up abruptly, my chair scraping across the floor.

I paced the tiny office back and forth, all my instincts telling me to leave, *go home.* My head was telling me to sit back down and finish the job in hand. To stop being so emotional.

I did sit back down. That was me all over, seeing the job through to the bitter end. There were papers in there referring to a separate court case involving Matthew's mother.

She was convicted of perverting the course of justice. She'd lied to police about Matthew's whereabouts at the time of the murder, giving him a false alibi by saying she was with him. The case went into detail about the mother's relationship with her son. It sounded very strange, almost sexual. She certainly 'loved her boy'. A history of abuse and incest is fairly common to see in the childhoods of murderers. If that's all you ever know growing up, it's not surprising that murderers inflict the same kind of abuse on their victims later in life.

As for Matthew's report, I'd be lying if I said there wasn't a part of me that wanted to give him a really bad write-up after reading all of that, but I couldn't. The guy was doing what was asked of him. He was no better or worse than most of the criminals on D wing. I had to remain impartial because – as hard as it was sometimes – that was my job.

It didn't mean I couldn't shake his story from my mind though. The whole drive home my brain was spinning with graphic images. With the words of the judge. Mostly, though, with the pain I imagined she must have felt in those last dying moments.

I pulled in at the service station in Camden, which had become my nightly routine. Service station, microwave meal – or a ping-ping as I called it – and then home. They must have known my face in there by then.

Even the newspapers on the rack made me feel queasy. I couldn't bring myself to read their headlines; I wanted to shy away from the world and all its brutality. I swung around into the booze aisle. Hovering there for a moment before deciding to pull a bottle of red from the shelf. To hell with it, I needed something to take the edge off.

I suppose *home* was never somewhere I wanted to rush home to. It was a two-bedroom maisonette split over two floors in Bakersfield, next door to my old prison. It had been built in the seventies and was nice enough. Clean and tidy but lacking character and ambience. It was more practical than cosy. Somewhere I could get my head down at night.

Only I couldn't that evening. I must have stayed up watching TV for hours on the sofa trying to wind down. Even my favourite detective, Inspector Morse, couldn't calm me.

You'd probably think I had my bellyful of crime working in a prison, reading files like those of Matthew Waldram, but I am addicted to watching crime dramas. The clue gathering, the problem solving; I loved to race the detective to the finishing line. I found the whole thing soothing – watching something that fascinated me from the comfort of my couch. But that night, it wasn't doing it for me.

I plonked the plate in the dishwasher, my uniform in the laundry basket. I brushed my teeth, and WHACK the images were back with a vengeance.

It tossed my thoughts into even greater turmoil. Suddenly I was not only haunted by a dead woman but also by immense rage – anger at myself for not being able to block it out. What was wrong with me? I'd always been able to in the past. Was I going soft? *For goodness' sake, Vanessa, get a grip*, I screamed internally. Of course it was the most normal thing in the world to feel affected by Matthew's file, but you're not encouraged to think that way in the prison system. Perhaps I saw it as a sign of weakness.

The night was spent tossing and turning with images that could rival the worst kind of horror film until I woke in a cold sweat. Three hours later I walked onto the wing and unlocked Matthew's cell as I would normally.

'Morning, how are you?' I asked, in my usual impartial way.

He was rubbing the sleep from his eyes as he said: 'Yeah, I'm alright, gov.'

Part of me despised him but I would never have shown him that. I couldn't let how I was feeling cloud my professionalism. And plus, it wasn't for me to judge him. He'd been judged.

The nightmares lasted for several months. To try and overcome the insomnia I kept telling myself, 'stuff and nonsense', you know, like French and Saunders used to do in their sketch of the two old women in Barbours. Stuff and nonsense, get on with it, get a grip.

And then one day, it lifted, just like that, and I was able to sleep again. Of course it didn't really go; horrific things like that can't just vanish into thin air. They build up into what is now well recognised as post-traumatic stress disorder. Unfortunately, I only found that out much later.

Chapter 9

DRUGS ON A WIRE

HMP Wormwood Scrubs:
September 2003

'You went from milking cows to locking people up?' one of the officers on D wing exclaimed. We were on our break and he'd asked me how I'd ended up working in the nick.

'Yep, that's pretty much it in a nutshell,' I nodded, taking another bite of my sandwich.

'You could argue there's not much difference between the two. Some of the animals you get in here ...'

Before we could get stuck into an involved discussion about animal-like behaviour, my phone started ringing. It was Steve Smith on the fours. He's passed away now bless him. A brilliant officer. He got on very well with prisoners but didn't suffer fools; he was shrewd as anything around them, the perfect combo. My lasting memory of Steve will always be when I first met him – unlocking a cell door with a fag in his mouth. Everyone could smoke back then before the ban was put in place in July 2007.

'Boss, boss,' you got to come up and see this.' He sounded breathless.

When someone phones in like that you don't mess around and say, 'What is it?' You just get off your arse and go have a look. He wouldn't be ringing me unless it was something significant.

Every day, while the prisoners were out working or on courses, the officers carried out a 'fabric check' on every single cell on the wing – a 'locks, bolts and bars' as it was called. They checked that everything was secure, that there wasn't a gaping hole in the wall and a ladder hanging out the window. It's not a search as such, just a nosey around the cell to see what's what.

As I clinked my way up the stairs to the fours, I hoped what was about to be unveiled was an Aladdin's cave of contraband. Phones, drugs, maybe even a few weapons for luck. Sadly no matter what we did, they still found a way into the prison, and drugs were becoming a serious issue on D wing.

You can tell when a wing has a drug problem. The place has a vibration, an underground current. Gatherings on association, murmurings as you walk along the landings. Prisoners quickly disappearing into their cells when they see you coming. The smell of cannabis wafting past your office as you're trying to do some work was a particular give-away. Trouble was, we were struggling to catch them red-handed. Phones 4u was one of the few getting nabbed for contraband, but he wasn't dealing the drugs, they were coming from somewhere else.

DRUGS ON A WIRE

Cell 445 belonged to James Taylor. He was a drugs pusher, serving life for killing someone in a fight. White, six foot one. Average build. Huge great big tattoo of an eagle head on his right arm. I hadn't had much to do with him: he kept his nose out of trouble most of the time. It's always the quiet ones! Anyway, he was out at a workshop, so we had the place to ourselves.

I stepped inside the poky cell and crossed my arms.

'Go on then, let's have it,' I said, half expecting Steve to begin with turning over the mattress. Instead, he led me to the window.

'Over here, gov.' His eyes were sparkling.

Back then, every cell had a small barred window which the prisoners could open. Nowadays they are fastened shut with a ventilation hatch.

Part of the check was banging on the windowpane to check it hadn't been taken out and put back.

Steve was pointing into the sky. I followed his finger and frowned.

'What exactly am I supposed to be looking at?'

'Look closer.'

Squinting, I had another go but couldn't see anything except for crisp blue sky, a few clouds and the odd pigeon.

I shrugged. 'I give up. What's going on?'

Steve threaded his hand through the bars and hooked his finger around what at first looked like thin air.

'See it now?' he said, tugging at something. Blink and you would have missed it, carving up the autumn sky, glinting in the sunlight.

'Bloody hell!' My mouth fell open as he pinged the fishing wire. One end was tied to the bars, the other …

'Where does it go?' I gasped.

Steve gave it a little shake. Our eyes followed the glint – over the twelve-foot prison wall, up some more to the rooftop of the neighbouring Hammersmith Hospital. It was a zip line, all the way into cell 445.

'We need to get security in here, now.' I unhooked my radio.

There were now three of us gathered around the window, staring in awe at the handiwork.

'Well, I'd never.' Security Principal Officer George Maxwell shook his head. He pulled out his camera and took a picture of the wire, which would be used as evidence in Taylor's adjudication. Maxwell was a character and a half. Very old school, he reminded me of Mr Mackay off *Porridge*, because he was Scottish, because he had a moustache and because he walked like the TV character. I could imagine him striding up the landings shouting: 'Fletcher!'

The question we were all wondering was *how*. How had this line been set up? It was pure genius. Something James Bond would come up with. Forget your dead pigeons and your tennis balls – yes people used to, and still do, hide drugs in dead pigeons and sports balls and chuck them over the wall. That zip line trumped them all; it was banging.

My theory? It was catapulted in stages, over the wall and up a further hundred foot to the roof of the hospital, obviously with the help of someone on the other side. The fact it was such fine fishing wire made it practically invisible to the naked eye.

'No wonder we had a drugs epidemic on D wing! God only knows how many parcels of heroin had zipped down that line, straight into the hands of James Taylor,' I scoffed.

'Indeed,' George nodded. 'Time I had a chat with security at Hammersmith. I'll leave you to deal with Mr Taylor.'

I locked the cell so no one could come in and tamper with it. Meanwhile, George Maxwell scooted across to the hospital to speak to their security team about how this could have happened. As it turned out, the roof had public access, and it wasn't alarmed. Anyone could have gone up there, hung a little bag on the zip line and whizzed it over to the fours on D wing.

When James Taylor came back from his workshop, I was waiting for him. Me and two officers, in my office. I won't lie: I was looking forward to the confrontation. There is a sense of immense gratification when you catch a prisoner red-handed. This was a big find for us. What's more, it was going to help clean up the wing, something I was feeling increasingly passionate about.

'Tay-lor,' I bellowed as soon as I saw him skulk past. 'Come in here, now.'

He came immediately, not a hint of apprehension on his face. 'What is it, gov?' he said innocently.

I pushed back into my chair, limbering up to deliver the news.

'I've got a bit of a problem.'

James glanced left to right at the officers flanking him, eyeballing him. 'What do you mean?

'Well, we found something in your cell.'

He shrugged. 'Don't know what you're on about.'

'You have absolutely no idea what I might be referring to?'

Shrugging again. 'No idea, gov.'

I snorted.

This pleading of ignorance went on for a while. I gave him several chances to fess up but when it was clear he wasn't going to budge I laid it out straight for him.

'We found a line going from your cell to Hammersmith Hospital.'

He'd mastered the blank expression.

'I'll give you ten out of ten for how ingenious it was, but unfortunately for you …' I paused, just as Simon Cowell does before delivering his verdict to contestants. '… you're going to the Seg.'

And still he didn't say a word. Not how it was done, who had been helping him on the other side. He knew when to keep his mouth shut. James just looked at me as if to say, 'For fuck's sake.'

He got fourteen days' punishment down the Seg on cellular confinement. Just an hour a day out of his cell to exercise in the yard, alone. That's a harsh punishment. Imagine being locked up in a cupboard-sized room for twenty-three hours straight, with no TV, no social media to scroll through, nothing to entertain you, for fourteen days.

Prisoners were allowed to see the doctor if they were feeling unwell or struggling with the anxiety of being banged up, but the punishment would continue to be enforced unless there were extreme circumstances that warranted stopping it. If there wasn't a punishment for bad behaviour, then the prisoners would be running riot.

For a while things settled on D wing. However, it's a well-known fact that as soon as you shut one door another one opens. Another prisoner steps right into the previous shoes. Try as you might, it's virtually impossible to stop drugs coming into a prison.

George Maxwell and I had to come up with a plan to catch them off guard.

Chapter 10

ACE VENTURA: PRISON DETECTIVE

HMP Holloway: 1987

Drugs were never a major issue in Holloway. Yes we had them, but if we found a piece of cannabis the size of your little fingernail, we were doing well. I put that down to the fundamental differences between women and men. Female prisoners aren't on the make so much. There is huge potential to earn money selling drugs in the nick and men are quicker and much more interested in capitalising on that market. Women are more focused on surviving their sentence, while their thoughts are with the family they have left behind.

However, when we did find them, nine times out of ten they were hidden in the food packages.

The laws have changed now, whereby only clothes, paperback books and magazines are allowed to be given as gifts to prisoners, but before about 1988 family and loved ones were allowed to send remand prisoners food packages. Anything from their favourite chocolate bar to a chicken korma. It was a treat on top of their three meals a day and their canteen allowance. The ruling dated all the way back to Victorian times, when prisoners had to rely on family and friends on the outside to bring them food. If you had nobody, you basically went hungry living off bread and water.

For obvious reasons, the law was an utter ball ache for the staff because every single item of food, no matter how small it was, had to be searched for contraband. Even if it was a Mars Bar – because we all knew it was easy enough to reseal an opened one of those and make it look like it hadn't been tampered with. We would have to open the chocolate bar up, cut it in half, look inside, prod it about a bit, and when we were satisfied it was clean, send it up to the wing.

At that time Holloway often had a disproportionally high number of West African and Nigerian prisoners. Most of them had been done for being drug mules. One woman was even caught at Heathrow airport carrying a dead baby stuffed full of drugs. Precious was her name; she was pulled over when someone noticed something suspicious, i.e. the baby wasn't moving. I did feel for these women as most of them had been victims of abuse, enslaved by some drug lord out in Africa who threatened their family's life if they didn't bring the drugs over to the UK for them. They were probably promised a few thousand quid for the risk, but in reality would have ended up with only a couple of hundred and a twenty-year sentence for bringing a kilo of heroin over. Whatever their circumstances, they had broken the law, so that couldn't go unpunished. However, that didn't stop me having empathy for their situation.

What I also felt sorry for was me, and the rest of the officers who were lumbered with the task of riffling through their local delicacies – goat and fish-head curry. Yuk! That fishy smell I'll never forget as long as I live. Or those glassy eyes glaring up at me from that swampy soup. Imagine the workload for us though: if there were two hundred prisoners on remand at Holloway, half of those would receive packages. That's a hundred meals to search, every single day. Ball ache.

We didn't have a special room dedicated to food searches. It was a few tables in an office and a team of us delving in and out of dishes. No gloves, no proper hygiene. We looked in one with a spoon and then looked in the other. It wouldn't be unreasonable to say that the Mars Bar might have a bit of a fishy aftertaste after we were done with it.

It often turned into a bit of a competition – who could find the most drugs in a day. I've always been quite competitive, so I took delight in announcing my discoveries. It was such a shitty job, it kept things light-hearted when we were knee deep in fish curry.

The most cleverly disguised drug smuggle, without a doubt, hands down, went to the individual who tampered with a Kit Kat.

From the outside, the nation's favourite chocolate bar looked perfect, as if you'd just picked it up from the shelf in

Sainsbury's. I did my usual tearing open of the foil, snapping it in half. Nothing. I was about to give it the all-clear when, suddenly, something struck me as odd about it. I held it up to the strip light. Why was the colour of the chocolate on the top different to that on the bottom?

I had a hunch I might be onto the biggest find of the day. That flame of competitiveness ignited inside. I kept it under my hat while I picked up the knife and carefully scored the other way this time, lengthways along the biscuit.

Bingo.

There, flattened lengthways and the size of a pea, was a piece of silver foil.

The other officers were going to be green with envy. I unwrapped the package and, just as I suspected, found a small amount of a white substance, which later tested positive for heroin.

The craftsmanship that must have gone into that! They even stamped the Kit Kat sign on the bar. I was positively glowing inside when I broke the news to the rest of the room.

'Look what I've found!' I announced.

Just as I suspected, there were a lot of murmurings and 'Damn I wish I'd had that bar' comments.

The one downside of my victory was the paperwork. It was an absolute pain because for every discovery you had to fill out a report before bagging it up for evidence. Once that was done, though, there was one more small reward to come: delivering the news to the intended recipient of the Kit Kat, who would no doubt have known about what was coming and very much been looking forward to their care package.

This wasn't Carly Jones's first run-in with the deliveries. In fact, pretty much every week her mum tried to smuggle drugs in for her. She was a master of invention, her favourite trick being slicing open the stems of flowers and hiding the heroin inside a beautiful bunch of fuchsias. We'd intercepted her attempts so many times it was a wonder she even bothered trying any more.

Carly Jones was a colourful inmate. She swore like a trooper and her presence was always felt on the wing. She was in and out of Holloway like a jack-in-the-box, mostly for drug-related crimes, stealing from shops, nothing particularly serious, but she was never in prison long enough to ween herself off her addiction. Sadly there were a lot of women like Carly in Holloway. Women for whom the system was not helping. I will address this later, my views on drug-related crimes and the problems with rehabilitation, but for now, Carly Jones and her Kit Kat …

She was sitting on the bed in her cell when I arrived. I peered through the hatch first and then unlocked her door.

'Oh, hello, miss.' She looked up at me, a little startled.

'A word if you don't mind, Carly.'

She was fidgeting with the cuff of her sweater, pulling it up over her hands. She had this nervous disposition about her, as many of the drug addicts had. Her eyes were hollowed, her cheeks cut like glass, her black hair messy and wild around her bony shoulders. She looked fragile and ill, like someone who was possessed, and I thought she may have been if it weren't for the gob on her. Despite her state, Carly always had something to say, some smart-alec reply.

'You had a parcel come in today.'

Her eyes lit up, although she managed to keep the rest of her expression blank.

'Unfortunately,' I went on, 'there was an illicit item inside. So … you won't be getting it now.'

'Oh right.' She continued to play dumb. Of course she knew.

'And don't expect any more food in.'

There came the eye-roll. The dismay. 'For fuck's sake,' she spat. A thump of her fist on the mattress. I left her to her tantrum and headed back down to the search room.

Catching Carly might not seem like a massive deal; it was only a pea-sized wrap after all, and she was hardly a big drugs pusher. But it was all part of something much greater – intelligence gathering. We now knew that 'Carly Jones consistently attempts to get drugs in'. She would be flagged up on the system. She would be watched more closely, as would her associations with other prisoners who might be trying to do the same thing. Small brushstrokes which would eventually lead to the unveiling of a bigger picture. Intelligence gathering is the key to keeping a prison safe. I had no idea at the time it would play such an important part in my life.

As for the food parcels – they were eventually stopped because of the security risk. As well, the searches were taking up too many man hours and the prisoners were considered to be fed well for the £2.02 spent on them each day – not much less than the £2.87 spent on hospital patients. Asides from books and clothes, family and friends can also give prisoners money. It's put into an Inmate's Personal Cash (IPC) account. Families can also order and pay for newspapers to be delivered to the prison through local newsagents.

While we are still on the subject of food, if I said to you, 'Giant African snails', what would you think? Probably not, yum, that's tonight's dinner sorted then. That didn't cross my mind either when I saw the huge creature slithering across my desk, leaving a slime trail behind.

It was 1991 and I was working in reception, which is where inmates are 'welcomed' into the prison, where their warrants are checked over, where their property is searched, where they are handed their essentials like toothbrush, deodorant, toothpaste, shampoo, razor – the Human Rights Act allowed for that – and the bog-standard WRVS clothes if they didn't have any clean clothes of their own. Unlike male prisoners who have to wear prison-issue uniform once they are convicted, women prisoners, whether convicted or on remand, had the right to wear their own clothes. However, we often handed them out because a worryingly large proportion of the women coming into Holloway were homeless, arriving in rags and infested with lice.

Reception was also where prisoners were discharged. It wouldn't be unusual to see figures like eighty coming in and ninety going out on a daily basis – a huge turnover. There was another group of prisoners who would pass through reception, and that was the women on the enhanced wing. Enhanced meant trusted. They were criminals but they weren't violent. Generally, they were well behaved. No surprise that a lot of the enhanced wing were West African, the women who had been caught for drug-muling.

Every Sunday, the enhanced wing were granted a temporary release licence, whereby they could leave the prison for a couple of hours to walk into town – Holloway – for food shopping. They would have a big meal together in the evening.

We didn't worry about them escaping, doing a run for it while they were at the market, because, quite frankly, where were they going to go? Most of them didn't have any family in the UK. They didn't have any money, well, maybe £20 in their back pocket for shopping, but how far would that get you? They'd also been risk assessed. If in the unlikely circumstance they did do a runner, we would call the police who'd track them down with a fair amount of ease.

I'd been in the job for more than four years now, promoted to a senior officer – one of the youngest SOs in the country – and a few weeks into my eighteen-month stint on reception. As part of your training you were moved around the prison and you could put in for a transfer if you needed a change of scenery. It helped grow your skillset and, quite frankly, keep you sane. The only transfer I'd asked for was to the great outdoors. I'd come from doing six months mowing the lawns in the gardens, which was heavenly. Reminded me of all the fresh air I used to get milking cows in the countryside.

Reception – because of the to and fro – was a lively place to work. Except on Sundays when nothing much at all went on, the only traffic being the enhanced prisoners on day release.

This one particular Sunday I was in the property office, heading up the searches being carried out on the prisoners' belongings. Much like the security checks they do at airports on your hand luggage. The ladies on the enhanced wing had just returned from their shop down the market. They'd been strip-searched and their bags had been run over by the well-trained nose of a passive dog who can sniff drugs off a mile away. It didn't matter how trusted they were, they were always searched.

A female officer, new to the job, appeared at the door of the property room. She was clutching a plastic bag. Her eyes as big as saucers.

'Is everything okay?' I asked.

She was a slim girl, blonde, hair pulled back into one of those chignon buns and couldn't have been much older than twenty-two. Wet behind the ears, as they say in prison. Without a word, she carried the bag at arm's length to the table, plonked it down and gave me a look that screamed, *Do something*.

My eyes flitted between her, the bag, and then the *ginormous* snail that poked his head out of it. When I say ginormous, I mean the size of a small football. A huge great big thing, sliming onto my desk.

I recoiled in horror.

'What is it?' the officer asked me.

For the first few seconds I was frozen with surprise. 'I don't know!' I finally replied. Obviously it was a snail but nothing like I'd seen before. 'Where the hell did you find it?'

'One of the women brought it back from the market. She says it's for their supper tonight.'

'Come again?'

'They want to eat it.'

After I'd recovered from my initial shock, my abhorrent feelings against animal cruelty kicked in. 'They are not eating this,' I said, protectively. 'It's a living creature. They are not taking it upstairs to the kitchen to murder it.'

'Well, what should I do with it?!' the officer exclaimed.

'I don't know, ring London Zoo, see if they know anything about it.'

It was making tracks, oozing slime everywhere. 'But in the meantime, get it off my table!'

The poor officer gingerly scooped it back into the bag with as little contact as possible.

She was back at my door quicker than I expected. I don't know what I thought the zoo keepers would say, but it wasn't: 'London Zoo want me to bring them the snail.'

For Chrissake. I was trying to do a job and losing an officer on an already skeleton staff was far from ideal. At the same time, I didn't like the thought of any harm coming to the snail.

'Okay, we'll call you a cab,' I agreed. The zoo was only five minutes up the road in Camden after all. I couldn't see the delivery taking much time. We put the snail in a large cardboard box and let it ooze away in there.

The officer went off with the creature and I was left dealing with a very irate Nigerian woman.

The prisoner who had bought it was beside herself. Distraught I'd taken her delicacy away, she was ranting and raving. She was quite a large lady, thick set, with really long pointy fingernails that were painted scarlet red.

'What was it?' I tried to get an answer ahead of the zoo.

'Food for tonight,' she replied, without a second thought for the snail.

'It's absolutely not!' I exclaimed. 'That's not why you're given temporary release, so you can go pick up animals and cook them alive.'

Her English was broken but her gestures were easily translatable. She was shrugging and waving her talons around; she just didn't see the problem. I suppose in her culture, it would be as normal as me having fish and chips.

'Supper' turned out to be very rare, endangered species of giant African snail that can grow up to 20 centimetres long and live for up to ten years.

In Nigeria, they are a delicacy and are often called Congo meat. I discovered the horrible process by which they cook them. First they boil them alive in hot water, extract them from their shell, slice them up and fry them until they are crunchy, or they're chucked in a stew with peppers and served up with rice. They were becoming increasingly endangered because of jungle deforestation.

I stopped her temporary release. She was removed from the super-enhanced wing. I couldn't have prisoners going around buying endangered species on the black market.

That was a crime in itself. She'd clearly picked it up from some dodgy market stallholder.

Meanwhile, the giant snail found a very happy home at London Zoo. Who knows, maybe it found a mate and its offspring are there today, sliming away? I like to think so.

Chapter 11

WHO LET THE DOGS OUT?

HMP Wormwood Scrubs:
September 2003

'If we've found this, who's to say there's nothing else,' PO George Maxwell said of the zip-wire find. It was a fair point. We needed to act fast.

Hammersmith Hospital security team were working well with us. We were in constant communication. They had alarmed their rooftop, cut it off from public access, but great as that was it wasn't our main concern any more. That delivery route was dead. We now needed to concentrate all our efforts on finding the drugs that had come in via the zip wire.

There was only one real way of achieving such an ambitious goal and that was to carry out a drugs bust. We had to surprise them. If those lifers knew that we were about to check their cells for gear we'd hear half the wing flushing their toilets at the same time.

So how were we going to catch them off guard? We needed to bring in the dogs.

Active dogs and passive dogs. Two types, two very different hunting noses. Active dogs are noisy. When they get a whiff of contraband they start barking and going nuts – they are used to search areas. Passive dogs are used to search people; they don't disturb anything. If they find something suspicious they sit quietly, and far less aggressive, calmer creatures. Often you'd have a more hyperactive breed like a springer spaniel for an active dog and a labrador for a passive dog, although that wasn't a written rule.

We had two beautiful hounds in the Scrubs. Alfie was our active dog, a liver-and-white springer spaniel, and Monty was our black labrador passive dog; we later had Harry who was also a black labrador. During my time at the Scrubs we had many different drug dogs. Their average working lives were between four and six years. They were then retired from service and found a new loving home or the dog handler could apply to keep them on as a family pet. In all the years I worked in the prison service, never once did I meet a handler who didn't want to keep their dog. I knew some officers who had four or five waiting for them when they got home. They cared deeply for their dogs and couldn't let them go.

As good as they were, it wasn't nearly enough nose power to tackle D wing. We were going to have to call in the troops – i.e. dog handlers and officers from nearby prisons.

There is very much a 'let's club together' spirit in prisons. I scratch your back, you scratch mine. We'd struggle to operate if we couldn't rely on each other in moments of crisis. Drugs on D wing may not have been a pandemic but it was a serious problem. Don't forget, the problem might start in one place but it doesn't take long to ripple throughout the entire prison.

It was 5.30 a.m., pitch black outside and freezing. Almost forty officers from the Scrubs and nearby Pentonville and Wandsworth, the National Dogs Teams, plus eight dogs and their handlers, plus another senior officer, an orderly officer and the night-shift officers who wanted to help out rather than knock off home, were huddled inside the visitor centre, which is typically, as the name might suggest, used for prison visits. It was the only place officers could come into the Scrubs and not be seen by anyone else in the jail. If someone on a wing spotted or heard a load of staff and dogs rocking up they'd alert the entire prison – by clanging and shouting out of their windows. The noise reverberates everywhere in an old building like ours.

The officers were assigned into pairs. One would search one way around the cell, one would go the other way. Even though we had a bunch more officers, there still weren't enough to tackle all 244 cells – that would need 488 men and women. We had to make a shortlist – pick out who we thought the big players were, the prisoners most likely to be dealing in drugs and contraband. Obviously Phones 4u was up there on the list. We also had to bear in mind that the prisoners we suspected most wouldn't be the ones stupid enough to hold on to the contraband. Often they passed it on to some patsy to look after it. The drawing up of a mental flow chart of what was going where was needed. Some officers were better at it than others. Without blowing my own trumpet too much, I felt I had a good grasp of the traffic flow. I put that down to the way I interacted with the prisoners, making time to chat to them, finding out what made them tick, reading the atmosphere on the wings. Eyes in the back of my head, that's what I had. We narrowed the hit list down to about thirty.

I'd had at least four fags and two cups of coffee already to get me going. As senior officer on the wing, I was one of the few in charge under George Maxwell's direction. My nerves were rattling with adrenaline, caffeine and nicotine. We couldn't mess this up, especially since we'd ferried in a fleet of other officers to help. The key was to fly under the radar until the very last moment.

'Listen up everyone.' George began his briefing. 'The aim of today is to uncover as much contraband as possible. I don't need to remind you to search everywhere inside the cell. Leave no stone unturned.' He stroked his moustache as he spoke. 'Make sure the prisoner is strip-searched then removed from the cell before you start your search and if they give you any trouble shout out for support. We are in this together.'

There was a communal nod and murmur of yes.

'One more thing. We have one shot at this. Not a sound please.'

Easier said than done: around thirty-five officers and eight dogs trying to quietly make their way through the vast echoing Victorian corridors. Can you imagine what a challenge that was in itself?

I drained the last of my tea and got to it.

As I led the way to D wing it made me think back to my childhood dream of joining the forces. Is this what it would have been like, marching in a squadron? I felt a mixture of excitement and trepidation. There was a high probability we'd get some backlash from the prisoners, especially if they were fearful of what we might find. These were violent and highly unpredictable criminals. The most dangerous in the prison. Anything could happen.

I turned around and hissed, 'Stop stomping! And shh with your keys. Hold on to them in your pocket.' The dogs were of the excitable kind, so the handlers were trying very hard to stop them barking. So far, so good on that front.

We tried again. This time practically tip-toeing in our boots. I could hear the pads of the dogs' paws on the floor, we were being so quiet. As we drew closer not a word was spoken; everything was communicated with hand signals. We came to a halt outside the doubled-barred doors of D wing. This was it. Showtime.

In we crept, filing through onto the wing while the prisoners slept. The officers began to break off, scaling the stairs and crossing the landings. In twos, they parked themselves outside the doors of the cells we wanted to bust first. On three, they would unlock and storm in. I gave our prison dogs a good luck pat and then splintered off, positioning myself in the central passage on the ones, ready to oversee all of the confiscated contraband.

The officers on the fours were the last to take up their post. As we waited for the order an eerie silence fell across the wing. It was so quiet you could have heard a pin drop. Then – chaos.

'Okay, now!' George Maxwell shouted.

It sounded like thunder, rolling across the building as the officers charged at the same time.

'Stand up! Put your hands where we can see them.'

'Fucking hell!', 'Fuck off, you cunts!' and 'You've got to be fucking joking!' A barrage of expletives bellowed across the wing. Followed by the sound of dozens of toilets flushing at the same time. And those prisoners whose cells weren't being busted open were banging on their doors with their fists and feet. The noise made the dogs start barking. Chaos.

Mattresses were overturned, belongings clattered to the floor. The dogs were going berserk with the scents they were picking up.

My eyes darted up and down, back and forth, watching the prisoners being hauled from their cells. Most did what they were told, while others resisted and had to be restrained. You'd never seen so many pissed-off men in one room at the same time; well, if you don't count England losing at yet another penalty shootout at the football.

I was grateful not to be in the thick of it. Not because I was afraid of being assaulted, but the operational side of the bust interested me much more. I was looking forward to uncovering the contraband, to finding out who was stashing what. I'd never cared much about that kind of thing while I was at Holloway; I did what was asked of me and went home. Something about working in the Scrubs was making me feel more alive and invested in my job – igniting a part of me that *actually cared* about the prison. A desire to want to clean it up.

I had a couple of officers helping me with the evidence gathering. As soon as the prison officers found anything, they would bag it up and bring it to me. It didn't take long for the first haul to arrive.

Our job was to tag and file it. To write a description of what it was, to log it in the book and then sign it, so there would be a trail of paperwork that could be used for adjudications or, if needs be, used as evidence in a court of law.

We found two very deadly shanks (knives) made out of plastic toothbrushes. One where the handle had been shaved into a point. The other had razor blades melted into the end. Under a prisoner's pillow we discovered pool balls that had been missing for a couple of months. Pool or snooker balls and large batteries in a sock are a popular weapon for prisoners to attack each other or indeed staff with. Placed inside a sock and hurled around, they can be lethal – smash your jaw, shatter your cheek, knock out your teeth. We also uncovered a wealth of cannabis and heroin plus a dozen or so mobile phones.

Some of the hiding places were ingenious – a chunk cut out of the Koran, inside three wraps of heroin. Phones and drugs were taped under the sink, taped inside the rim of the toilet, stuffed into a pillow; one prisoner even managed to hide drugs in his bedframe. A weapon was found taped to a prisoner's leg. He must have slept with it like that all night long – couldn't have been comfortable! Drugs were also found buried in a pot of body cream and behind a false back of a wardrobe. A stash of heroin was weighted down into the bottom of a squash bottle. Just as with the zip wire – the imagination and ingenuity these guys had was staggering. I couldn't help but think, if only these prisoners would channel that intelligence into doing good they could make something of their lives.

The search took most of the day it proved so fruitful. Those who were caught were punished by, you guessed it, being sent down the Seg. The more serious the contraband, the longer their spell in solitary. We were over the moon with how successful the operation had been and it had earned us some serious brownie points with the number one gov.

There was only one thing that cast a shadow over our day. That alerted us to there being a serious problem on D wing – *even* more concerning than drug smuggling. It was something one of the dogs sniffed out. When I tell you, you'll probably wonder what I'm on about. That's nothing in comparison to finding class-A drugs, knives and shanks, surely, you'll say. But what old Casper the spaniel upturned had far-reaching implications; it reeked of something much more dangerous – corruption.

A bottle of whiskey. Jack Daniel's to be precise. Sniffed out in Kevin White's cupboard on the threes. Drugs, weapons, phones can be thrown over the prison wall, but a glass bottle, not a chance. Someone had passed it through security and brought it into the Scrubs. Which meant only one thing – we had a bent member of staff on our wing.

As an SO, I didn't have much to do with the investigation; that was led by the security team. But I knew who the member of staff they suspected was and *why* he suddenly became a prime target – because the prisoner in whose cell we found the whiskey grassed him up.

It wasn't long after Kevin had returned from serving his punishment in the Seg that he came knocking at my door asking to see someone in security. He claimed he had a bit of information, something they'd be very keen to hear. I read that as him wanting to fess up about the whiskey bottle for whatever reason. The guy wanted a good old moan about how the member of staff we suspected was on the take and had short-changed him out of a deal.

Kevin told the security team how two days ago, a package containing drugs and money had been thrown over the wall by 'a mate'. It had been picked up by one of the 'red bands' – they were the trusted prisoners sent out every day to tidy up the rubbish from the grounds – who had handed it, with the best intentions, to this bent officer, who proceeded to open the parcel and pocket the cash for himself. Kevin White said he went nuts when the officer eventually gave him his package. 'He's done me out of 300 quid! I want something done about him,' he complained to the security team. Completely missing the point that he'd implicated himself in the process. Not the sharpest tool in the box. A good illustration of the selfishness you see in male estates. Nothing mattered to Kevin more than getting his gear.

Of course the member of staff denied it and, sadly, Kevin's statement wasn't enough to throw the book at him.

WHO LET THE DOGS OUT?

It was a prisoner's word against a member of staff's. In order to sack a member of staff for corruption you have to prove they did it on the grounds of probability. After a long, drawn-out investigation, the security team couldn't nab him. I didn't envy their job; it was challenging and exasperating. The officer left of his own accord in the end, but that wasn't something I got to see as not long after the drugs bust I got called in to see the number one gov.

Chapter 12

A SHADOW OF HIMSELF

HMP Wormwood Scrubs: October 2003

'Boss, the number one gov wants to see you.'

I looked up from the newspaper I was having a quick squiz through. 'What?'

Steve grimaced. 'Yeah, he said he'd like you in his office now.'

Dread gripped my stomach. *Nobody* got called to see the head of the entire prison unless you were in for a bollocking. This could only be bad news. I was being moved on to another prison. *Not again*. It was the run-in with the budgie, I knew it. He probably thinks I'm a right old joker, not taking my job seriously. I was panicking and catastrophising the entire walk to his office. Even though a year and a half had passed, my sudden transfer from HMP Holloway had left me feeling vulnerable to it happening again.

The number one gov could be found in the same building as the security office, the prefab building adjacent to the prison entrance. First floor, his name on the door: Keith Munns.

I knocked twice, my nerves, rattling. I didn't want to be moved on again. Eighteen months ago, I'd never have said this, but I was really loving working in a men's prison. The Scrubs and the lifer wing had become my home. I felt like I was *doing* something with my life. Achieving things.

'Come in,' he said.

Deep breath, Vanessa.

The Gov's office was palatial compared to everywhere else. A book-lined room with an oval boardroom table and cabinets filled with leather-bound books, journals of the Scrubs dating back to the 1900s. The Gov stood up from behind his huge oak desk to greet me.

'Ah, Vanessa, come in, sit down.'

Sit down? I've only ever stood in front of the Gov. This did not bode well.

Keith Munns was a tall man with grey hair and wore glasses. A northerner. Well-spoken but with a Manchester accent. He had a bit of a twinkle in his eye, taking the edge off his formidable title. He was very popular with the staff.

I noticed the piles of paperwork to the side of his computer. If I thought I had a lot to deal with, it was nothing in comparison to him. I couldn't even begin to imagine the level of responsibility his job entailed, the amount of problems he had to deal with on a day-in, day-out basis. Just the thought made me shiver. I'd never want to be a governor I decided as I sat in front of him, awaiting my bollocking.

I wanted to break my rising anxiety by cracking some jibe about football. In the few interactions I'd had with the Gov we'd always ended up bantering about our rival teams. He being a Man. United fan, me being an Arsenal supporter. Now didn't seem the time though. I blew out through my cheeks. 'You wanted to see me, sir?'

'Yes I did. I need you to do me a favour.'

Oh. Not what I expected. My heart sang.

'Anything,' I said, beaming.

'I want you to move to A wing.'

It sank as quickly as it had risen. A wing was predominantly for remand prisoners yet to be convicted. Volatile. Violent. A shit-hole, basically.

'I've got some issues on A wing.' His tone turned serious. 'I need you to sort them out for me.' He went on to explain there wasn't enough discipline being installed. There wasn't enough consistency. Staff morale was generally very low.

'I'm really happy on D wing though, sir.' I didn't want to move; I loved being with the lifers. I'd spruced that wing up and it was ticking over beautifully under my watch. I suppose that's exactly why the Gov wanted me on A wing, and although it was a massive compliment, it was still a bitter pill to swallow.

'I know that, and I've seen what a good job you've done on it. But,' he stressed, 'I really need you to go to A wing.'

Well, if the number one gov says, *I really need you to*, then *you do*.

I nodded. 'Okay, no problem. Thank you for the opportunity.' I rose out of my seat.

A SHADOW OF HIMSELF

The Gov thought A wing needed a woman's touch, so there I went.

There wasn't anything particularly remarkable to report from my time in A wing, so I'll skip on through it. In a nutshell, I did what the Gov asked of me: I cleaned it up. I wasn't there that long, six months tops, but in that time I did have the pleasure of watching over a TV celebrity.

He was almost unrecognisable when he arrived – I had to do a double take. If I say Jefferson King you probably won't have the foggiest who I'm on about. If I say Shadow from the ITV show *Gladiators*, hopefully a lot of you will know.

In its heyday, everyone rushed home to watch *Gladiators* on Saturday night, me included. It was bigger than *Blind Date* and *Noel's House Party*. Shadow was one of the favourites on the show because he was unbeatable and menacing. Nobody wanted to fight him – he was so strong and scary looking. He reminded me of a panther, sleek, muscly and with those piercing eyes.

The day he walked onto A wing he was quite literally a shadow of his former self. He was emaciated – thin and scrawny, his cheeks and eyes were hollowed out. He was almost skeletal. The result of becoming a drug addict. Crack cocaine and heroin, I believe.

The story I heard was that he was fired from the show after being caught taking cocaine in a nightclub. His life fell apart after that. He couldn't cope with the fall into obscurity, when all the fame and the glory had gone, so he turned to drugs to numb the pain. He was in the Scrubs for dealing drugs and, by the looks of things, had become hooked on his own supply.

He kept his head down from the word go; he didn't want to draw any attention to himself from the other prisoners. I sorted a few things out for him but apart from that I didn't have much to do with him because he mostly kept his nose out of trouble. He just wanted to serve his time and get out.

He would have been on a drug-replacement maintenance course to wean him off his addiction, overseen by the prison doctors. He wasn't alone. A lot of the men on A wing were drug addicts, inside for doing some sort of crime to feed their habit, from shoplifting to burglaries to armed robberies.

That's the thing about druggies: they'll do anything to feed their habit, even sell their own grandmother for a fix. They can't focus on anything except where that next hit is coming from and it doesn't matter who they'd have to hurt or what they'd need to do to get it. Drugs make people selfish and that's one of the things I hate most about them.

Numerous prisoners would come up to me on association complaining, 'Guv, I'm withdrawing from drugs, you don't understand what it's like, I'm dying,' and I'd reply, flippantly, 'You can't die from not taking drugs!' Which is true: you can't die. You can from alcohol withdrawal: that can be very serious as your body can pack up. But drugs, no. When I started in Holloway there wasn't any methadone maintenance course; they used to make the addicts go cold turkey. It was called the detox unit for a reason.

My response to those inmates could sound harsh but I suppose I struggle to feel sorry for addicts because, at the end of the day, it was *their choice* to take the drugs. It's not like we don't know what the dangers of taking them are, so if someone chooses to go down that path then they have to accept the consequences.

It's all very well explaining away their mistakes, saying poor such and such, they've had a hard life, they were abused as a kid, they were beaten up by their partner; and yes it's dreadful, truly it is, but there are plenty of people out there who have been through equally terrible things and have managed not to turn to drugs. And what about the innocents they've hurt along the way? That sweet old lady of seventy-five who they beat up and robbed blind for drug money – what about her? She worked hard all her life, lived through two world wars and after all that ended up dying alone in a pool of her own blood thanks to a drug-crazed person who put their need for a fix before anything else.

Back to Shadow. Yes, it was sad seeing him looking so ill and ravished by his addiction, and I can only imagine what it must have felt like to have suffered such a fall from grace, but how he chose to deal with it, i.e. getting hooked on heroin or whatever it was, was a choice *he made*. If he wanted to stop he had to find the willpower to do it, to be forceful in his decision.

It all comes back to what I mentioned earlier – dynamic security, rehabilitation, turning a negative into a positive, what I originally hoped to achieve when I joined the prison service. We should be helping these prisoners wean off their addictions and teaching them skill sets to find jobs, educating them, so they don't fall back into the same old cycle of drugs, crime and prison.

The problem is they're often let out back onto the street before the doctors have had a chance to get them off their habit. The average 'stay' of a prisoner in Wormwood Scrubs was six weeks. What on earth can you do to help someone in six weeks? Nothing. You can send them on any course you want but they don't have enough time to address their drug taking let alone the bigger problem: *why* they are taking them.

From what I witnessed, the why was very different for men than women. In Holloway, the women who had turned to drugs often did so to blot things out. Most were either prostitutes or victims of abuse. They'd fallen into a toxic spiral which had taken hold. There were men at the Scrubs whose why was also to forget the sexual abuse, but more often than not I was hearing how peer pressure from other men was the main cause of their addiction

A large part of me believes prison isn't the right place for drug addicts, simply because we don't have the time and the resources to put them back on track. We've all heard the stories of prisoners coming in non-addicts and leaving addicts, and sadly there's more than a grain of truth in that. There are many prisoners who get introduced to drugs while serving time. The boredom of being locked up doesn't help their inability to say no.

What would I do about the problem? I think the government needs to establish some sort of halfway house.

Somewhere secure, which isn't as relaxed as an addict anonymous group but also isn't as unforgiving as a prison. A place where they are counselled and closely monitored for the weaning-off process. How would it work? Joe Bloggs, a heroin addict, who's shoplifted a load of stuff from Marks & Spencer with the view of flogging it, is given a stay of execution. Instead of getting a twelve-month prison sentence, of which he'll serve six, he's sentenced to half a year in a drug rehab centre. If, however, he reoffends once released, there'll be no second chances – he'll go straight to jail next time.

These halfway houses – I don't think they should just be for the addicts. There's a lot of bad people in prison, but there's also a lot of people locked up who shouldn't be there. We need to look much more closely at *why* we're putting people behind bars. Serious crimes, absolutely: for those who murder, rape, abuse, etc., prison is the place for them. But for those who steal a bottle of whisky from Safeway or a sandwich from British Rail because they're homeless and starving (I had a woman like that in Holloway), I honestly can't see how it's cost effective to lock them up for that.

The problem is, as always, money. An effective drugs strategy costs the government. Building secure rehab centres, employing staff, it's all expensive, and the way things are currently structured, there isn't the budget for it. Whether the government will start allocating more money to these projects is anyone's guess. What I do know is – there's got to be something better than prison.

Chapter 13

AUNTIE ROSE

**HMP Holloway:
November 1994**

While I'm on the subject of famous people, I'd like to dip back in time to when I had to look after a very high-profile prisoner, someone who made Shadow pale in comparison.

I'd be surprised if there was anyone in Britain who hasn't heard of Rosemary West. One of only two women in the UK serving a full life sentence, for the murder and torture of ten women between 1971 and 1987, including her eight-year-old step-daughter. The other is Joanna Dennehy, who killed three people and attempted to kill a further two on a rampage across Hereford. Myra Hindley was also serving a full life sentence before she died of respiratory failure in 2002.

As senior officer, I'd been assigned to manage the Seg. At the time of Rose arriving at Holloway, she'd been charged with the killings, but her husband, Fred West, a builder, was considered to be the mastermind behind the murders. Rose was seen as the abused wife who'd been emotionally and physically coerced into going along with it. A bit like what Myra Hindley first argued – Ian Brady had *forced* her to watch him torturing those kids.

The TV and papers had been full of grisly stories of what they'd found at the 'House of Horrors' – 25 Cromwell Street in Gloucester – building up to what was going to be the trial of the decade. Fred had been sent to HMP Winson Green, Birmingham, awaiting his court appearance. When I heard the news that Rose was being sent to the Seg at Holloway for her own protection under Rule 43, the first thing I thought was: *Oh crap. That's the last thing I bloody need.*

As far as I was concerned, celebrities and high-profile prisoners were a pain in the arse. Everything, and I mean everything, you do in relation to them comes under much higher scrutiny. That's a lot of pressure for the staff. All Rose West needed to say was, 'I've been treated badly', and the world's media would be jumping all over the story, wanting to print something on how we were persecuting her before she'd even been convicted. Any opportunity to scrutinise the prison system. The British press never seem to want to report about the good we do; it's always about the mistakes we make and where we're failing, or at least it feels that way.

Apart from fretting I was about to be thrust under a microscope, I was also anticipating the Seg was about to turn into Piccadilly Circus, as the world and his wife would be wanting to visit Rose. Doctors, nurses, probation officers, psychologists and nosy staff coming and going. It was going to make my job of keeping it a secure unit a lot harder.

You might ask: why the Seg and not put her on one of the wings? Well, for many reasons, but mostly to protect her from being attacked by another prisoner. She would have been deemed a trophy for violent inmates. Do you remember at the start of the book I mentioned Carrie Webber? The vigilante who liked to take a piece out of prisoners she deemed deserving of her punishment? Just imagine what would have happened if she had got her hands on Rose. It would have been a blood bath. The wings weren't a safe place for her, which is why I got the job of looking after her.

Absolutely no chances were taken: Rose didn't even pass through the reception building where the court warrants were checked. The prison bus pulled up right outside the Seg where I was waiting to greet her. I was flanked by two officers when the van doors swung open.

She wasn't handcuffed; she stepped onto the tarmac wearing those famous big bottleneck glasses. Her dark hair was short and curly and it was fair to say she was quite a large lady, size 18 to 20. She was clutching two HMP plastic bags' worth of her belongings. She didn't look the least bit shell-shocked or like the monster she'd been pegged as. More like some sweet old bag lady you might see walking through the streets.

'Hi Rose, I just need to go through your warrant with you.' I got straight down to business.

PISSD or 'pissed' as I liked to call the procedure. 'P' stood for prisoner.

'You are Rose West?'

'Yes,' she said nodding, quite chirpily, all things considered.

'I' stood for information or the offence. 'S' stood for sentence – in her case, not convicted. 'S' and 'D' were for signed and dated, which was done by the court officials. Once the formalities were over, I led her to her cell. I'd already sorted which one she was having, the cell nearest the office, so we could keep an eye on her and anyone who rocked up to see her.

Her belongings were taken off her and checked over for all the usual things: drugs, phones, weapons. There was a lot of canteen food stashed inside, which she must have picked up at the police station.

'Would you like to follow me.' I showed her to her cell and told her we'd get her out in a while to go through things and asked her if she'd like a cup of tea while she settled in. No flippant or sarcastic comments from me. I was minding my Ps and Qs because, as I'd predicted, the world and his wife were there. Everyone had come down, from nurses to psychologists, to assess 'the monster'.

It was going to be three to six months until she appeared at Winchester Crown Court over her charges, so until then she was under my watchful eye and care.

There were six other officers as part of my team, which dropped to three in the evenings. As I've said, the Seg was not somewhere you wanted to be if you could help it – believe me. The cells were small narrow cubicles with a tiny barred window, and don't even get me started on the smell. It was a place of punishment at the end of the day, so dirty protests from unhappy prisoners were a common occurrence. And when it didn't stink of shit, there would be water everywhere, from where some other prisoner had flooded her cell in protest. The noise could also be excruciating – constant banging and shouting; you could barely hear yourself think at times.

The twenty-three out of twenty-four hours' lock-up didn't apply to Rose though. She was there purely for her own protection – entitled to all the normal privileges she'd have on a wing.

Every morning we'd unlock her door. Let her have a shower, give her an hour of exercise. She'd walk around the Seg yard. Sometimes we got her out to clean the corridors. We'd give her a toothbrush to scrub the radiators and she seemed quite happy with having something to do. I think she was pleased to be out of her cell. She'd make tea for the staff, chat away, never about anything meaningful though. Nothing about Fred or the case, just chit-chat. Someone, i.e. her lawyer, had clearly told her to keep her mouth shut.

One of the first things she did was put in an application to the number one gov for a pair of knitting needles and some wool. They were granted, which may sound strange, but at the end of the day, what damage was she going to do with blunt knitting needles in the highest security unit in the prison? You could cause more harm with a razor and some twirled-up toilet roll, Carrie Webber style – back to her again I know, but she's a good case in point. I think granting Rose the knitting stuff also had to do with keeping her happy and busy as after all she wasn't meant to be in such solitary confinement; she was down there for her own protection, as she'd done nothing wrong in the prison. Human rights and all that. And she had to hand them out of her cell at night.

As soon as she had her stuff, she got to work knitting. Morning, noon and night. At 8 a.m., when I went to unlock her and say 'Morning, Rose', there'd she be again, knitting. Suffice to say, nobody knew what the hell she was making, it was just one long thing of knitting. She would stare into the distance while she did it, but you could tell that behind her glazed expression, a lot was going on. As if her brain was busy. On what, I dread to think.

She soon got the nickname 'Auntie Rose' from all the staff because she knitted, because she looked like your old auntie you'd pop round to see for tea and cakes, and because she had this sing-song way about her. She'd say 'Mor-ning' in that chirpy way. We didn't mean any harm by calling her that; it's something that happens in prison, everyone gets nicknames. I suppose it's a form of dark humour, our way of disassociating with the brutality of the world we are operating in.

So Rose West was Auntie Rose, and she bumbled along as if nothing had happened. Quite often when people are charged with horrendous crimes, they shut down. They can't eat, they barely communicate as the reality of their punishment, as the threat of life imprisonment, sinks in. Not Rose: she would eat whatever was put in front of her just fine and she'd even say it was nice. She would chat away to you, just like it was another day at the office. It was as if she'd completely separated Rose West, the serial killer, from Rose West, Auntie Rose.

She didn't even flinch when the number one gov came down to deliver what you'd think would be the biggest shock of her life.

It was New Year's Day afternoon, and I had the pleasure of working that shift. Rose must have been with us a couple of weeks now and was in her cell.

The Gov appeared in my office.

'Happy New Year!' I said cheerfully.

'Not so happy.' He flashed me a somewhat stressed look. He went on to reveal that Fred West had topped himself at lunchtime at Birmingham's Winson Green prison.

'Bloody hell,' I gasped. I didn't envy him having to deliver that bombshell. Rose was going to be devastated. After everything they'd – supposedly – done together. He must have been her everything.

How wrong I could be.

'Let's get this over with then.' The Gov told me to follow him to Rose's cell. I unlocked the door and stood back to let him go first. Rose was on her bed and looked up, surprised as I was to get a visit from the number one on New Year's Day.

He cleared his throat. 'I'm afraid I have some bad news. Fred has killed himself.'

The full story was that he'd hung himself in his cell with a noose made from bed sheets after lunch. He'd jammed his door shut to stop anyone coming in to save him.

I think she blinked a couple of times and then said: 'Oh right.'

Oh right? Oh right?! She didn't even flinch.

'Is there anything we can do? Is there anything you want to ask me?'

She shook her head. 'No, I'm okay.'

The Gov left as swiftly as he'd arrived and I followed him out. I gave Rose a final glance before shutting the door but nothing had altered in her expression. No tears, no nothing, just that glazed stare. The level of control and disassociation was staggering.

If you want my opinion, I think that was the moment Rose West thought she was going to get off scot-free. It was widely considered that Fred topped himself to protect Rose, hoping his suicide would be seen as an admission of guilt and that the case would be dropped against her.

You just knew there was something much more calculating going on upstairs in her head. Behind the Auntie Rose smiles and sing-song voice she was quietly working out her every move, like a chess player. Her tactic was slow and steady wins the race.

What makes someone a murderer? Well, that's the 64-million-dollar question, isn't it? And a question that fascinates me. I truly believe that in order to be good at a job like mine, you have to develop an ability to read people. As I mentioned earlier, from what I'd seen and from the reams of crime books I've read, murderers have no emotion. No idea of what empathy is. And very often, the murder they're charged with won't be the first time those killing tendencies have come out. They've probably killed or tortured animals in the past, they've been a bully, they've shown they can hurt people and things and not feel anything when doing it. There would have been a build-up, a warning sign at some stage. Even something small, like not expressing any emotion when losing a parent.

I'm sure if you studied Rose's behaviour over the years leading up to when she first started killing, there would be lots of signs. The fact she could compartmentalise for one.

There was no change in Rose's behaviour after she heard Fred was dead. She carried on just as she had before. We had a communal TV for the prisoners being held under Rule 43. Every evening at 6 p.m. I let them out to watch the BBC News together in the association room.

In the weeks leading up to Rose's transfer to HMP Winchester for the start of her trial, she would watch the news with a Jamaican woman who was on remand for drug-related and gangland offences. Kalisa had turned QE – Queen's evidence – against a prolific drug gang. A *grass* as they were better known in the nick. She had a price on her head and, just like Rose, was in the Seg for her own protection. They would sit together, quietly, content in each other's company – interestingly, it was the only time Rose didn't knit – while stories of her case dominated the headlines.

Don't ask me how Kalisa didn't manage to put two and two together, but for some unknown reason she didn't work out *who* she was sitting next to. I suppose Rose's appearance had changed somewhat from *that* mugshot of her with the big glasses and a dark mop of hair. Or perhaps Kalisa was also blindsided by the Auntie Rose act. Rose knew how to get what she wanted. She had Kalisa getting up to make her cups of tea. It was done in such a pleasant manner though, in such an insidious way, where you know you're being manipulated but there was nothing you could do about it. No doubt Rose had used that skill set to get Fred to do whatever she wanted.

I would sometimes hover in the background, catch the headlines, make polite chit-chat, intrigued by the effect Rose had on Kalisa.

On the day Rose left my watch in February 2005, we exchanged only a few words. I kept it as formal as her arrival at the Seg.

'See you, Rose, look after yourself.' Something off the cuff and meaningless.

The following day it was business as usual, I got Kalisa out of her cell to watch the six o'clock news.

'Just you tonight then,' I said as she got settled in front of the box.

Kalisa had a thick accent; sometimes it was hard to understand her.

'Oh my God, that terrible Rose West, look what she's done,' she commented on the main story. The coverage of Rose's trial had ramped up now it was getting close to the trial. 'Let justice be served,' she cried out. Suddenly being very vocal of her contempt.

One of the officers on the Seg, Jessica Murphy, exchanged glances with me.

'What you on about?' I exclaimed. Equally baffled by the situation.

'That dreadful Rose West, she killed all those women,' she carried on.

My brow crumpled. 'Who the blimmin' heck do you think you've been sat next to for all that time?'

If Kalisa could have gone white, she would have gone white. She was in absolute shock.

'Miss, miss, that's not true, tell me it ain't true.'

'Yeah it's true, her name was Rose, for Pete's sake. She had those bottleneck glasses.'

'Oh my God,' Kalisa howled.

Jessica and I were in tears we were laughing so hard. How could she not have worked it out? It was moments like that which offered a glimmer of relief in what could otherwise could become a very dark environment to work.

Rose West went on to stand trial at Winchester Crown Court in September of that year. Fred's suicide didn't save her bacon: she was given ten life sentences for the rape, torture and murder of those women and she was taken away to a Cat A prison. The court case revealed how it was in fact *her* that was the driving force behind the killings – she had Fred wrapped around her finger. The news didn't surprise me at all. Nor did it shock me to hear in the years that followed that Rose West was branded 'supremely manipulative' in whichever prison she was transferred to. Coaxing staff into doing her favours. Rumour had it, she also had multiple affairs with prisoners, including Myra Hindley, would you believe. Two of the most manipulative women in jail. I shudder to think how that power play worked out. No surprise, then, that the affair was short-lived.

None of it surprised me. All the signs were there in those months Rose West was with me down the Seg.

Chapter 14

BAKING THE TRUTH

Saffron Walden, Essex:
Now

I'm lucky the café upstairs has such good coffee. I pour the double shot of espresso into the buttercream mixture. The blender whirs, drowning out Radio 2 as I whiz it up into frothy perfection.

Coffee and walnut cake. That's what today's pièce de résistance will be. It's unusual for me to have just one cake on the go, though. My personal best is fourteen plus two batches of scones. I'm confident I'll beat that one day. My competitiveness in the kitchen reminds me of the food-search days at Holloway I mentioned earlier, when we all tried to outdo each other on how many wraps of heroin we could find.

Five minutes of high-speed whisking later I check on my buttercream. 'Not quite there yet.' I lick the spoon. Not light and creamy enough. I add a splash of milk, an ingredient that takes the mixture out of the everyday, as Mary Berry would say.

I'm so lost in my baking bubble, for a moment I forget I'm not alone.

A new lad has started at Angela Reed. Luke: he's twenty-two and hails from Essex. He's training to be a sous-chef and he's spent the morning perfecting his chicken Caesar salad to impress the boss.

He's very sweet and polite but a right old chatterbox. He hasn't stopped asking questions since I revealed I used to work in prisons many moons ago. I didn't give him any details, but he's fascinated by meeting someone who's worked on the other side. This was the fourth morning in a row that he's come in, said hello and hit me with blizzard of hows and whys and 'Do you mind if I ask you …'

Usually I'm very cagey about my past. I've kept myself to myself in the town, flying under the radar, but there's something endearing about Luke that makes me want to open up a little. He has a quiet determination. Maybe I recognise myself in him.

I get the sense he's building up to something today. He looks thoughtful as he sprinkles a handful of Parmesan shavings over his towers of iceberg lettuce. I was waiting for his usual follow-on of questions but it doesn't come. I can hear his brain ticking over.

'I don't mind you asking me,' I reassure him. Maybe there's something cathartic in it for me to chat about what happened in the Scrubs, because as soon as there's a pause, I'm willing him to go on.

'How are you going to get the walnut flavour to come out in the cake?' he eventually says.

I look at him sideways. 'Is that what you really want to ask me?'

He shakes his head lightly. He's got a kind face. His eyes smile with him but they also hide a story or two. I've seen many like it, lined by life experiences.

Luke has short hair and a goatee, George Michael style. He's wearing his kitchen whites and looks proud to be in them. I know that feeling. How wearing a uniform can suddenly give you structure and a sense of belonging.

He sighs deeply and finally stops going around the houses.

'My brother's in prison.' His voice is low, his words weighted – dragging him down.

I think I half-expected it. There's not much I haven't seen or heard or can't anticipate. 'Oh really?' I reply.

'Do you mind if I ask you for a bit of advice?' Luke goes on.

'Fire away,' I say and smile. Even though I'd packed my past away, I was enjoying revisiting it with the aim of helping. Most days I forget I'm harbouring a wealth of information.

'My brother's just got five years for armed robbery, and I' – he pauses – 'I'm not sure I –' he stops again. 'He wants me to visit him but …'

I start spooning the buttercream into the piping bag, helping relieve the intensity of our conversation. Luke is clearly struggling.

'You're not sure if you want to?' I finish his sentence.

He shrugs a little. 'Yeah, I guess.'

'I can relate to that.'

'You can?'

'Of course.' I smile, without revealing I'd seen this dilemma played out a thousand times over.

'We've been through so much together and for him to end up this way, after everything I did to protect him, it's' – he shrugs again – 'I feel let down.'

'Do you want to tell me a bit about what you two went through?'

Those lined eyes harden a fraction as Luke reveals he passed through twenty-five foster-care homes with his brother growing up. Twenty-five! Can you even begin to imagine what it must have been like to be shunted around like that? The experience was crippling for both of them. Luke was the youngest but the strongest of the two brothers and did everything in his power to help and protect his brother.

'It wasn't enough: he was filled with anger, hating the system, feeling let down by everyone and anyone, so he turned to crime. He went the same way as my dad.' He stares off into the distance. 'And my other brother.'

'Jesus. I'm sorry, Luke.'

He's fighting to hold it together.

'Firstly, you need to pat yourself on the back,' I say. 'Considering your family are career criminals I think you're amazing for not following the same path.'

'You do?' He perks up.

'Yes I do, you should be incredibly proud about how you turned out.' He is bringing out the mother hen in me.

'Thank you.' He looks away, bashfully.

I've met so many criminals who took the path their brother went down because it was the easier option. Criminals who have blamed everyone and anyone for their life choices except themselves.

There is always a choice. Even if life throws all its shit at you, you still have the power to decide which side of that black and white line you stand. Luke was clearly a strong, resilient lad who had fought hard to better himself and I admired that. After everything I'd seen, I took my hat off to him.

'Do you think I should visit my brother?' he asks.

I couldn't answer that for him. 'Do you want to? It's going to be difficult either way. Whether you go or don't go.'

'My family say I should go.'

'And what do you think?'

He sighs deeply. 'I don't want to.'

'Maybe you should listen to your gut then. You know, you can always write to your brother.'

He looks shocked. 'Can I?'

'Of course. What jail is he in?'

The relief visibly washes over him. I talk Luke through the next steps while piping rosettes across one half of the cooled coffee walnut sponge. Carefully I sandwich the two slabs together and then start on the icing. Smoothing the buttercream across the top. Swirling more rosettes around the edge. Finishing off with a sprinkling of walnuts.

If you hadn't guessed, baking is *my* therapy. It's helping me process the past. With every stroke of buttercream my soul is being soothed. You can't walk away from prison life unscathed. I thought I could, but it turns out not even I'm superhuman.

Chapter 15

ANOTHER RUNG ON THE LADDER

HMP Wormwood Scrubs: May 2005

Perhaps there were nods to my creative side when I worked in the Scrubs; I just didn't know it at the time.

No sooner had I cleaned up A wing, the number one gov moved me onto B wing. The smallest unit in the Scrubs, with room for just one hundred and seventy-six men, Keith Munns felt it was the perfect-sized area to be transformed into an induction wing for all the new prisoners. It would, essentially, be a holding pen where the newcomers could get up to speed with what they were entitled to and what we would be expecting from them.

I don't know where on earth the idea came from; it just suddenly popped into my head. *Passport*.

I was going to create a mock travel document for all the prisoners. They'd get a stamp every time they completed a stage in their induction, every time they passed a workshop.

For example, had they had their property returned? Yes? Tick. Had their valuables been listed? Tick. Had they received their pin number for the pay phone so they could have access to call their family and legal team? Yes. Tick. Had they been briefed about all the educational courses on offer? Did they know what workshops they would be attending? There were sections that covered citizens' advice and how to reach out for emotional support – the Samaritans were on hand if they needed help.

The scheme worked a dream and the prisoners appreciated the structure. Keith Munns and the number four governor, head of operations and security, both pulled me aside to have a word in my ear about promotion. They said I should, with a stress on *should*, apply to sit on the principal officers board. 'You're practically doing a PO's job anyway,' the number one said.

He was right. A PO was the most senior officer in charge of a wing and I'd pretty much been running D, A and B since I stepped foot inside the Scrubs. As a PO you're answerable to the number five gov of that particular area. Aside from carrying more authority, the promotion obviously came with a pay increase.

I wasn't overly fussed with it all, even the pay rise. My work ethic up until this point had been to show up, do my job to the best of my ability and don't take the piss with sick days. In fact, I could count on one hand the number of times I'd taken a day off. I lived simply and wasn't the slightest bit materialistic. One look at my flat and you'd know that! I suppose I'd never pushed for promotion because I'd failed to see how good I was at my job. It was only when people at the top started telling me, encouraging me, to aim higher that I even slightly considered I might have what it takes. Even this is hard for me to say. I hate blowing my own trumpet. It makes me feel exposed, uncomfortable and vulnerable. Believe it or not, I'm actually very shy. The person I was in prison, my tough, fearless persona, was a front to do my job well. Underneath, I'm a big old softie. Especially, as you already know, when it comes to animal cruelty. Any sort of pet rescue show on TV reduces me to tears within seconds.

So I sat my PO interview and, to my surprise, I flew through. I moved from B wing to the orderly office to reception to, finally, the security office.

Located next to the entrance of the Scrubs, it was busy, bustling, and contained some of the most sensitive of information. For example, intelligence gathering on prisoners we suspected were up to no good. That could be anything from a terrorist who was trying to plot attacks from behind prison walls, who was converting other inmates to extremism, to your bog-standard drug dealer trying to get their missus to smuggle a wrap of heroin in on her visit.

First impressions? It wasn't welcoming. The door to where the senior officers sat was always shut. You had to knock to enter and no sooner had you stepped inside, than a counter as high as your chest stood between you and the staff. Barrier after barrier had to be overcome before you could speak with someone on – what was probably – the most important team in the entire prison.

ANOTHER RUNG ON THE LADDER

Security is a hub of information and in order to have the intel flowing in from the officers and staff on the wings, the eyes and ears of the jail, the environment needed to be welcoming. The way it was set up was intimidating. It screamed *stay out* rather than come in. Not the way I envisaged a successful information hub should be run.

Out of all the wing clean-ups, I felt most passionately about giving this place a make-over. The governors had been right. The promotion had given me a boost of confidence and an injection of drive and vision. I instinctively knew that improving security was the key to cleaning up the Scrubs and I very much wanted to be part of that.

The counter was first to go. I then rearranged the entire office to make it open plan. I got rid of some staff who weren't pulling their weight. I made a separate room dedicated to incoming intel – with the door left open of course. Another office was created for the sole purpose of listening in to prisoners' phone conversations – pin phones as they were called. We were allowed to listen in on all calls except those made to a prisoner's legal team. I had a small army of clerks who worked tirelessly on the job. And it was a big job.

When a new prisoner enters a jail he/she is allowed to write down ten numbers of family, friends, a significant other they'd like to be in contact with plus the number of their legal representative. Those numbers have to be checked over thoroughly to make sure they're not dodgy, e.g. the woman they were arrested for abusing or whoever else they might want to scare into retracting their statement. The pin clerk would ring every single one of those numbers saying something similar to: 'Joe Bloggs has just come into custody at HMP Wormwood Scrubs and he's put you down as one of his contacts. Are you happy to receive calls from him?' It's either a *yes*, tick by their name, or a *no*, I never want to hear from that wanker again – score through their name. The paper is handed back to the prisoner and he can see who still wants to know him. This is probably all computerised now, but back in the day it called for intensive man-hours. The turnover was ninety new prisoners a day – that's hundreds of numbers that needed checking. On top of that, the clerks had to listen into conversations being dialled out from the landings. Of course they didn't tap into every single call – we'd have needed three hundred staff to make that possible – it was just the ones made by prisoners we suspected were up to no good plus maybe twenty randomly selected calls. There were two phones on each landing, so six to eight on a wing. Queues for the phone were never an issue because that was one of the few privileges prisoners had access to throughout the day.

On top of needing restructuring, the security office was crying out for a woman's touch. It was dank and dirty and by the looks of things hadn't seen a hoover since Victorian times. I sorted that out pretty sharpish and while I was at it had a load of blinds for the windows installed. Goodness knows how anyone managed to get any work done with the sun streaming into their eyes like that. The place was as hot as a greenhouse. The number five gov granted me permission to give the place a refit. New desks, new chairs, new filing cabinets. It was money well spent because everybody knows, a tidy place is a tidy mind. If you create an environment where people are happy working, they'll work a lot harder and they'll be more invested in their job. Which is precisely the attitude needed in a security hub. Most of all, I wanted to welcome people in. I wanted to say: 'Come in, sit down, have a cuppa, what's been happening on your wing? Who's been wheeling and dealing? Talk to me.' I wanted information. Information. Information.

I'd finally found a department that had impact. Where the decisions we made would significantly improve the prison as a whole. Somewhere I could make a difference. I wanted to take our ranking up from a two to a four. I wanted to help put Wormwood Scrubs on the map as one of the best-run prisons in Britain.

I'm not going to lie, there were some eye-rolls when I made 'my suggestions'. Nobody likes change. One particular officer was very put out and in the end he asked for a transfer to another department. I respected his decision. I understood where he was coming from – annoyed that some bright spark had come in and wanted to change things that had been done since time immemorial. Yet in the same breath, if he couldn't embrace the good I was doing it was probably for the best that he moved on.

Phase two of my new dynamic security team was getting *us* out on the wing instead of being sat behind a desk pushing paper around. 'Talk to staff. Talk to prisoners,' I briefed them. I wanted my team to walk the wings and for the prisoners to go, 'Eh up, security's here.' For them to feel we had a presence in the jail and there would be trouble if rules were broken. I only had a small troop – two SOs, two officers and a couple of admin staff. Ironic, considering its importance, we were one of the smallest departments in the Scrubs. I didn't let that faze me though; it was enough to start making an impression.

It was the closest I'd felt to being in the forces and I was loving every second of it. Up until this point, I'd been tested but I hadn't been challenged. This was a proper challenge. I was springing out of bed in the mornings. My brain was constantly whirring with ideas on what we could do to strengthen our security. How were we going stop these drugs coming in? Our greatest problem by far.

A mandatory drug test on the prisoners revealed a whopping 30 per cent were using. We had one of the highest rates in the entire country. Not good! Contraband was being smuggled in via various channels. Through family visits. Through corrupt staff. Through zip lines from hospital rooftops! That tried-and-tested method of lobbing them over the prison walls was winning out. We were having twenty to thirty parcels chucked over every single day.

Twenty to thirty parcels a day! And only half of those were we able to intercept. Try as we might, we couldn't always get to them in time. If they landed when the prisoners were in the yard picking up rubbish then that was bye-bye package. Never to be seen again.

Clean-up duty was awarded to 'red bands' – prisoners we'd cherry picked for being 'trustworthy'. We hoped their moral compass was stronger than the others and they'd feel compelled to hand in any packages they found. There were also small incentives to help with their decision-making. That said, you can't trust anyone, ever, least of all in a prison. Which is why so many parcels were slipping through the net.

If the package fell into the wrong hands, the prisoner would either keep it for himself, or it would be delivered to the intended recipient specified on the parcel. Moving drugs around a prison happened within the blink of an eye. Often the prisoner carried the 'delivery' from A to B 'internally'. Yes, it is where you're imagining! It never ceased to amaze me what new transport method they'd conjure up. Hidden among the food on a kitchen trolley headed for the wings. Stashed in a loaf of bread being carried to a workshop. They'd tried it all.

The delivery boy might receive some of the drugs as a thank you or be paid off in another way. Once in the wing, the drugs and the problems they created would spread like a virus.

We were mostly dealing with cannabis and heroin but sometimes cocaine. Our largest package to date had contained a bar of cannabis that was twenty centimetres long and two inches thick, as well as fifteen wraps of heroin plus six mobile phones. A bloody great big thing chucked over the wall. How the suppliers expected that not to land with an attention-grabbing thud, I don't know.

Apart from the drops, you could tell the Scrubs had a drugs problem by a) the amount of mobiles we were finding

– phones were mostly used to make drug deals – and b) the amount of bullying and assaults going on.

Spooning – I'll spare you the graphic details but essentially it's when a gang pins down a prisoner and uses a spoon to try and fish out drugs they think he might be hiding up his rear end. Spooning assaults mostly took place in the shower or in a prisoner's cell on association hour. As you can imagine, it causes severe internal haemorrhaging which often needed hospital treatment.

You know your wing's got a drug problem when a prisoner is begging for you to move them down to the Seg for their own protection. The Seg! The last place on earth you'd want to be voluntarily! These were prisoners who'd got themselves into serious debt with a dealer and were facing a beating or even death if they remained on the wing. Payment for drugs is mostly done on the outside. A family member or a friend will be given the account details of where they need to transfer the money, and if for whatever reason they don't make the payment, Joe Bloggs on the inside was toast.

I wanted to stop things before they happened. No more of this reactive security. I wanted *dynamic* security.

Wherever I'd been posted I'd *reacted* to problems. I'd been putting out fires. Now I had a chance to stop them starting in the first place. A chance to make a difference. The words on the Underground poster that had called to me all those years ago were now ringing through my ears.

If you improve the security, you make it a safer place for everyone: for staff, for visitors and for the prisoners. Drugs have a far-reaching effect, far beyond the prison walls. For example, if the prisoner is an addict they might be putting huge pressure on their family to bring drugs in during a visit. The family might then get into all sorts of problems trying to source the drugs. The problem swells until it becomes a tsunami of debt, violence and even murder.

It was rare to catch me sitting behind my desk. I led by example. Whenever possible, I was marching up and down those wings. The cocky comments from the prisoners dried up. Before long I was getting, 'Watch out, lads, security's here.' They knew better than to mess with me.

I also made my presence felt outside of the wings. I walked around the grounds to see what was what. When I say grounds, I mean the strip of land sandwiched between the wings and the prison wall. A refuse tip might be a more accurate description. Piled high with plastic bottles, food, anything and everything the prisoners could lob through the gap in their cell window. They did it to try and piss the staff off, like naughty children antagonising their teacher. Between the crap you might be lucky enough to spot a drugs package. Or, if you were really lucky, bear witness to it flying over the wall.

The memory is so vivid it could have been yesterday. It was a bright sunny morning in spring. The sky was clear and blue and there was a slight easterly breeze. I was doing a perimeter check with one of the two security officers on my team. I think we may even have been chatting about the weather when, suddenly, a pigeon fell from the sky and landed six feet in front of me.

THE GOVERNOR

Thud.

On its back. Wing splayed. I nudged it with my toe. Dead as a dodo.

'Two guesses what he's carrying and it's not a paper message,' I said to the officer.

Drones weren't yet a thing back then. Dead pigeons stuffed with drugs were all the rage. Tennis balls were also a popular choice of conduit. It was common knowledge we kept dogs and trained them in the yard, so the dealers – repeatedly – hoped we might overlook a stray ball.

I stared at the pigeon by my foot. The stiches across its stomach were clearly marked out. Not the best craftsmanship. I was in no hurry to touch it.

'Are you going to pick it up?' the officer asked.

'Nah, you are.' I let him have the honours. 'Because you're going to do the paperwork on it.'

He grimaced. 'Thanks, boss.'

Barely a year after stepping foot in the security office I rose through the ranks to become deputy head of security and operations, number five gov for short. Sixteen years I'd grafted in Holloway and in that time I'd been promoted only once. Within six years of starting at the Scrubs, in a men's prison where I'd initially assumed the odds were not in my favour, I'd zipped up the career ladder. What that says, I don't know. I work better with men? Maybe. Whatever the reason, the news knocked me sideways. I'd become something I'd never in a million years dreamed I'd be.

I was a governor.

Chapter 16

LAW AND HOARDER

HMP Wormwood Scrubs: October 2006

'It's like a clown's pocket!' My eyes were bulging at the amount of drugs and phones that came out of her. How was that even possible? A whole shopping bag's worth of contraband, stuffed inside her. I thought I'd seen it all until that day.

The sting operation began with a tip-off. I hadn't wasted any time in my new role as deputy head of security to begin waging our war on drugs. I'd set up an intel office, separate from the security office, and appointed a principal officer to run it: Mark. He was a great bloke who had a sharp eye for detail, which was exactly the skill set I needed to run covert operations and intelligence gathering. He was also friendly and approachable, someone the staff could come to with information, which was precisely what happened.

An officer on a wing had heard murmurings that a solicitor was bringing drugs in for their client. We didn't know who this solicitor was, if they were male or female, but we did have the prisoner's name: Jeremy Northbridge. We also had a record of everyone who had visited him since he'd arrived at the Scrubs.

My eyes scanned over the names Mark had just handed me.

'Katherine Shawcross.' The eyebrow went up. 'Get on to the solicitors' firm she claims to be with and see if it's kosher.'

Shawcross had visited Northbridge half a dozen times over the past few months. If the tip-off was to be true then that was a whole lot of drugs that could have been smuggled in.

Mark nodded. 'Sure thing, gov.' He was excited as I was to catch her out. A bent solicitor would be a big coup for us.

One phone call later and we had our answer. The London law firm was the real deal but she wasn't. Katherine Shawcross had been faking her credentials; they'd never even heard of her.

Gotcha, I thought. All we needed to do now was set up the sting operation to catch her red-handed.

'Visits' were another very common way family, friends, dealers and significant others would try and smuggle contraband into the jail. The handover is often done either at the beginning or the end of the meeting and carried out in a whole manner of ways. Quite often it's through kissing. Sometimes it's slipped in a drink the family member has purchased from the canteen. The prisoner will swallow the drugs and wait for nature to take its course. Another more revolting technique would be a handshake followed by the prisoner shoving the drugs that had been passed to them down their trousers and up their bum. You'd think it would cause a spectacle, but oh no, they are incredibly rehearsed and speedy in their delivery. They can get it up there within a blink of an eye.

The social visitors area was situated just inside the main prison. It was a large rectangular room filled with tables and plastic chairs and a blue mottled carpet that had seen better days. The canteen hatch was to the side with shelves full of sugary snacks and drinks. Visitors could buy prisoners treats up to the value of twenty pounds.

The room was closely guarded and watched by officers, often with sniffer dogs. There was also CCTV: we had several cameras that could zoom in on the tables where the prisoners would sit across from their loved ones.

Solicitor visits were different though. As their conversations with their client were private, they didn't have to be 'in sound of a prison officer'. They were allowed the privilege of sitting in the sound-proofed booths downstairs in legal visits. The booths were also closely watched, but Katherine Shawcross had clearly viewed this as an opportunity to be exploited. She'd underestimated my department.

The records had her booked in for another legal visit the next day, between 6 and 7 p.m. We'd be ready and waiting this time.

I got on to the police liaison officer to help arrange for back-up. Justin worked for the Met Police but he was based in our security office. Every prison has its own liaison officer in the police, acting as the go-between. It was a line of communication I was continuously fighting to improve since I'd stepped up as governor. For some time it had felt like a one-way street, the police taking our intel and not giving much back in return. Justin and I were working to change that. He was now passing me back intel on prisoners beyond what we could see on our records. For example, Joe Bloggs might be serving time for murder but he also had a long string of arrests on suspicion of drug dealing. Knowing Joe Bloggs had a dodgy past in narcotics would give us a head start on who to keep an eye on if dealing became rife on his wing. I'm sure you can see where I'm going with this. A two-way street with the police was essential to improving security in the Scrubs.

Justin was just the sort of copper you'd want to work with. Apart from being on the same page as me he also had a dry sense of humour. He was about my height. Square set. Dark hair with a lovely broad smile. He didn't waste any time giving Hammersmith Police the heads-up about Katherine Shawcross. Justin asked for a couple of uniforms – officers – to be there when she visited, ready to make an arrest if we found drugs on her.

We could do strip searches but we weren't legally allowed to carry out internal searches. Nor would we want to, I might add! So it was best to leave that to the Old Bill. They were the ones who would make the arrest, so it was easier to leave the evidence gathering to them. Plus, in strip-searching a solicitor – we couldn't be a hundred per cent certain she wasn't – we could have been on very dodgy territory. She'd be scrutinising our procedure for failings and we could end up with a lawsuit on our hands even if we'd done everything by the book. Not worth the extra hassle.

A male and a female police officer turned up at the Scrubs half an hour before Shawcross was due to arrive. We briefed them on the situation and they took position alongside us.

Jeremy Northbridge was brought down from the wing. We couldn't have him thinking anything was amiss and cottoning on to what was going on. One last-minute call to his 'solicitor' and it would be game over for us. Evenings were reserved for legal visits only, so it wouldn't have looked suspicious that there wasn't anyone else in the waiting room with him.

So while Northbridge waited for Shawcross, his drug mule, the police officers, Mark (my principal officer and right-hand man), plus another couple of officers and myself, all took position in the foyer. The foyer was where every visitor was routinely searched when they entered the jail. If we could find the contraband on Shawcross, we had her bang to rights.

'Where the hell is she?' I checked my watch for the gazillionth time. It was ten past six and I was starting to think that, despite our covert efforts, someone had tipped the alleged solicitor off.

'Yeah, it's not looking good.' Mark's brow had furrowed into two deep grooves.

'Let's give her five more minutes.'

Just as the words left my mouth, the visitor door swung open.

Katherine Shawcross didn't look anything like I was expecting. Put it this way, I was more convinced than ever she wasn't a real solicitor. She was dirty and dishevelled wearing clothes that looked more nightclub ready than courtroom. She was dressed in a micro skirt and a cheap crumpled blouse. Her hair was greasy, bleached yellow with two-inch dark roots showing through. Her lips were painted bright red with lipstick. The only thing that was missing were fishnet stockings.

She wobbled into the room on high heels with all the grace of someone who'd had too many on a night out. I also noted that there was no obvious place she could hide drugs on her. Her handbag had already been placed in a locker, which meant, if she was concealing them, there was a very high probability they were stashed somewhere *inside* her. Didn't bear thinking about.

The coppers stepped forward, boxing her in on both sides.

'What's going on?' she said, her eyes skipping between the officers.

We had a dog and his handler there as well. Monty. Our star black labrador. He immediately sat down next to her indicating she was good for it.

Panic filled her eyes. Shawcross turned on her heels, but we were ready for her. Mark and I closed in on her from behind. The police officers were in front, boxing her in. She had nowhere to go.

'Katherine Shawcross, we are arresting you on suspicion of the possession of drugs with the intent to supply …' Mark began.

'Wha-a …' she stuttered.

'You do not have to say anything, but it may harm your defence if you do not mention when questioned something which you later rely on in court. Anything you do say may be given in evidence.'

All the colour drained from her face. Her pillarbox red lips moved, but this time no sound came out.

I couldn't disguise my Cheshire-cat grin. It was hard not to feel contempt for someone who was trying to bring drugs in. I thought that would be job done, but no, the female officer spoke up.

Pointing towards the side office, she informed Lisa: 'We're now going to strip-search you.'

Cripes! I didn't expect that. I thought they'd first take her back to the police station. Not do it here, now. For legal reasons, the officer needed another female official to be present while she conducted the search. Her colleague, being a bloke, wouldn't do, so she turned to me for help.

'Would you please be there?' she asked.

One look at this bogus lawyer and where she might be hiding her stash and I knew it was going to be a messy job. I've never been good at hiding what I think. My face must have spontaneously contorted into a grimace before the words left me. 'Umm, I'd love to, but …' I looked over to the two officers who'd patted her down when she first arrived. 'I'm going to pass that lovely job on to my operational support grade.'

Donna flashed me a look. 'Thanks, gov!'

Katherine looked just as mortified. All three ladies disappeared together into the side room while I had a bit of banter with the boys. Five minutes later they re-emerged, their faces a mixture of horror and astonishment. I wasn't quite sure what to expect.

The policewoman – who was wearing latex gloves – was holding a supermarket carrier bag at arm's length. Donna slid to my side and whispered in my ear: 'You're never going to believe this,' she started, slightly giggly with shock. 'The officer pulled out that carrier bag and inside is what's known as a nine bar, which is approximately 250 grams of cannabis, a couple of mobile phones, some wraps of heroin ...'

'What?' I looked at her. 'All of that, inside her?'

'Yes, gov.'

'Bloody hell.'

'I know, gov.'

Words failed me. I mean, how? How is that even possible?' Nature had a lot to answer for.

There was no chance I was going anywhere near that bag to have a look.

'Thanks very much for letting me do that,' Donna added sarcastically.

'Christ almighty,' I chortled. 'It must have been like a clown's pocket.'

The police officer handcuffed Shawcross and arrested her again, this time not on suspicion of, but for possession of, drugs and mobiles with intent to supply.

We bagged and tagged the evidence as a favour to the police – they obviously weren't keen on having to carry the soiled shopping bag all the way back to the station, so the least we could do was to put it in an evidence bag for them – and away she went to Hammersmith Police Station. No longer a threat to Wormwood Scrubs.

Once Shawcross was at the police station, faced with the fear of being sent to prison, she started to sing like a canary. Informing the officers of everything she'd been up to with the hope of a judge giving her a more lenient sentence. Justin, our liaison officer, let me know that our sting operation didn't just put an end to her bringing drugs into the Scrubs but that we'd also busted a much larger operation. Shawcross had been pulling her bogus solicitor act on three other prisons across the country – HMP Gartree in Leicestershire, HMP Norwich in Norfolk and HMP Strangeways in Manchester. She'd got around!

'Nice one.' I patted myself on the back.

Katherine Shawcross's boyfriend, Jeremy Northbridge, was serving life for murder. I think the police said something about her claiming to be under his spell, that he forced her to become a drugs mule. Or maybe the dealer she owed the money to gave her the prisoners' names and said he'd knock what she brought in to them off what she owed him. Dealing to prisoners is a lucrative business and a quick way to make a buck. A crappy old phone that's worth ten quid on the outside is worth about three hundred on the inside. Who knows how she got herself entangled in such a depraved mess, nor did I really care beyond the fact she had compromised the security of the jail. What I did know was that she was going to see what it was like on the other side of the bars. Victim of drug addiction and of a toxic relationship she may have been, but she'd also broken the law and that was her choice to make.

As for Northbridge, he'd been stuck in the waiting room the whole time the Shawcross drama had been playing out. I wish I'd been a fly on the wall – watching his panic build as he stared at the hands on the clock going around. It was quite possible he was facing a beating if he didn't supply whoever he'd promised on the inside. There's always a food chain when it comes to drugs.

His expression was as skittish as Katherine's when he saw Mark and I appear at the door. I'm not going to lie, we took great delight in telling him his supposed solicitor had been arrested and would no longer be visiting him or anyone else. What's more, he'd be heading down to the Seg that night.

'We believe you've been dealing drugs and you'll be moving from Wormwood Scrubs, ASAP,' I stated.

I had to move him on, for a number of reasons. Firstly, his safety was now compromised. Those prisoners who were expecting a delivery off him would come looking for their pound of flesh instead. The safety of anyone else involved could also be at risk if he stayed on. Being a lifer, Northbridge didn't have to worry about having his sentence extended. However, his dodgy dealings would certainly not do him any favours when it came to report-writing time.

He didn't take the news well; he started kicking off, calling us every name under the sun. The usual insults. Mark quickly dealt with him before things escalated. With the help of an officer, he grabbed Northbridge while a third officer held the prisoner's head to protect it. He was flailing this way and that, putting up such a fight he could have easily caused himself an injury. Northbridge was cuffed and taken to the Seg.

Everyone was on a high at what we'd achieved and I was chuffed to pieces, for the staff as well as myself. Katherine Shawcross got six and a half years for being a drugs mule. I wasn't there for the sentencing, I didn't have the time to spare, but I heard the judge wasn't impressed by the amount she'd been dealing and the frequency of her visits or the fact she'd even gone to the lengths of using headed paper from law firms to gain access to special solicitor visits. Justice was served.

Chapter 17

THE BOY THAT CRIED WOLF

HMP Wormwood Scrubs: 8 January 2007

Something didn't feel right.

My hairs were standing on end. My gut was screaming *this could be a trap*. But what could I do? My hands were tied. If I didn't say *yes* and the prisoner died I could be done for corporate manslaughter. This was one of the toughest decisions I'd had to make in my new job as governor.

It was creeping up to lunchtime. The windows in the office were fogged up with condensation from the bitter cold outside. The sky was concrete grey, pressing down on us, threatening snow. I was fed up with winter already.

The phone ringing broke my gloomy thoughts. It was Andy, the principal officer on E wing. From his first word he sounded harassed and worried.

'Boss, we've got a prisoner down here who urgently needs to go to hospital.'

Prisoners being rushed to hospital wasn't out of the ordinary in a place where suicide attempts, self-harm and drug overdoses were a fairly frequent occurrence. Some of these prisoners had serious health conditions that could erupt at any given moment despite their treatment care plan with our medical team. Sometimes you just get sick and there's no way to prepare for it.

But every time I heard those words, a wave of stress steamrolled through me.

'Can you tell me more? What's wrong with him?'

'I dunno. The doc doesn't know yet. He says it's serious. He's rolling around screaming he's in pain.'

'Who is it?'

'Ryan Faulkner.'

The name didn't ring a bell.

'Okay,' I replied. 'I'll get back to you.'

It was my job now to risk access the situation before we gave it the all-clear. I asked one of the officers in my team to have a look into Faulkner's file. Why? Because escorting a prisoner to hospital was a big deal. It instantly thrust us into a vulnerable position – we were no longer working from a controlled environment. Now there were hundreds of risk factors involved. As deputy head of security the things at the forefront of my mind were: a) Could this prisoner harm a member of the public? b) Could this prisoner try to escape? Hopefully his file would shed some light.

The officer didn't have to say anything as he carried the bulging Manila file towards my desk. His eyes said it all.

I licked my forefinger and thumb and got stuck in.

'What the …?' *You're having a giraffe*.

Possession of firearms, which he was serving a minimum of five years for, was a red flag for starters. I winced as I read on. There were a seismic number of security breach reports. He'd been abusive to staff. He'd been caught with mobiles, with drugs, and …

My breath caught in my throat.

We'd had some fresh intel that Faulkner had been planning a prison break. What's more, he had previous – he'd escaped custody, not once but twice before, including breaking out from a prison van. In May 2000, following an appearance at Tower Bridge Magistrates' Court for armed robbery, Faulkner had somehow managed to get out of the van while it stopped in traffic on Tower Bridge Road.

Wow. This guy was Harry Houdini.

The intel about him planning his next escape could have been a load of rubbish. It could have been gossip – a prisoner trying to settle a score or trying to get Faulkner moved to another prison. It happens a lot with rival drug gangs. But let's face it, it wasn't looking good, especially when the prisoner in question was suddenly struck down with a mystery illness and needed to urgently be taken out of the prison.

This was too big a situation to be handling on my own. I rang my boss, the number four gov, who was in the office above me. I explained the hospital situation and asked for some guidance.

'He's writhing around in agony,' I said, with a raised eyebrow. The scenario reminded me a little of the way footballers fake their injuries to be awarded a foul. We all know it happens. In my experience, it's often the ones who aren't obviously in pain – the quiet ones – who need the most urgent medical attention. I wasn't saying for sure Faulkner was making it up, but coupled with his history and the intel we had, it was definitely raising too many eyebrows. My boss, Caroline Nauman, thought so too.

'I'll come down immediately,' she said, hanging up.

The number four gov, the PO and I were all crowded around my desk, taking it in turns to flick through the concerning material in the file. We all wore the same look – severe mistrust. I turned to Caroline.

'What do you think we should do?'

Before she had time to reply, the phone rang.

'Governor Frake.' I was still getting used to saying those words. It was growing on me, the job I'd initially feared had become my reason to bounce out of bed in the mornings. Even in testing times such as this.

'It's Doctor Blake calling about Ryan Faulkner.'

Understandably, from his point of view, he wanted to push for a decision.

'We have to get him to hospital now,' the doc insisted.

Caroline and the PO were listening in intently.

'Can you tell me what's wrong with him?' I pressed for details.

'He's in a lot of pain, we just need to get him to hospital to be checked over properly.'

We were still no closer to the truth. Here was the perfect example of where prison staff and medical staff often collide. Doctor Blake was looking at Ryan Faulkner as a patient. I was looking at Ryan Faulkner as a dangerous prisoner who could be a serious security risk. My job was to keep the Scrubs secure. Dr Blake's job was to keep the prisoners fit and healthy. On the whole I got on well with the medical team and tried to see things from their perspective. But this stunk to high heaven. He was also trying to override my authority.

'Can't you give him some paracetamol?' My irritation levels were rising with the lack of information.

Dr Blake got shirty with me. 'I'm qualified to do my job, he needs hospital treatment.'

'Has he vomited?' I kept my cool, I kept digging.

'Not as yet.'

'Well, we're still discussing whether we should let him go.' My eyes met Caroline's, who nodded in agreement.

Doctor Blake broke the news: 'I've called the ambulance.'

What? 'It isn't your job to do that, it's control's,' I barked. He absolutely should not have gone ahead with such a risky decision without the say-so of the security department.

'Well, I've done it now. I need to get back to my patient.' Arrogantly, he put down the phone.

I gritted my teeth as I turned to Caroline to explain the situation.

There wasn't time to get into an argument with the doc. I had to keep my composure, we had to act fast, round up all the outside support we could get to manage the situation. I asked one of the officers on my team to contact Hammersmith Police, to tell them there was a prisoner we had concerns over who was about to be transported and could they please send some officers down to assist with the escort. Meanwhile, I spoke to the head of security at the hospital. We'd built up a good rapport since the drugs zip-line incident, so I felt confident we'd get them on board. I warned him of the situation. I used the words 'extremely concerned' and asked if he'd put extra officers on standby in the A&E department. He said of course and got straight to it, which gave me a fraction of relief.

I got back to the E wing orderly, Andy, to check up on Faulkner's condition. To my horror, he replied: 'Gov, I don't think there's much wrong with this geezer. I think he's faking it. But the medics are convinced.'

I dropped my head into my hands. My anxiety ratcheting up. 'I hear you. Anyone making a big display of rolling around in agony is suspicious in my book,' I replied. 'But if the doc's made that decision, we can't go against it.'

We couldn't. What if Ryan Faulkner died? Apart from a loss of life being a tragedy, all hell would break lose. We'd be done for corporate manslaughter. My hands were tied.

'But, gov?' The orderly was as fearful as I was.

'You're just going to have to do your job – help oversee him into the ambulance. You better jack up a three-man team.'

Usually we only send out two staff on an escort, one of whom would be handcuffed to the prisoner. It was lunchtime, I only had a skeleton crew working, but I couldn't take any risks with Faulkner, so I pulled another officer from the lunch patrol.

Andy rustled up the team for me. One woman and two men: John, Steve and Jenny, the SO who would be in charge of the escort. She nipped in to the security office to get kitted out with handcuffs and a mobile phone. Jenny appeared as tense as the rest of us. Nobody wanted this to go ahead bar the doc.

'What have the police said?' I asked my officer for an update.

He shook his head forlornly. 'They say they're busy, they can't give us any men but they'll send a patrol car to pass by the hospital.

I lost it.

'Did you tell them how serious this could be?' It was very unusual for us to call on the police for help with an escort and they would have known this.

'Yes, gov, they have no men to give us.'

'For fuck's sake!' Dread rose in my throat. I have a sixth sense about things, and I'm rarely wrong. This is what concerned me the most.

All we had now was our team for the journey and the hospital security team on arrival. The distance of travel was only three hundred metres but that was irrelevant – anything could happen in that time.

The ambulance entered the jail, drove through the courtyard and parked up at the back door of E wing. The two paramedics used the lift to get Faulkner down from the fours. He was handcuffed to Steve and all three officers sat with him in the back of the ambulance.

I went to check on my team just as they were leaving. The ambulance had stopped to wait for the gates to slide open. I was so stressed I didn't even feel the cold wind lash against me.

John unlocked the back door of the van and I was able to get a good look at Faulkner. Five foot ten. Medium build. Fair complexion. Brown hair. Brown eyes with a distinctive scar on his forearm. He looked pained – his brow was furrowed, he was breathing rapidly but he'd stopped his writhing around. Steve was sitting next to him, their wrists handcuffed together. We don't cuff prisoners to beds or chairs – that's a load of old nonsense made up by TV shows.

Warily, I asked John. 'Are you all okay?'

He nodded. 'All fine, gov.'

'Well, you know what to do.' I gave him a final nod and slammed the door shut. The ambulance inched forward, passing through the gates into the outside world.

Andy, the orderly officer, moved to my side, blowing into his hands to keep warm. He'd been there from the start, watching the drama unfold on the wing. We shot each other a sideways glance.

'I'm not happy about this,' he said, his breath puffing into the icy air.

I stared off into the distance, watching the huge gate slam shut.

'Tell me about it.'

Chapter 18

AMBUSHED

HMP Wormwood Scrubs:
8 January 2007

I'd been smoking like a trooper, watching the clock, drumming my fingertips on my desk – failing miserably at getting through my workload. I couldn't concentrate properly while I waited to hear back from Jenny and the team.

Half an hour had passed and she still wasn't picking up her mobile.

Something was wrong. Very wrong.

'Anything?' I called across the office, hoping she might have dialled one of the others. They all shook their heads sullenly.

Finally, the main phone on my desk rang. I couldn't pick it up quick enough. 'Jenny?' I almost shrieked.

It was the control room at the prison entrance. Where they have all the TV monitors with CCTV footage.

'There's been an armed escape. Faulkner has gone.'

Everything around me suddenly slid into slow motion.

'We've called the police. The staff are still at the hospital.'

As if I was underwater. The words – slow and distorted.

My worst nightmare had come true. I felt physically sick, like someone had smacked me in the stomach.

I couldn't give a toss about Faulkner; all I cared about was the staff. Armed escape meant firearms. Gun to your face. Finger on the trigger. I didn't know if they'd been hurt. I didn't know what state they were in. Another punch to the gut. This time from guilt: we'd been the ones to send them out.

Guilt swapped to anger – at the doctor for insisting Faulkner went to hospital, and then at myself for not doing more. I didn't know what else I could have done but that doesn't stop you hating yourself. All reason went out the window as panic set in.

The world around me sped up as I came to my senses and I leapt out of my chair. I burst into Caroline's office. She looked startled.

'He's gone,' I blurted. 'Armed escape.'

She stared at me in disbelief and then came the 'Fuuuck!'

Her chair went flying, smashing against the skirting board with the force of her jumping up. We legged it down the corridors. Officers leapt out the way, pinning their backs to the wall to let us pass. We threw our prison keys in at the gatehouse. All 'sign out' procedure went out the window.

'We're going to the hospital,' I shouted over my shoulder.

The icy air burned my lungs as we sprinted as fast as our legs could carry us. Never had I regretted my nicotine habit as much as during that three-hundred-metre sprint to Hammersmith Hospital.

The ambulance was still outside A&E. The back doors thrown wide open. It looked like a horror scene from a motorway crash. The ambulance driver was sitting on the back steps of the vehicle, sobbing, her head slung into her hands. The face of the hospital security guy was ashen. Wavering, like a tree in a storm, as if he was about to pass out at any moment. A dozen or more people had crowded around, rubbernecking. I searched the crowd. My heart was beating so fast I could hear it.

John, Steve, Jenny – Oh thank God, they were all there. They were alive.

My breath was fast and shallow from running. I tried to calm my heart as I rushed to their side.

Something was very wrong. As I closed in on the group huddled by the A&E entrance I noticed Steve's hands were violently trembling. John and Jenny were chatting at high speed, yet they weren't making any sense. It was clear that all three were in a dreadful state of shock.

It was hard to know what to say. Any words that left my mouth would have little impact on soothing the situation.

'Are any of you hurt?'

They all shook their heads lightly.

'Do you want to tell me what happened?'

Steve tried to speak but the words got trapped, dying in his mouth. John stepped in.

'We didn't know what was going on,' he blurted. 'We pulled in at the hospital and then something rammed into the back of us.'

'I thought it must have been some crazy driver rushing into A&E,' Jen spoke up. John nodded.

'Yeah and then the shouting started. Someone was yelling at the ambulance driver to open up the back and that's when we knew.' His voice quivered.

'Take your time,' I reassured him.

He breathed out. 'We knew it was coming, we braced ourselves for the doors to open.'

I almost felt like I'd been there with them; the tension was palpable.

'There were two men wearing balaclavas. They knew enough to not bother asking Steve. One of them pointed a gun at my face and said if I didn't give him the keys to the handcuffs he'd blow my brains out and the brains of everyone else around me.'

I drew a sharp breath. 'Jesus.'

'So I gave him the keys,' Steve said hesitantly.

'Of course you did!' I gave him a reassuring squeeze on the shoulder, 'No prisoner is worth your life.' I don't think it was possible for me to hate Faulkner more.

'Did he go willingly?' It might not have been Faulkner's mates breaking him free but a rival gang who were after him.

'Oh yeah, he went willingly,' John scoffed. 'He got in the Volvo and they sped off down the road.'

Steve had one half of the handcuffs still dangling from his wrist. He looked the most traumatised of all. Words were failing me.

'The police have been called. Maybe they will bother to make an appearance now,' I said, my tone laced with bitterness. I wanted to lash out at everyone and anyone who had failed me.

I did my best to try and calm down the team, offering my age-old remedy of a cup of tea – the hospital vending machine's finest brew. I waited with them for the police to arrive. Their statements were hopefully going to help catch those fuckers – Faulkner and his accomplices.

Those steps back to the Scrubs were made with a heavy heart. I wouldn't have wished my worst enemy to go through what Jen, Steve and John had suffered. Trauma like that can have serious long-lasting effects. For starters, you'd never want to go on an escort again – you'd be constantly looking over your shoulder for an ambush. For a gun barrel to be pointed between the eyes. It was impossible for me to guess how the team would recover; all I could do was be there for them.

It only took a few days for the cops to catch Faulkner. He was hiding out in a house in the Docklands area of East London. They still had to track down his mates who had abandoned the silver Volvo in Ealing. Faulkner was immediately made an E list prisoner – E for escape artist – and moved up to a Cat A prison, HMP Belmarsh to be precise. He would be made to wear 'patches' to make him stand out in a crowd – yellow stripes on a green boiler suit. I was relieved I didn't have to look him in the eye ever again.

A huge investigation into what happened followed. Thankfully no one at the Scrubs was found culpable. What else could we could have done? We were damned if we did and damned if we didn't. One thing I was thankful for though – that my path never crossed with that doctor's again. He resigned not long after the inquiry. Just as well.

Meanwhile, I had to carry on as normal.

I didn't *feel* normal though. It was like I was lugging a dead weight around my neck, which was strangling me with guilt, with lingering anger towards the doctor and perpetual worry for the wellbeing of the staff. It was dragging me into the ground with every footstep I took while patrolling the wings and the perimeter.

I had to keep my chin held high. That was the thing about my job as governor: I couldn't let it be seen that I was carrying the weight of the world on my shoulders. In the blink of an eye there could be another crisis – a suicide by hanging, an assault, a riot. Whatever it might be, I had to be ready for it – look confident and show I'd be able to make a high-stakes decision. I had to be titanium whether I wanted to be or not.

Caroline and I thought Faulkner must have used a smuggled mobile to tell his gang he was on the way to the hospital. That's what I meant when I said phones were some of the most dangerous weapons of all in a prison. The bane of our lives.

The best way to make good from bad was to learn from your mistakes. I needed to focus our attention on developing *even* more strategies to prevent phones coming in. To up the ante in our never-ending battle.

Chapter 19

RUM BUGGER, RUN

HMP Holloway:
15 May 1994

E-list prisoners in HMP Holloway didn't have a special uniform to make them stand out from the crowd back in 1994. These prisoners marked as those likely to attempt to escape were allowed to wear their civvies, as were all the women. To this day, female prisoners can still choose not to wear the prison-issue uniform. It's all thanks to a law that was passed in 1971. Research found that women prisoners responded better to rules if they were allowed to wear their own clothes. I suppose, psychologically, it makes them feel more free and connected to their former life, which in turn has a calming effect.

It was a summery Sunday afternoon. The sun was blazing, the sky was turquoise blue and all the ladies at Holloway, myself included, were wearing short sleeves to keep cool. I was the senior officer on duty in the control room, comms as it was known, which was the hub of the prison. It looked just as you might imagine, with CCTV screens and a big map of the prison mounted on the wall with little bulbs that lit up if an alarm bell or a fire alarm was pressed. The switchboard was navigated from comms and we had a microphone to communicate with the radio stations throughout the prison – walkie-talkies, etc. It wasn't called the control room for nothing – all movements of prisoners and vehicles went through us. If that wasn't enough, we also had a police radio that allowed us to listen in to their conversations. That could come in very handy because it alerted us to any major incidents in our area that we would need to monitor.

One officer was watching the screens while I logged the free flow of the prisoners coming and going from their various wings to exercise. We had a giant whiteboard to mark down and keep track of all the movements. It was twenty something years ago, remember; now it would all be computerised.

The entire jail had been tipped out into the four exercise yards to make the most of the glorious weather. We liked to get the prisoners outside as often as possible as it improved the general mood, which made them easier to manage.

Melanie Myers was what you could describe as a 'rum bugger'. Up to all sorts. So much so, she'd only been at Holloway for a month but she was already marked as an E-list. She was only nineteen years old and was facing spending the best part of her life behind bars.

Melanie had been charged with murder – for stabbing a taxi driver to death in the course of a bungled robbery. The teenage boy she'd been in the car with had been given the lesser charge of manslaughter. Apparently they'd both blamed each other for doing it but Myers was said to have been the one who stabbed the poor driver through the heart. From what I heard the evidence was stacked against her and she was likely to go down for it. Violent and wily as a fox, Melanie wasn't someone you wanted to let out of your sight.

Prisoners who were on the E-list were escorted everywhere by at least one officer carrying a radio and a logbook. Location? Time? Where are you moving the E-list to next? All these things had to be noted down by the officer, and consistently so.

Melanie had a memorable face thanks to her sticky-out Mickey Mouse ears. She was mixed race with black hair, was five foot ten and had one of those mouths that naturally turned down. The officer escorting her to the exercise yard radioed the control room. 'Hello, MJ, it's Alpha One.' MJ was the unique call sign for the prison. As the control room, you were that title.

'Go head, Alpha One,' I replied.

'I'm moving the E-list prisoner book number one to Bravo wing exercise yard.' Bravo being B wing of course.

I logged it down and that was that.

The women were out in the sunshine for a good hour. It was around 3 p.m. when the officers began bringing them in, wing by wing. Yard by yard.

I was now manning the switchboard. A call came through from a man with a strong Irish accent.

'Hi there,' he began merrily. 'I'm not sure whether you know this or not, I'm in the Holloway Castle' – i.e. the local boozer – 'and I've just seen a prisoner jumping over the wall and going past the pub.'

My first thought: *This guy's had a few too many Guinnesses to drink.* Prank calls were a common occurrence. 'Can you ask Myra Hindley what time she's coming out to play,' was a classic, even though Myra hadn't been at Holloway since 1974. Another firm favourite was the character Deirdre from *Coronation Street.* When she was sent to prison in the soap series we used to get an endless stream of calls asking for us to free her. 'Free Deirdre!' 'She shouldn't be locked up. Why can't you let her out.' That kind of nonsense. People with too much time on their hands.

So when a drunk rang in to say he'd seen a prisoner escape, you can understand I had my doubts. That said, I would never turn a blind eye to anything that could be a potential security risk. Even if it sounded like a prank.

I radioed around the entire prison asking the senior officers on every wing to hurry up, lock up and do a head count.

I had a lot of huffing and puffing in my ear.

'Just do it,' I stressed. 'I want to know if there's anyone missing.' Another load of 'What! Are you kidding?' Believe it or not, escapees were rare, hence their reaction.

'Quick as you can.' It was better to be safe than sorry.

Not long after I'd put the order in I received a frantic call from Alpha One. She was breathless. Manic. On the verge of hyperventilating.

'I've got three missing. I've got three fucking prisoners missing!' she squealed. 'And one of them is the E-list!'

Bloody hell. The guy down the pub hadn't been seeing double.

I needed to alert Scotland Yard pronto.

We had a direct line from the control room to the police station. The phone was bright red in colour and as soon as you picked up the receiver it dialled you in. We called it the bat phone. For obvious reasons. Every day it was tested to make sure it worked.

My heart was going as I waited for a detective to pick up.

'Scotland Yard.'

I don't know why, but you could always count on whoever picked up the bat phone to be grumpy.

'It's Senior Officer Vanessa Frake from Holloway Prison. We believe we've had an escape. We have three prisoners who are unaccounted for. We've had a call from an alleged witness [alleged because I didn't know if he was pie-eyed] from across the road in the garden of the Holloway Castle pub and he believes he saw at least one prisoner jump down from the wall.' I paused, cringing. 'One of whom is an E-list.'

How embarrassed did I feel having to tell Scotland Yard that a prisoner that had been earmarked for likely to escape had escaped. My cheeks went almost as red as the phone.

'Bloody hell!' came the reply.

As the police raced over to us, the circus inside the jail got under way.

After conducting another head count, after making sure every single prisoner was locked up, we needed to search the jail from top to bottom.

The police arrived within minutes, no exaggeration. They got to work securing the perimeter of the jail and scouring the entire neighbourhood and beyond. Our job was to make sure Melanie Myers and her gang weren't hiding somewhere inside. We couldn't be certain the member of the public was telling the truth. He could have been part of an alternative escape plan for all we knew.

The contingency plans, which were overseen by the duty governor, the number one governor Janet King and the area manager, were full on. You couldn't even escape to the toilet it was that hectic. It took about three hours to conduct a thorough search of the jail and its grounds, bearing in mind we had half our usual workforce as it was a Sunday.

Once we'd confirmed they really had done a runner, well, there wasn't a lot else we could do. It was up to the Old Bill to catch them. From there on in, it was about collecting endless statements and signing off the paperwork. Witness reports that later came in said they spotted Melanie and the two other women make a call from a pay phone near the prison and then *walk* north along the Camden Road.

I spent the evening running around like a headless chicken. I didn't get to leave work until after 11 p.m. I'd clocked in at 6.30 a.m. I was knackered.

It took a little while to work out how the three women, who were all on remand, had managed to get away, because they'd pulled off the seemingly impossible. They'd broken a glass door at the back of the swimming pool – yes, Holloway had an actual pool for the women to exercise in!

From there, they'd somehow managed to clamber up onto the roof of the pool building. As the wings were joined together in a hospital layout, they scuttled across the roof-tops until they reached the prison wall, which the end wing backed on to.

Back then Holloway didn't have barbed wire on top of its wall. The council had forbidden it as it was deemed unsightly for the residents living in the neighbouring houses. No wire made it a hell of a lot easier for the ladies to clamber down.

That said, it was still twelve foot high and Melanie was injured when she landed. We know this because she was eventually caught four days later when she checked herself into St Bartholomew's Hospital in central London with a back injury. She checked in under another name but by then her mugshot had been plastered on every news channel going, so she didn't stand a chance of not being identified.

The other two women, Jean Jarvis, who'd been charged with burglary, and Stephanie Osbourne, who was on remand for supplying drugs, were eventually caught.

All of the staff on duty that day, including the officer who let Melanie and the two other women out of her sight, became part of a huge internal investigation commissioned by the then director general of the prison service, Derek Lewis, and overseen by a governor from Long Lartin high-security jail.

No one person was found to blame. The escape was made possible thanks to a catalogue of failures including the general lack of security and the fact there was no barbed wire on the prison walls. The officer who failed to count the prisoners off the exercise yard was ordinarily a very competent officer. It was a daft mistake to make, but one many of us could have fallen foul of. It served as a good example to us all – never take your eye off the ball. She was mortified though and was ribbed about it for months to come.

As for the barbed wire: the council immediately approved planning permission for it to be installed.

Chapter 20

WHO'S THE BOSS?

HMP Wormwood Scrubs:
November 2007

Mobile phones in prisons – I've spoken about the immeasurable harm they can cause. I've mentioned certain prisoners, i.e. Phones 4u, who ran a little sideline supplying them. What I haven't done is explain one of the main 'channels' by which they were entering the prison. I also need to reveal the devices we used to detect them. As governor number five, this was now my bag. Unfortunately, it was an area that often boarded on grotesque, shall we say.

All new prisoners are told to sit on the BOSS – Body Orifice Security Scanner when they come in at reception in order to check if they are concealing a phone or a weapon. The BOSS looked like an electric chair. Gun-metal grey, solid and clunky – all it was missing was leather straps to tie you down. Perhaps not the most welcoming of sights when you first arrive in a prison.

The regulars, i.e. the prisoners who were in and out of the Scrubs like jack-in-the-boxes, knew exactly what it was and what it was used for, and would try everything in their repertoire to outfox it. No one can beat the BOSS chair though. *No one*. If there's a phone somewhere hidden on or in your body, thanks to its very expensive technology that can detect metallic objects, it *will* find it and that red light *will* go on.

How do the prisoners try to smuggle them in? There's no delicate way of putting this – they stick them up their backsides. And you wouldn't believe the size of the phones and how many of them they can stuff up there.

As you can imagine, the rear orifice doesn't always appreciate having a tonne of metal thrust up there. An issue I'd never really had to deal with until I was governor.

Patrick was a traveller, a jack of all trades, someone who, from what I could tell, had their fingers stuck in too many pies. He was in the Scrubs for theft; it wasn't his first time in the nick – we could call him a career criminal. Thanks to the new dynamic security I'd put in motion, my office was gradually becoming a hub of flowing information. We'd had some intel come in to suggest Patrick was in possession of an illegal phone. Since he'd passed the BOSS chair on entrance, he'd clearly acquired the device post-arrival at the Scrubs.

The first line of response would be to search Patrick's cell. I counter-signed the SIR – Security Information Report – listing a load of stuff I wanted to happen such as having his phone calls monitored and having his interactions with other prisoners watched. I insisted the searching of his cell must be carried out by my team and not the officers on Patrick's wing. Why? It keeps things neutral and doesn't compromise the day-to-day relationships between prisoners and wing officers. Otherwise resentment and mistrust builds, creating unnecessary tension.

The security-led search with two of my staff went ahead that morning. I was at my desk when the call came through from the wing twenty minutes later. It was Gareth with an update.

'What you got for me?' I asked, hopeful they'd nabbed him.

'Bit of a problem, gov,' Gareth replied. 'As soon as we busted his cell he rushed into the toilet. He came out a few minutes later.'

'No toilet flush?'

'No.'

'And no sign of it in the toilet or his cell or on him?'

'No.'

I'm no Sherlock Holmes but it didn't take a super sleuth to work out that the phone must be concealed somewhere *inside* Patrick. Three guesses where.

'Take him down the Seg and put him on the BOSS chair,' I instructed. The chair had wheels and could be moved around the prison. Nine times out of ten you could find it in the hallway at reception or in the Seg for moments like this.

I had a gut feeling that probably wouldn't be the end of it. A career criminal like Patrick wasn't likely to give that phone up easily. I could have counted down the minutes until my phone rang again.

'Yes, Gareth?' I answered.

'Gov, I'm at the Seg, the BOSS chair is going off like nobody's business. He's still denying it though. Can you come over?'

'With pleasure,' I replied. It always amused me when prisoners thought they could beat the BOSS.

The Seg was a two-minute walk, if that, from my office. Past the chapel, a Grade II listed building, the largest prison chapel in the whole of the UK. It was truly a work of art – built by various prisoners between 1874 and 1891. The inside, such as the murals and the stained-glass windows, were also designed by prisoners. The Seg was the stand-alone wing next door.

I welcomed the stretch of my legs. I'd been cooped up behind my desk all morning putting out fires. Since becoming a gov, my workload had quadrupled. There was always someone needing something done.

One last long glorious breath of fresh air into my lungs and I prepared myself for the possibility of being hit with the stench of a dirty protest.

'Morning, gov.' Gareth greeted me at the door with a slightly weary expression.

To my delight, the Seg was in a relative state of calm and freshly fragranced with disinfectant. The BOSS chair was on the landing on the ground floor, sticking out like a sore thumb. Patrick was standing next to it looking somewhat uncomfortable. He was very tall, six foot five, and had a slight stoop because of it. White, mid-thirties, with brown shoulder-length hair which he wore in a ponytail.

Gareth pulled me aside to whisper in my ear.

'He's definitely got it stuffed up there – he was walking funny on the way over here.'

'I'm not surprised.' It always amazed me how they even managed to get it up there in the first place. 'Stick him on the chair,' I said.

Patrick shot me a look.

To which I responded: 'There's no point giving me daggers – it's your own fault you're down here.'

He gingerly lowered himself down, wincing as he touched the seat. No sooner had his bum touched the metal than the red light began flashing.

I folded my arms, sighing with impatience.

'Look, Patrick, we know you've got a mobile phone.'

He looked away.

'You're not going back to your cell until you hand it over.'

We were legally not allowed to 'retrieve the phone'. And, just as with the bogus lawyer, nor would we want to. Usually when caught bang to rights, the prisoner would remove the phone himself and hand it to some poor member of staff.

'I'm not giving you anything,' he grumped, like a petulant kid.

'Right then. I'll sign you up for good order and discipline and you can stay down here until you come to your senses. No skin off my nose. It's your choice how long you're down here for.'

He wasn't particularly happy with my decision. I left him chomping at the bit.

'Make sure you stick him on the BOSS chair first thing every morning,' I instructed the Seg staff. They strip-searched him and put him in a cell while I wrote up a report for him to stay down there for as long as it took to retrieve the phone.

It was impossible to calculate how long Patrick's digestive system would hold out. There was also the possibility he might shove the phone straight back up where it came from – doesn't bear thinking about the details – but eventually he would crack. They always did. There is only so much solitary confinement one person can take.

Two days later I got the call from the Seg, only it wasn't the conversation I was expecting to have.

'Gov, Patrick has still got the phone but he wants to give it up,' the officer on duty told me.

Something wasn't adding up in that sentence.

'Well, tell him to hand it over then.'

There was a pause.

'He would, only he can't get it out. It's stuck!'

For fuck's sake. This was all I needed. A security breach that had escalated into a health risk. No wonder the guy was wincing. Jeeez.

'Okay, leave it with me,' I groaned.

I got on to the healthcare department where the doctors and nurses were based. Our healthcare department was H1 and H2 the other side of the prison. H1 housed prisoners with mental-health issues, H2 was offices and clinics. Prisoners who were ill or who had mental-health problems would have around-the-clock medical care.

The on-duty doctor was as surprised as I was to receive the news we had a prisoner with a phone stuck up his arse. Not the doctor who had dealt with Ryan Faulkner, who had since left. I'm biting my tongue to stop myself saying anything further about *him*. It was a woman and she immediately went to see to Patrick. Rather her than me.

The news of the obstruction had circulated around the office. Jokes were being cracked. The usual dark prison humour that got us through the day. I mean, in what other job would you be dealing with such a crisis?

I'd prepared myself for the worst. Our medical staff were unwilling to remove such items from prisoners as we didn't have the facilities to ensure their safety if something went wrong – i.e. we couldn't perform surgery!

The doctor called me back with those dreaded words: 'He's got to go to hospital.'

As you know, and with good reason, I hated sending the prisoners out. That said, Patrick was hardly a cunning escape artist. He could barely manage to hide a phone let alone have the nous to plan a prison break. I was confident he hadn't engineered for his mobile to get stuck up his bum.

I let Andy the PO get on with sorting the escort to Hammersmith Hospital.

I'm sure you'll be glad to hear the phone was successfully extracted. It was a Nokia 3310, the one you could play that Snake game on. It was bagged up and returned to the Scrubs, as was Patrick (returned, not bagged up). The phone was passed on to Justin, the police liaison officer, who passed it on again to the anti-corruption team in head office where a whiz team of hackers would download the phone's information and examine it for intel. Mobile phones are your biggest footprint. They show what you've looked at, what you've read, what you've said, where you've been, who you're in contact with, and these are just the basics.

I'm glad pulling that phone apart wasn't my job though. Imagine being the one to have to touch those keys. Yuk.

Chapter 21

WHAT A SHAMBLES

HMP Wormwood Scrubs:
April 2008

'You've got to be fucking kidding,'

I stared at the front page of the *Sun* newspaper in disbelief.

'How the fuck did this happen?'

I was raging. This was going to reflect terribly on all of us. My department would look bad. The officers in charge of the wing would be crucified. The entire prison was going to appear a joke – which was a crime in itself. We'd been working so hard – and winning – at turning the Scrubs into one of the most secure jails in the country. Then a prisoner takes a picture of our resident celebrity drug addict in his cell on an illegal mobile phone, sends it to a tabloid paper and BAM, we're front-page news. Slaughtered for our supposed slack security.

'The pictures are the most high-profile breach of prison security of their type since an image of Soham murderer Ian Huntley

in his cell at Woodhill Prison, near Milton Keynes, was taken by an undercover reporter.'

It wasn't fair. If you hadn't guessed, or heard my use of expletives, I was livid. I hated the journalist for reporting the story, I hated the press for once again jumping on the bandwagon to paint the prison system in a bad light. And I hated Pete Doherty, lead singer of Babyshambles (and then later, The Libertines), boyfriend of supermodel Kate Moss, for turning my morning into a circus.

Yeah, I really disliked him. He was a cocky so-and-so from the moment he stepped foot inside the Scrubs twelve days earlier.

For months leading up to his arrest, Doherty had been flaunting his drug use left, right and centre, thinking he was above the law because he was some sort of rock star; I say 'rock star' in inverted commas. The papers had been full of stories about his heroin use and his tempestuous relation-ship with Kate Moss. Finally the cops had had enough, and the judge presiding over him had sent him to the Scrubs for three and a half months as punishment for repeatedly breaching bail conditions imposed for drug possession convictions. He'd been given a drugs treatment and testing order for possession of drugs including heroin, crack cocaine, cannabis and ketamine, but he'd failed to take the court-ordered drugs tests.

Doherty had been to prison only once before. In September 2003 – when he served two months of a six-month sentence for breaking into the flat of fellow band member Carl Barât. However, he'd appeared in court more than fifteen times since 2004 but somehow always managed to avoid serving time. In September 2004 he was given a four-month suspended sentence after pleading guilty to carrying a flick knife.

Justice had been finally served. He was now my problem, as deputy head of security and ops. Just as with Rose West, I had to keep him out of harm's way. He was likely to only serve half of his sentence, so if I could get through those six weeks without any negative publicity, that would be ideal.

We had half an hour to prepare for Doherty's grand arrival. The court gave us the heads-up that we'd be receiving him while he was en route to us in the prison van. Part of my remit was handling the security at reception, so I called an emergency meeting with the number four governor – my direct boss – as well as my PO and the duty doctor. We all agreed that with such a prolonged history of drug abuse, Doherty should be placed on the detox unit located above the Seg. There he could be observed closely while on our methadone maintenance course. His safety and health came first.

It was a small unit with around-the-clock nursing care. The maximum number of inmates at any one time was around fifty. We didn't think there would be a problem having him on a wing – he wasn't a murderer or a child sex offender, so the risk of someone wanting to take a pop at him was low.

To make sure nothing personal about Doherty would be leaked to the press, I insisted that all his paperwork, which included his case file with photos and addresses and case details, would be sent directly to the security office after he was signed in. I would keep it under lock and key in my desk drawer.

To protect him even further, we let him forgo the whole reception formalities, and a team went through his warrant and property with him in the detox unit.

I didn't have much to do with him on a day-to-day basis, as I had a whole prison to look after. The staff on his wing would give me regular updates though and the feedback was always the same.

'He's up to all sorts. A total pain in the arse,' the detox unit officer said.

I rolled my eyes. 'What's he done now, for Pete's sake?'

Just as he flaunted his heroin use on the outside he was flaunting our rules on the inside.

The officer informed me how Doherty was always the last to be locked up at night, larking around, flashing a cocky wink when he was asked not to do something. He was demanding this, that and the other – expecting special treatment because he thought he was something special. Diva behaviour is bad news for a wing because it inspires and incites the other prisoners to think they can get away with the same.

'The prisoners are crowding around him, like flies to shit,' the officer said. 'I've had to replace his name card five times already because he keeps taking it down and signing it with his autograph.'

Above every cell door is the prisoner's name. It wouldn't

have surprised me if Doherty was trying to make a bit of cash on the side by handing out signed autographs. Why somebody would pay for that, God only knows.

I sighed out deeply, rubbing my forefinger across my brow as I thought over what to do next. 'If he keeps behaving like a twat, we'll have no choice but to move him.'

'Yes, gov,' the officer replied.

A couple of days later, the *Sun* newspaper story broke. On top of publishing a picture of Doherty in his cell, they also reported on how he had been supplied with heroin. A prisoner told the journalist he'd been buying gear with IOU notes while he waited for his prison wage to go into his account.

'We can't believe how much he's still clucking for it. They put him inside to force him to give up but Pete always has a need to feed his habit,' said the 'anonymous' prisoner.

It was 7 a.m. when the security officer handed me the paper. My hands were trembling with rage as I held the red top between them. It's virtually impossible to stop drugs coming into a prison. A story such as the *Sun*'s completely misled the public about the good work we'd achieved. The public would be reading the report thinking we allowed prisoners to walk up and down the wing taking photos and jacking up as a matter of course, which simply wasn't true. We worked so hard managing very difficult circumstances, managing extremely difficult prisoners, taking innumerable measure to prevent situations like this, and all of that effort was blown out of the water in thirty seconds when a reporter got hold of a story like this.

WHAT A SHAMBLES

I tossed the paper down on my desk.

As for Doherty – no doubt he had somehow got his hands on some gear. If you ask me, he never had any intention of using his time in jail to clean up his drug habit. He had zero inclination to use his sentence for doing good. All he wanted was to maintain his drug habit and be the rockstar junkie that everyone expected him to be.

I stood up abruptly from behind my desk and called out to the orderly officer.

Doherty thought he could waft in and out of prison. Well, now he was going to find himself wafting down to the Seg.

'I want him moved ASAP before the prisoners are unlocked,' I ordered.

It was the first time I'd had any one-on-one interaction with Pete Doherty. Until this point I'd managed the situation but let the officers deal with him. I was so furious I went to speak to him in person to get some answers.

The overwhelming smell of disinfectant rushed up my nose as soon as I entered the Seg. Followed by shouting and banging. The usual sounds of someone kicking off about being locked up.

'Where is he?' I had on my unimpressed face. The senior officer on duty didn't even have to ask who I was after. News travels fast around a jail.

Doherty's cell was next to the staff office so they could keep a keen eye on him. The officer unlocked his door and I had to bite my lip to restrain my anger.

He was on his bed wearing a prison-issue grey tracksuit bottoms and a light-blue T-shirt. His back was resting against the wall. One arm casually hooked over a raised knee, his hair dishevelled. He looked like he needed a good scrub in Dettol.

Doherty glanced at me sideways. I thought I'd be polite and introduce myself.

'I'm Governor Frake.'

He cast me a look as if to say, 'And …'

'And,' I finished off his silent question, 'I'm here to inform you why you've been moved to the Seg.'

I told him about the picture in the national newspaper and the reports that he was still using. He didn't look particularly surprised or interested in what I had to say.

'It's unacceptable,' I said. 'I gave you the benefit of the doubt but you've made it impossible for me not to move you down here.' Hands folding across my chest. 'Who was the prisoner that took the picture?'

He shrugged at me, grunted and mumbled something incomprehensible. Doherty was cocky but in a sullen petulant teenager kind of way.

'So you have nothing else to add?'

He shrugged again. Blinking a couple of times through those puffy dark-ringed eyes of his. His whole persona screaming: *Do you know who I am and who the fuck are you?*'

'Fine. Make yourself comfy. You won't be going back to the detox unit, you'll be staying here on good order and discipline for breaking prison rules.'

'I'll speak to my solicitor about that,' he piped up.

'You speak to who you like.' My turn to shrug. 'Enjoy your stay.' I left him sulking in his cell.

There was nothing I could do to reverse the damage the newspaper article had caused. What I could do, however, was send a few shock waves through the detox unit. Drugs were clearly rife in a wing dedicated to eradicating them. After some digging, intel gathering and powers of deduction, we worked out who Doherty's partners in crime were and devised a strategy to catch them red-handed.

'Time to get the dogs in!' I announced.

We were going to bust every single cell door in that unit just as I'd done in the lifer wing. Six a.m., we'd catch them off guard. No stone left unturned.

I'll spare you the details of another wing raid. The process was much like the last. Dogs barking, prisoners effing and blinding, multiple toilets being flushed at the same time. Despite the usual resistance, the operation proved fruitful. We found an array of phones and heroin wraps, while four of the prisoners we suspected to be involved with Doherty were indeed caught red-handed. They were promptly shipped out to various jails across the country. News of the raids was announced in a press release, which bought us back some good PR. Meanwhile, Doherty served out the remainder of his time on the Seg without any further drama.

I'd been out twice already that morning to warn the press they were on private property. It was Doherty's release day and every paparazzo and reporter going was camped outside the Scrubs. They were allowed on the pavement by the entrance or they could stand in the road if they so wished, but quite a few had ignored the warnings and slipped past the barrier to stand under the towers of the famous gatehouse.

'Out, now!' I pointed.

'And who are you?' they taunted me.

'I'm one of the governors. This is private property – if you don't move I will call the police and have you arrested.'

It would have made my day to see some of those cocky paps carted off. They were rude and disrespectful and all they cared about was getting the front page. Never mind us, who were trying to keep the prison safe and secure. Until Doherty set foot on that pavement, it was our job to protect him.

Doherty had dressed up for the occasion, wearing a black suit and tie, and a string of Catholic rosary beads draped around his neck. His belongings were slung across his back in a black gym bag.

The wooden door of the discharge gate slid open. Doherty swaggered through it, puffing away on a fag as he walked towards the huge crowd that had gathered.

He couldn't wait to hold court with the reporters. I, however, wasn't the slightest bit interested in what he had to say. He'd been my responsibility for twenty-nine days, and as soon as he had officially left the Scrubs, I turned and made my way back inside – to get on with doing my job.

Chapter 22

BENT OFFICER

HMP Wormwood Scrubs:
7 August 2008

'There's a line. A black-and-white line. There's no grey areas. You're this side and they are that side and never the twain shall meet.'

Those were the words spoken by my tutor at training school and I've never forgotten them. Corrupt prison staff are the lowest of the low as far as I'm concerned. Just as prisoners see sex abusers as scum, that's how I view bent officers.

Some people put on a uniform and assume it gives them power. For them to go on and abuse that power is despicable. It undermines the integrity of the system and their profession and it also puts their colleagues in a dangerous and precarious position because they are jeopardising the safety of the jail.

Since becoming a security governor, corruption was one of the things I was most passionate about wanting to weed out. You're always going to get bad apples in every basket, but I was cranking up the pressure on my staff, on myself, to root them out.

Anger, disappointment, I felt it all as I read through the latest piece of intel that had come in. It didn't altogether surprise me. There was something about her. It was hard to put my finger on it. Perhaps it was the way she interacted with the prisoners – in too friendly a manner. Being gruff and rude to prisoners is wrong, but being over-friendly is equally wrong and, moreover, dangerous.

Often the signs are there from the start, especially when it comes to female staff having affairs with prisoners. It kicks off with something seemingly innocent. Heavy make-up. More black eyeliner and mascara than usual. Red lipstick. A dark bra that shows through their white shirt. All these little signs communicate the same thing – look at me. I need to be noticed. Pay me attention.

Prisoners notice everything. They look for chinks in your armour. Weaknesses that they can use against you. They search for the non-verbal clues. They look for a difference.

It doesn't even need to be a change in clothing or make-up; it could be something as small and insignificant as adding a personal key ring to a key chain. They all signal the same thing to a prisoner: I'm willing to break the rules.

To them, a member of staff who breaks the rules equals a person who may be manipulated and possibly corrupted. A member of staff they can keep in their back pocket, some-one they can manipulate to smuggle in contraband. They're a member of staff who will get them their drugs. I'd say 90 per cent of the romances that develop between prisoners and staff have nothing to do with love, well not on the prisoner's side. They see the member of staff, male or female I hasten to add, as a meal ticket to getting what *they* want. Usually the member of staff craves attention so desperately, they fall for it. And that's how corruption mostly begins.

How it ends? Generally, not well. If we caught them, the prisoner was looking at an extended sentence and the staff member faced a significant amount of time behind bars. Let me tell you, prison is not the place you want to be if you're a bent member of staff or cop. As you can imagine, they are seen as a trophy target, a chance for the prisoners to get their revenge.

Making money from selling drugs and phones to prisoners or organised crime rings is another major motive for corruption. A member of staff can earn anything up to a couple of thousand a month. I suppose for those who had no morals it would be a nice little earner on the side.

Organised crime wasn't what I was dealing with here though. This was about a perverse kind of love and obsession.

For a month or so I'd been receiving intel that we had a bent officer among us. Someone who had been bringing drugs into the Scrubs for a prisoner they were having an affair with. Finally we had a breakthrough. I had a name.

Patricia Ollivierre, an officer on B wing, had been working in the jail for several years. A single mum of two. Thirty years old. A whole future ahead of her. So in God's name why she would want to risk it all for some nasty bit of work, I couldn't fathom.

It baffled me why someone would fall for a murderer or a rapist or someone who had abused kids. They were hardly a catch. Maybe it's the forbidden fruit element of it all, the bad boy appeal, goodness only knows.

Corrupt staff always make the same mistake though – they forget how prisoners love to talk. They're the worst kind of gossips. They've got nothing else to do with their time and showing off gets them kudos. While *she's* fantasising about their so-called romance, *he's* bragging about how he's got her wrapped around his finger. A conversation between a prisoner and his mate in the cell next door might go something a little like this:

'Can you get me some cannabis?'

'Yeah, it will cost you fifty quid for half an ounce. I've got a member of staff in my back pocket, they'll get it for me.'

'Nice one, mate. Who's that then?'

Next thing you know, word gets around that Patricia Ollivierre is supplying drugs and, unfortunately for her, that intel works its way back to security. All I needed now was the name of *him*.

When I received the news about Patricia, I was also busy rolling out a brand new scheme that could change the future of the Scrubs.

I was constantly pushing for the jail to be the best in anything to do with security, so when the opportunity to become the first jail in the UK to pilot a piece of technology that could detect mobile phones arose, I jumped all over it. 'Yes please, we'll sign up for that, thanks very much,' I told the London Prison Anti-Corruption Team.

I was proud of the rapport I'd built with the anti-corruption team at headquarters. The communication between us and them had been somewhat fractured when I started in security. Much like the office, which I had to rearrange upon my arrival, everything was there to work with but it wasn't running smoothly. Now I had monthly meetings with the task force to discuss who we suspected of corruption and what measures they would be implementing to catch corrupt staff in the act, i.e. surveillance operations. We also now had Justin, the police liaison officer, stationed in our security intel office, who was the go-between for us and the police.

The mobile phone detectors worked in much the same way to how you get caught watching TV without a licence. They pick up a signal – *if* the phone is switched on. The device looked like a walkie-talkie. It was small, black and flashed green when it picked up a signal. The number of flashing bars would increase the closer you moved to the phone or decrease if you stepped away from the signal. Perfect for walking past the cells on the landings.

After all the dramas we'd been through I couldn't wait to trial them – to wipe the smiles off those prisoners' faces who thought they could get one over on us. A bit of payback for all the harm mobiles had caused.

I rustled up a team. It was soul lifting to see how many volunteered for the trial. Fifteen officers forfeited a night in with their family or loved one or an evening on their own relaxing to come back into work at 9 p.m. and help me clean up the Scrubs. Nothing gave them more of a buzz than finding a phone because it was such a victory – a one-up to us. I bought them all sandwiches and drinks from the mess as a token of my thanks. I always felt staff worked better if you kept them well fed.

I kept the operation as hush-hush as possible. Only a few people knew what we were up to that evening – the duty governor being one of them – so as not to risk the operation being sabotaged.

All it took was for one prisoner to get wind of it before-hand, or to hear us coming on the night, and he'd make sure the entire wing knew. 'Security is on the wing,' he'd yell as loud as he could. Prisoners would jump up, start banging their doors, screaming out to the other wings. You might as well not bother then. So stealth was the name of the game.

We looked like a cartoon with our big burly 'warders', as the tabloid papers liked to call them, creeping around on tip-toe clutching mobile detectors, studying for signals.

I was with them the entire time, walking the landings, supporting, directing. As the officers hauled the prisoners they'd caught with a signal out, I'd chat to them while their cell was turned over.

'Nice night for a search,' I'd remark, rocking back on my heels.

The cells were searched professionally. All the rumours you hear and all the TV shows you watch where ransacking takes place are a load of nonsense. Two officers systematically make their way around the room and meet in the middle.

Most of the prisoners were fine about it. They understood it was part and parcel of prison life. None of them got aggy – aggravated – so we put off their move to the Seg until the morning.

We had a good night. We managed about ten cells before the operation was sabotaged by too many lairy prisoners. Six mobiles, cannabis and heroin were handed to the evidence officer who bagged and tagged them. The next morning, the phones were sent to the anti-corruption unit to be analysed for anything that could be a security threat. The information was downloaded and cross-referenced with their criminal database, which also had a record of all the prison staff's phone numbers. You can probably see where I'm going with this.

Long story cut short. One of these phones contained something very revealing. A bit too revealing if I'm honest.

Chapter 23

THE COLONEL'S SECRET

HMP Wormwood Scrubs:
8 August 2008

The morning after our bust and I was feeling a little less perky than usual. I'd clocked off at 1 a.m. and was back at my desk for 7.30 a.m. I rubbed my eyes, yawned and then there was a knock at my door.

'Patricia!' I exclaimed. The officer standing in front of me was none other than our prime corruption suspect. *What did she want?*

'Nice to see you. Come in.' I painted on a smile. 'Please …' I nodded to the chair. 'Sit down.'

She seemed agitated, aggressive even. As she was taking a seat, she blurted: 'I've heard I'm under suspicion.'

Bold as brass. Challenging me. Nice touch, Patricia. Try and fool the governor into thinking you're innocent by broaching the accusations head-on. What did she think? I'd suddenly form a new opinion of her, thinking she was innocent because someone who was guilty wouldn't possibly ever draw attention to themselves? If she was

214

playing a game, I don't know how she ever imagined she'd beat me.

'Suspicion for what?' I replied.

She tilted her head. Her eyes locking onto mine, trying to read me. I felt the weight of her gaze. Patricia was a well-built lady. Huge dark eyes and a helmet-style haircut that was gel-fixed to her scalp.

'Well, I don't really know.' She shrugged. 'I just want your assurance that I'm not.'

Still challenging me.

I pressed out another fake smile, cleared my throat and lied: 'Patricia, do you think you'd be sat in front of me if you were under any sort of suspicion?' I added a snort and a shrug for good measure. I was hardly going to tell her she was under surveillance. That would defeat the entire purpose of her being put on it. I needed her to act normal. To go about things as normal, as that's how we'd catch her out.

She nodded hesitantly. 'I suppose not.'

'You don't need to worry.'

I'm not sure she believed me, but she left looking less agitated. My mind, however, was now even more made up that she was guilty.

I filled out a security report that I'd had the conversation with her, which was immediately winged up to anti-corruption. This case was heating up by the second. A few days later the task force called an urgent meeting. They'd retrieved all the data from the phones we'd found, and whose number should be on there? You guessed it.

I shook my head with disgust and dismay as I read through the saucy text messages between Patricia Ollivierre and Blake Riley. A prisoner on B wing where she was posted. He was serving eight years for rape. As I said, hardly a catch.

Blake had contacted her 153 times. She had called him 29 times and sent him four text messages. They were pretty damning.

'Keep positive babes and don't let things get you down, you have got this far.'

'You don't know, they might just bust your door down soon and you can hit the road and no one is looking more forward to it than me. Love you sexy, kiss kiss.'

In another Ollivierre told him: 'It feels like someone is dangling you in front of me but I cannot touch you.'

She'd also gone to the lengths of contacting Blake's solicitor to chase up paperwork he needed for his ongoing appeal case.

I filled up my glass with water from the jug and took a sip. There were three officers from the anti-corruption team sat around the boardroom table with me. A printed-out photo of Blake's appendage in a state of arousal was pushed across the table. Eugh.

'Nothing to write home about,' I quipped.

It got a few sniggers from the Met officers.

'What are we going to do?' I locked eyes with them in turn.

We had enough to arrest Patricia for misconduct in a public office, but she'd be out for that in no time, if she was given a prison sentence at all. We needed to get her for possessing drugs with intent to supply. Drugs that compromised the security of the Scrubs and put everyone in it at risk. Staff like Patricia Ollivierre destroyed all the good I was trying to do. She was supposed to be on our side. She'd abused her position of power. I wanted her to pay for what she'd done.

'We're going to catch her red-handed,' I announced.

We needed to catch Patricia with the gear if we were to stand a chance of putting her behind bars. The decision was made to run a close surveillance operation on her, and Justin, police liaison officer, arranged for several officers from anti-corruption to follow her. They would watch where she went, what she did and who with. At some point she was going to meet up with her supplier.

It was a week later when Justin called me with the heads-up. He was over at head office and had the surveillance pictures in front of him. 'We're certain she's in possession of the drugs as we speak so you best get the dogs ready.'

'Roger that,' I said excitedly.

I was standing in the control room, my eyes glued to the CCTV screen that was zoomed in on Patricia. She was in the car park, clambering out of her car. Under her left arm was a bucket of KFC. In her right hand a carrier bag of what I assumed was chips to go with the bargain lunch meal.

I looked to my PO Mark. 'Get the dog on her. I'll meet you down there.'

It was obvious what she was playing at. Patricia was hoping the fatty deep-fried chicken drumsticks would mask the smell of the drugs and put any dog off the scent. She knew she was under suspicion, so was taking extra precautions.

Mark and I plus two officers and the dog handler were waiting to greet Patricia and her takeaway as soon as she stepped foot inside the foyer.

It wasn't out of the ordinary for us to conduct searches on staff. They were carried out fairly frequently as part of our baseline security audit requirements. It was much like an airport check. The officer passed through a metal detector portal and all bags went through an X-ray machine. A metal detector wand was then waved over them and they were given a rub-down search.

In Patricia's case we set the dog on her first – the most trusty weapon in our arsenal.

'Patricia.' I greeted her with an officious smile.

She hesitated as she saw the welcome committee.

'Over here please if you don't mind – we just want to walk you past the drugs dog.'

Monty's ears pricked up.

Patricia looked skittishly from left to right as the two officers closed in on her.

'What for?' she said.

'You've been selected. This way, if you don't mind.' I gave her no option.

She stiffened as Monty approached her in his usual gentle manner. His tail wagging. His nose twitching as he got to work sniffing. Within seconds he sat down, indicating he'd picked up a scent. All eyes in the room were now locked on Patricia. I had to hand it to her, she put on a good performance.

Frowning impatiently, she snatched the KFC tub into her chest.

'Do you have anything on you that you shouldn't have?' I asked, giving her a chance to come clean.

She shook her head angrily. 'No!' Pretending to be insulted, peering into her pile of battered chicken. 'It's probably my lunch that's set him off.'

I chortled. 'Don't think so, Patricia.' *More like you're using the Colonel's recipe to disguise the scent of the drugs.*

We searched her, but didn't find anything. I suspected she was doing a 'dry run' to see if she would be searched. *Very clever.* However, the fact Monty had sat down indicated Patricia had recently been in contact with drugs. We needed to find the stash.

'Mind if we search your car?' I asked. I had to ask but it wasn't really a question. If she'd refused I'd have arrested her there and then.

She shrugged. 'If you like.' Cool as a cucumber. Cocky. Even acting annoyed that her lunch was turning cold.

I let Mark and the officers escort her while I returned to the control room to watch the show unfold from the surveillance cameras. I wanted it all on camera so a) it could be used in evidence, and b) to protect my staff. That way there could be no allegations made against them for planting evidence.

Mark brought dog handler Officer Price and Alfie, the liver-and-white springer spaniel, with him. Alfie was an active dog who searched places not people. Mark instructed Patricia to unlock her car. As soon as the driver's door was open, Officer Price gave Alfie the go-ahead. The spaniel leapt inside, nose to everything. Within seconds he was barking crazily at the glove compartment. He then sat down. Bingo.

'We've got a hit,' Mark radioed through to me.

'I can see that,' I said. 'Let's see what she's got on her.'

Patricia hung back with an air of attitude. That's another thing I've noticed about bent staff: they all seem to carry the same sense of entitlement. As if it's their God-given right to break the rules. It's not surprising if you think about it. To be corrupt you've got to have an inflated sense of your own importance – i.e. you think you can get away with it and you don't have much, or any, remorse about doing it.

Mark turned the catch on the glove compartment and a load of rubbish fell out into the footwell. Chewing gum wrappers. A half-empty Coke bottle. Crisp packets. Wearing latex gloves – so as not to contaminate the evidence – Mark swished his hand about, rummaging through the contents. It didn't take long to find what had set Alfie off.

I whistled as Mark talked us through what he was holding in his hands. Enough drugs to make a small mint. Seventeen grams of heroin and a fifty-one gram block of cannabis, to be precise. Goodness knows how much she'd already brought in and how long it had been going on for.

If it's possible to be buzzing and angry at the same time, that's what I felt. Victorious we'd caught her red-handed but furious at how someone we'd employed to prevent and disrupt the trafficking of drugs into prison had been doing precisely the opposite.

I listened as Mark read her rights.

'You do not have to say anything' – she folded her arms – 'but it may harm your defence if you do not mention when questioned something which you later rely on in court. Anything you do say may be given in evidence.'

'Bring her in,' I instructed Mark.

I watched the screen intently as they frogmarched her back to the security office. The whole time my mind replayed how Monty had sat during his search of her. Patricia *must* be carrying drugs on her as well. I wanted them found.

Patricia took a seat in one of the comfy chairs in the PO's office, still with a firm hold on her KFC. The rich, fatty smell engulfed the room. The office was walled with glass windows – which gave it a goldfish-bowl feel. Everyone in the main offices was pretending to get on with their work while watching the drama unfold. They felt as pissed off about the whole thing as I did.

I took the bucket from her and handed it to one of the officers to be searched.

'Can I have it back?' Patricia asked. Bold as brass.

'No,' I snapped. 'Not at this time. If you hadn't noticed, we're busy leading an investigation into *you*.'

'Can I go to the toilet?'

'No!' Her desperation to disappear to somewhere she could be alone was a red flag. I suspected the drugs weren't hidden in the food but that she had them on her.

'Gov, there's nothing in here,' the officer said, emerging from the KFC bucket, his gloves glistening with grease. Just what I thought.

'I've got my period,' Patricia protested.

'I'm sorry but you're still not going to the toilet. You have to wait for the police to arrive.' They were the ones who had to conduct the search. I didn't want her flushing away the evidence.

She sat sulkily as we waited for the coppers to show up. Sighing deeply. Shifting in her chair noisily. I was relieved when they finally arrived just to put an end to her tantrum-like performance.

There were a few uniforms led by a female officer. I briefed her on my suspicions. She read Patricia her rights again, arresting her on possession with the intent to supply. Then, in her most serious voice, she said: 'We are going to take you to the station where you will be strip-searched and subjected to an intimate search.'

Patricia's eyes widened in horror.

It's not something police do as a matter of course. I knew it was a bluff to get her to cough up.

And cough up she did, quite literally. Out of her mouth popped a clingfilmed wrap of 14 grams of heroin.

'Here you go.' She handed it over, much more sheepishly.

I couldn't help but laugh. The female officer winked at me.

What I think must have happened was that Patricia did have the wrap hidden in the KFC bucket but as soon as she spotted us with Monty on the other side of the entrance barrier, she slipped it under her tongue or in her cheek. That's why Monty sat down for her, because he could smell it in her mouth.

The policewoman pulled me aside. Out of earshot, she whispered: 'Do you want us to walk her out or do you want her handcuffed?'

She knew where I was coming from. How important a message I needed to make.

'Handcuffed!' I wanted her shamed. I wanted all the staff to watch a corrupt member of staff – who had put everyone's life in danger – staff, prisoners, visitors – being marched out of the jail. I wanted everyone in that jail to know what happens if you cross the line.

Serves you fucking right, I said to myself as I watched Patricia taken away. I wished I could have said it to her face but I didn't want to do anything to interfere with or jeopardise the case.

About half an hour later I got a phone call from one of the officers on Patricia's wing who hadn't been privy to the spectacle. They were still waiting for her to return with their lunch order. 'Gov, Patricia was supposed to get my KFC – what's happened to that?'

I chortled. 'I think you're going to have to go to the mess for lunch.'

* * *

I heard back from the anti-corruption team that their search of Patricia's house had been most fruitful. Apparently it was like an Aladdin's cave in there. Brand new TVs, PlayStations, computers, mobile phones. She had made a pretty penny out of Blake and possibly his mates too. She'd clearly been at it for a while.

I don't think she had sex with him, maybe a kiss and a cuddle and a grope. She wouldn't have had the opportunity to have full-blown sex. It's actually uncommon for that to happen because of all the other officers patrolling the wings.

Blake was moved to the Seg and I paid him a visit.

He was a stocky guy, not particularly tall but well-built if a little on the portly side. He was wearing his grey prison-issue tracksuit bottoms halfway down his bum, parading his boxer shorts. A look that always baffled and irritated me.

'You're down here for good order and discipline. It's initially three days to be reviewed after then. You may or may not know an officer has been arrested in connection with supplying drugs into the jail and, unfortunately, your name is in the frame.'

He never said a word. No expression. Nothing. Prisoners know when to keep their mouth shut. She clearly meant nothing to him.

The case against Blake and Patricia turned out to be a landmark one. Blake was charged and found guilty of corrupting an officer – the first time in history a prisoner has been sentenced for such a crime.

Mark and I were in court to see Patricia sent down for seven years. That's a lengthy sentence. The judge felt, as I did I when I had her publicly marched out of the Scrubs, that she needed to be made an example of to deter other staff from doing the same.

The story made the papers and in his summing-up Judge Andrew Goymer said: 'It goes without saying that for a prison officer to be involved in any way in the supply or potential supply of drugs is a very grave breach of duty indeed. Drugs don't grow inside prison, they get there because they are brought in from outside. A prison officer is employed to prevent and disrupt the trafficking of drugs into prison.'

I couldn't have put it better myself.

Chapter 24

WHO D'YA THINK YOU'RE TALKING TO?

HMP Wormwood Scrubs: April 2009

I imagined him parking the car outside the clothing store Next. Sitting behind the wheel, watching the hundreds of happy shoppers pass him by, his brain crowded with hateful thoughts as he decided on the opportune moment to strike – when he could cause the most damage to life.

Maybe he'd have been sweating in those last minutes he was deciding to blow himself up. Or maybe he'd have been buzzing with the excitement of knowing how many people he was about to kill.

BOOM. The car would have lifted off the ground as it exploded. The glass and metal shattering, firing shrapnel in every direction. Killing and maiming innocent shoppers who had come to the Arndale Centre in Manchester for a joyous day out.

WHO D'YA THINK YOU'RE TALKING TO?

Those that weren't hurt, those that could wrench them-selves off the ground, would run, screaming as they fled from the blast, only to get stuck in the terrorists' spider web. A squad of suicide bombers positioned across Market Street and St Ann's Square would have been waiting to pounce on all those fleeing.

Hundreds could have been killed if it hadn't been for SOI5, the counter-terrorist command at Scotland Yard, foiling the Al-Qaeda attack planned for the Easter weekend.

I closed my eyes and breathed out a huge sigh of relief as our police liaison officer, Justin, told me the news. He was calling from the counter-terrorism unit at head office where he'd been promoted to.

'Thank you,' he said, 'for giving us that piece of intel.'

I'd drilled it into my staff of all grades and areas – no matter how small or incidental it seems, log it. Write that report on what you overheard, what Joe Bloggs told you on A wing, because you never know what it could lead to. It might be a very small cog in a much larger wheel but it could end up saving countless lives

Running the security in a prison wasn't just about making sure criminals were locked up; it was also about policing from the inside to protect those on the outside. As you might imagine, a jail is a hotbed of activity. Criminals plot-ting from behind bars. That's why it was imperative to keep your ear to the ground, to gather as much intel as possible, and to make sure that information was communicated to the right people so we could do our bit to protect the public.

THE GOVERNOR

I had so much I wanted to say. My brain was bursting with praise as I made my way down the stairs from my new office.

As soon as I'd got the news from Justin I gathered everyone from security and intel together. It was important to tell your team when they did well – and this was a day to remember for ever.

I'd been promoted from number five gov to number four, so I was now in charge of all the security and operations for Wormwood Scrubs. Any breach fell on my shoulders. It was a huge responsibility but I was more than ready for it.

'Gather round, chaps.' I beckoned my team in.

There still weren't many of us, just a few extra admin support staff, but enough to make a huge impact. That much was clear.

'So I have some incredible news I want to relay from the police liaison. Thanks to some intel we gathered six weeks ago, we've helped foil a terrorist attack that had been planned on the Arndale Centre in Manchester.'

There was a chorus of gasps as I explained what Al-Qaeda had in store for our country. How the hit on the shopping centre was part of a worldwide attack where they had also planned to plant suicide bombers on the New York subway over the Easter weekend – with the aim of causing maximum damage and widespread panic.

'It's thanks to you.' I signalled to Allan, an officer I'd called over from A wing to be part of the celebrations

Allan had filed an SIR, Security Information Report, after he'd heard a suspicious conversation between two prisoners on his wing.

The first thing I did every morning – after my fag and cup of tea, strong builder's and two sugars – was check through all of the reports. This particular bit of intel hadn't sat right with me, so I'd immediately contacted Justin who was now based at Scotland Yard. I can't go into details but what I can reveal is that at the time I had no idea that small bit of info would help save so many lives.

'That's why the job you do is so important and I can't thank you enough for working so hard to tighten the security of this jail,' I went on. I felt incredibly proud of everyone involved.

There was an impulsive explosion of clapping. Everyone's eyes meeting each other's with an unspoken *well done*. The air was electric with gratitude.

I'd come across a number of terrorists during my years working in prisons. Back in Holloway, the ones we had locked up were mostly members of the IRA. At the Scrubs, it was Al-Qaeda and some hard-core animal rights' activists.

Prisoners charged under the terrorism act, TACT offenders as they were officially called, were watched closely. Again, I can't reveal the exact details of what went on but the security measures we implemented were far greater than with, say, a lifer. For example, every single one of their pin phone calls was listened in on, apart from conversations with their solicitor. Visitors had to be cleared first by the police. Their movements were continuously logged. What do they do on their association time? Who do they speak to? How do they respond to being told what to do? How do they react to female staff? Do they follow a religious belief? Do they take an active part in religious services? Who do they associate with? All these kinds of things were noted down by staff around the jail.

They could be inside for a whole host of reasons, from having been found with literature about some training camp in Pakistan to being part of a radicalised group to having very extremist views. They weren't all Muslims, I hasten to add; we also had some TACT prisoners who had far-right ideologies such as neo-Nazism and neo-fascism, that kind of rubbish. There was also anti-vivisectionists who had sent parcel bombs to research labs. These were offenders who didn't meet the Cat A criteria but still needed to be kept a close eye on.

There was one particular Muslim extremist who caused me a lot of grief. From day dot I had severe doubts as to whether he should be in a Cat B prison, and within no time at all he proved my concerns correct.

The police had been watching him for a while for suspected terrorist activity. When they conducted a search of his property they found a load of dodgy literature and immediately arrested him.

We initially had him on a main wing under close observation and pretty soon it became clear he was an out and out extremist. He refused the privilege of having a TV in his cell, saying it was infidel. He strongly disagreed with being made to wear a prison uniform as he was anti everything establishment. He didn't want a bed in his cell, just a prayer mat. He strongly disagreed with our imam's teachings in Friday prayers, citing them as too soft. The jail's mosque was in the multi-faith centre, a small rectangular building next door to the old chapel. Things reached boiling point a matter of weeks later when the prisoner completely lost it. He stood up and started shouting 'Allahu Akbar' – God is great – at the top of his voice, screaming the place of worship down even while the officers had hold of him and were carting him off.

The final red flag was when I started to get reports coming in of how he was trying to radicalise Muslims and other offenders on his wing. His technique was to scare them into conversion with the threat of being assaulted or murdered. 'Only by becoming a Muslim can the brotherhood protect you.' The intensity of his extremist behaviour was cranking up by the day. There was no pause button; it was all or nothing with him. As with all terrorists, to be honest.

I told head office I had serious concerns and that I felt he needed to be upgraded to a Cat A prison, like pronto. The definition of a Cat A prisoner is one who would pose the most threat to the public, police or to national security if they were to escape. I gave the nod to have him moved into isolation while we waited for a decision from head office. I could request the upgrade but I didn't have the authority to implement it.

He didn't like that, not one bit. Moreover, he hated the fact the decision had been made by a woman. To say he had an issue with the opposite sex would be putting it mildly. Part of his extremist views was the belief that women were the weaker, lesser sex who needed to be controlled. Men were to be obeyed. He'd refused to speak to any female staff during the entirety of his 'stay' with us. It must have really got his goat when I appeared at his cell to take him down to the Seg.

The orderly officer came with me and unlocked his door. He stood up from his prayer mat, his face half hidden behind a long straggly beard. His dark eyes narrowed as they locked onto me.

'What's *she* doing here?' was the first thing he said. 'I don't speak to women.' He glared.

I laughed. Who did he think he was talking to?!

'Well, it's immaterial whether you speak to women, because you've been put up for Cat A status,' the orderly told him. 'While we're waiting for the decision we're moving you to the Seg, so get your stuff together, you're going now.'

Never would I let a prisoner think they had affected me with anything they spouted out of their mouth. I think I might even have flashed him a sarcastic smile as the orderly led him away.

Head office agreed with my risk assessment and he was moved that same day to HMP Belmarsh in Thamesmead, south-east London.

Chapter 25

STARING EVIL IN THE EYE

HMP Wakefield, West Yorkshire: April 1994

He was known as the gay slayer. Strangling his victims and leaving their bodies in kinky sex positions such as strapped into a harness or tied to bedposts. He'd do bizarre things to the bodies like leaving cuddly toys in sex positions on their chest. He even slaughtered one victim's cat and attached the cat's mouth around the victim's penis and placed its tail in the victim's mouth. He'd call up the newspapers, confessing to what he had done but not revealing his identity, as if he was getting off on playing a game of cat and mouse. After his first murder he told the *Sun* newspaper he wanted to become a famous serial killer. Well, he certainly managed that. I'd never seen what evil looked like until I stared him in the eye.

A prison officer I'd made friends with at Holloway had offered me the chance to have a look around HMP Wakefield, a Cat A men's prison in West Yorkshire, otherwise known as the 'Monster Mansion' due to the large number of high-profile, high-risk sex offenders and murderers held there.

Her dad was one of the governors there and he'd offered us a special tour of the place. I jumped at the chance – I was new to the job and keen to glean as much as I could about the prison service. Martine and I took a day's holiday and set off at the crack of dawn for the 'Monster Mansion'.

HMP Wakefield is another Victorian institution, steeped in history, tradition and architecturally grand. What marked it out as unique was the clock tower that stood in the heart of the wings. It could have slotted into a picture postcard of a picturesque country village if it weren't for the CCTV cameras surrounding the clock face, angled down towards the exercise yards and wings.

The first thing that struck me about the place, apart from its vastness and the smell of unwashed men and overcooked vegetables, was how well they had the place under control. Come the end of association hour, the clock bell rang, ricocheting off the old walls, vibrating along the corridors. All the prisoners on the wing we were passing through immediately stopped what they were doing and obediently returned to their cell. Behind the doors, hands clamped behind their backs like soldiers, ready and waiting to be locked up. How the hell did they manage that? At Holloway it was like herding sheep. 'Oh miss, I forgot this.' 'Oh miss, I just need to get a toilet roll.' You'd go one way and they'd scuttle off in another direction until you eventually had no choice but to corner and grab them or threaten them with the Seg.

We should do this. Why can't we implement that? Even back then my mind was humming with 'home improvement' ideas although I didn't know at the time what to do with them. I stored them away in my mental filing cabinet for later.

After more sightseeing, we came upon the canteen. A shop where, once a week, prisoners could spend their money on treats. Crisps, biscuits, tobacco, rollies, pretty basic stuff.

An officer was manning the counter and half a dozen prisoners were queuing up. One of the bulbs on the overhead strip lights was flickering, casting a strobe effect across the small windowless room.

I felt his presence before I saw him.

The air suddenly felt close as if he'd sucked all the oxygen in from around us. I turned around and standing before me was a giant. I kid you not: the guy was six foot six and built like a brick shithouse. My eyes kept reaching up and up until I finally met his gaze. Although as soon as I had, I regretted it because those eyes of his were nothing short of evil. They were piercing blue, the whites bloodshot pink. All the hairs on the back of my neck instinctively shot up. I don't quite know how to put it into words other than I knew I was in the presence of evil. I'd never experienced anything like it before, or since.

Whereas he engulfed the entire room with his aura, I had ceased to exist to him. He looked straight through me as if I was invisible. I stepped out the way and let him pass.

'Who's that?' I turned to Martine.

'*That*' – she stared ahead – 'is Colin Ireland.'

As soon as she told me his name I knew who he was. The papers hadn't long been filled with his trial. He must have only been at Wakefield for a few months, yet he was throwing his weight about like he'd been there years. You can just tell by the way the other prisoners reacted, standing back, clearing the way for him to pass. They too must have sensed his evil.

Before his death in 2012, Colin Ireland was one of only a handful of men in the UK serving a full life sentence, never to be released from jail. All his victims were gay and he picked most of them up in a pub in Earl's Court in London. He checked with them first so see if they were into S&M so they'd be willingly tied up, making it easier to kill them.

He was said to be highly organised, and carried a murder kit of rope, handcuffs and a full change of clothes to each murder. After killing his victim, he cleaned their flat top to toe to erase any trace of where he'd been. He even stayed in their home until the morning in order to avoid arousing suspicion by leaving in the middle of the night. But despite his thorough efforts, it was a fingerprint match that led him to being caught in the end. While he was awaiting trial, Ireland confessed to all the other killings. Five in total over a three-month spree.

He'd left such an impression on me that as soon as I got home from Wakefield I jumped on the computer and began researching his case. I wanted to know *why*. Why do those things? Why murder anyone and then go on a mad killing spree over three months? What was the trigger? Was there anything about his childhood that made him turn? My search for answers proved fruitless. Sometimes there isn't a why though; some people are just born evil, I truly believe that. Either way, understanding the psyche of murderers fascinated me. I've said it before and I say it again, to be good at my job, i.e. read a situation before it escalates, I needed to understand what I was dealing with. Every one of these criminals I met informed me a little more – and formed me into the person I became.

It was rumoured that Ireland ended up killing again while he was in prison – strangling his cellmate who was a convicted child murderer. Two weeks later he was moved on to HMP Whitemoor in Cambridgeshire, I assume to a single cell! It was also rumoured he later confessed to killing ten more men but the police couldn't find any bodies to back up his confession. People said he might have made it up because he wanted notoriety, to be crowned the serial killer who'd committed the most murders. That would make sense and follow on from his need to ring the newspapers to brag about what he'd done. Narcissism: it's the trait, or should I say personality disorder, so many murderers have in common.

Chapter 26

HOOCH POOCH

HMP Wormwood Scrubs:
October 2009

I suppose when most people take a bath they relax, they let the day's troubles wash over them; they might even light a scented candle or two and listen to soft music. Somehow, as I stared up at the 1970s woodchip wallpaper, I found myself thinking about – bird netting.

It was a eureka moment.

Fuck 'em! I'm going to cover the entire outdoors area of the Scrubs in netting in order to catch all those bloody parcels being chucked over the wall.

I was so excited by my idea I couldn't languish in the bath a second longer. I hopped out, dried off, wrapped my dressing grown around me and headed straight for my computer to get to work on searching for a company that might be able to accommodate such a vast notion. It was 11 p.m. I never switched off from my job.

Drugs, as you well know by now, were the bane of my life. It didn't matter how many patrols we had doing circuits of the grounds, they were still coming through. Prisoners with mobile phones could quite easily watch the officers from their cell windows and dial up their mate with the package on the other side when the coast was clear. Unless we had dozens of officers standing outdoors, 24/7, we were never going to win. Before you ask, sadly there just wasn't the budget and the available staff for that.

I needed something that would physically stop the parcels landing – and what could be better than the netting they put across rooftops to stop birds nesting?

Drugs were on my mind because I'd had a day of it. I'd been on adjudications – deciding if and for how long prisoners should be sent to the Seg for – and most of the cases I'd reviewed were drug-related. On top of that, I'd had our monthly figures in for the mandatory drug testing. After seeing some impressive results since I'd become governor – dropping to under 10 per cent of prisoners being found with drugs in their system – it had suddenly shot up to 33 per cent. On top of that, I'd had intelligence come through that there were a lot of drugs about on our largest wings, A, D and C. I was pissed off and deflated. It was a never-ending battle and sometimes it was a struggle to stay positive.

As it turned out, netting an entire prison was not your typical DIY job. It was going to need a bit of help finding the right company and to get a quote. I had a skip in my step as I walked into work the next morning though. The first thing I did, even before my tea and fags, was approach my deputy's desk.

'Right, Mike, I've got a job for you.'

'Yes, boss,' he replied, thinking it would be a run-of-the-mill duty.

'I want you to research netting.'

His brow crumpled. 'What do you mean?'

'I want to cover this jail with netting to stop these bloody parcels coming over.'

He looked at me as if I'd completely lost the plot, like he needed to order the pink papers for the men in white coats to come and take me away.

'I'm serious.'

'O-kay.'

'I want you to get on it, Mic.'

'Okay, no worries.'

Mike was a very diligent man and I knew I could trust him with a task like that. By the afternoon he had an option for me: Ecolab. I gave the company a ring. I explained to the woman on the other end of the line that I was a governor and what I was after. I knew it wasn't practically possible to cover the entire Scrubs, but it's what I wanted. At first she thought it was a crank call, but a while later I'd managed to organise for someone to come and give me a quote.

Now all I needed to do was put it to the purse strings, i.e. the number one gov.

I knocked on his door. 'A word, sir.'

Keith Munns had retired but another northerner had stepped into his shoes: Phil Taylor.

He was a Yorkshireman in his fifties. Slim, grey hair and he wore square-shaped thick black-rimmed glassed. He was decisive, a strong character and very security conscious. He always listened to what I had to say.

Sometimes number ones aren't popular with the staff because it's a them and us mentality, especially if they hadn't worked their way up the ranks but had been parachuted in from an entirely different profession. We had one who had come from a managerial role in Sainsbury's. At the end of the day, a number one is more about the managing than the prisoners.

'Vanessa, lovely to see you.' He peered over his glasses. If I thought my job was hectic, it didn't even touch on what the number one had to manage in a day. He was constantly spinning plates. One of the most challenging things he had to do was constantly answer to the bigwigs over at head office.

I didn't want to take up his time. 'Gov, I've got someone coming in to do me a quote. I know the answer to stopping these drug packages coming over is netting, so …'

He looked at me. His shoulders rising and falling as he snorted. 'Well, good luck with that one.'

It wasn't a no, at least.

'Let me just get all the estimates together and I'll put it before you.'

'Okay.' You could tell he thought the idea was pie in the sky. And who could blame him. It did sound farcical.

Bird-netting man visited the jail the next day and Mike and I gave him the grand tour, showing him where the hotspots were – the back of A wing, the back of D wing, the side of E wing. He must have thought *What the?* as he examined the huge mass of space between the wings and the prison walls. He was professional to the final word though and said he'd manage it. To cut a long story short, he brought his team in, they measured the place up, ignoring all the insults from the prisoners shouting out of the windows, and a month later his quote arrived in the post.

I whistled as I read the numbers: £70,000. The number one was not going to like this.

I handed the boss the paperwork, which included the maintenance costs of £10,000 a year.

I studied his face as he read the proposal.

He hates it. He's never going to say yes.

He looked up and a huge smile broke.

'I love it,' he exclaimed.

'What? Really?' I was in shock.

'Yes, it's brilliant.'

Before we rolled it out we had to get Nick Pascoe, the area manager, to give it the all-clear and get us the funding. Wormwood Scrubs had, or did back then, a £25 million budget to spend on everything. I had to prove to Nick that the Scrubs' drug problem was so severe he needed to invest £70,000 in our scheme. *I could do that.* Nick had a bit of a soft spot for me. Not like that; he appreciated my diligence and perhaps my patience. He used to come into my office and chat at me for an hour at a time about himself, say it's great to chat with you today, and then leave. That was fine by me: I just sat and listened and grunted and oiled in the right places. It got me my bird netting, so I wasn't complaining! I say that with my tongue in my cheek of course because it was really my proposal that got us the go-ahead. The numbers of drugs offences spoke for themselves.

As soon as I got the green light I picked up the phone and rang Ecolab. Several months later – nothing moves fast in the prison service – we had our brand spanking new netting, AKA 'drug catcher'. When I say things move slowly that's because all the Ecolab staff needed to be security cleared and briefed, and one of the guys had to be security trained in how to use the keys as they were coming and going so much we couldn't be holding the door open for them every time. Nobody, and I mean no one, got a key without being security trained. 'You mustn't take your keys off the hook. You mustn't forget to leave them in your pocket when you go home. You mustn't give your keys to anyone else.' Not rocket science but the rules needed to be hammered home. Re-doing the locks on the entire prison would cost millions. I dread to think.

But once it was up, it worked liked a dream. I can't describe to you the feeling of watching those packages coming flying over only to land on the net. Seeing them bounce up and down like on a trampoline. All those prisoners watching from their cells must have been crying with frustration. Ha! Revenge is best served cold, as they say.

The next round of mandatory drug testing (MDT) results proved it was worth all the hassle and investment. The figure dropped to below 20 per cent and the month after, below 10 per cent, and it kept falling to 4 per cent. Four! Never in the history of the Scrubs had that happened before. Not only that, we had the lowest MDT rate out of all the London jails, helping to bring our security rating up from a two to a four. I was pleased as punch.

I didn't sit back and gloat though, because as I told everyone I'd gathered in the chapel for a security meeting, we may have won the battle but we hadn't won the war. As soon as that netting went up I knew it would cause a whole host of new problems. For every action there is a reaction.

'You will find yourselves under more pressure from prisoners to bring in drugs,' I warned the staff. 'They can't get it via their usual channels so they will turn to you instead.'

Prisoners are extremely crafty. Corruption isn't always about a member of staff having an affair with a prisoner. It can start with something as simple as a curry. I had one officer whose mum made him a korma every day for lunch. A prisoner on his wing he was quite pally with asked if he could try a bit one lunchtime. He shrugged and thought why not, no harm in that. Next day the prisoner asked the officer for a fag. Next day, could he pick him something up from the canteen? It's a form of grooming; the officer had no idea he was being played. A few weeks later the prisoner asked the officer if he could bring some drugs into the jail hidden inside his mum's curry. When the officer point blank refused the prisoner blackmailed him, threatening to tell his boss that he'd been carrying out favours for him. A sackable offence. So what does the officer do? With the fear of losing his job hanging over him, he begins smuggling drugs inside his mum's korma. It's as simple and insidious as that.

HOOCH POOCH

'Remember to stay vigilant, action what they taught you at training school. Do not give an inch,' I warned them. My words echoed up into the high ceiling of the ornate chapel.

Operation bird netting was one of a whole ream of changes I'd introduced. The mobile phone detectors were doing their job well. I'd had new metal detectors brought in – we used them to whizz over anyone coming in and out of the prison. The ones we'd been using up until now were so old they could have come in with the Ark. I was constantly on the look-out to trial new interventions, even the less conventional ones.

We also weren't strangers to using animals to control problems in the jail. We had the hawk guy come in with this bloody great big bird to scare off our pigeon epidemic. We had feral cats brought in to help control the rat population, which was a problem, and that's putting it politely. Sometimes I'd stare out of my office window and think the ground was moving, there were so many of them. They weren't just normal-sized either: they were rats on steroids. So big they could have had boots on them! Anyway, we brought in these cats we rescued from the Cats Protection League that we hoped would catch the rats, but they took one look at them and thought *no thanks*. I think the prisoners must have been feeding the cats because they used to just sit around in the grounds doing nothing all day. Not quite what we had in mind, but there you go.

So the idea of rolling out another animal-related scheme did fill me with cynicism. Saying that, I adored dogs, so when Tracey came to me suggesting we put our liver-and-white springer spaniel Alfie forward for the National Canine Security's new initiative where he'd be trained up to become a 'hooch pooch', a big smile spread across my face.

Hooch – an explosive, highly alcoholic home-brewed drink. Prisoners loved to make it secretly in their cells using anything that could ferment – such as a piece of fruit or a slice of stale yeasty bread combined with sugar from the canteen and water. They usually kept it hidden in a squash bottle behind their radiators to give it that extra heat for brewing. It was a huge problem, mostly for the effects it caused. It could give you super-strength, making prisoners aggressive, violent and, in worse-case scenarios, go blind or even cause death. It was that potent, being something close to 90 per cent alcohol.

So I signed off the paperwork and Alfie went to doggie school. If it worked, he'd be the country's very first hooch pooch.

Having a cuppa with the dogs at the kennels next to D wing was usually the first thing I did every morning before my daily 8 a.m. meeting. It was my little slice of heaven, an oasis of calm before the craziness of the day set in. We had two liver-and-white spaniels and two black labradors.

I adored them all but I especially love labradors. There's just something about them, their big soppy eyes, their willingness to please, and although I would hate to have to choose, Monty was my favourite.

HOOCH POOCH

Dogs played an incredibly important role in a prison's security. They were an extension of our team and worth their weight in gold. They aren't bred specifically for the job; they are often rescue dogs or they've been donated by people who can't look after them any more. However, to be chosen for the coveted role, they need to display a special instinct, and it's not what you think – having a nose for drugs. It's all about the tennis ball.

A prison dog has to show a strong desire to want to play or retrieve a ball. Why? Because that's how you get them hooked on the scent of cannabis or cocaine or, in Alfie's case, hooch.

Training begins with the handler throwing a ball for the dog every time they sit or come to heel, so pretty soon the dog associates rewards with tennis balls. The next stage is hiding drugs inside the ball, e.g. a wrap of heroin. The dog then associates the smell of heroin with the reward of finding his ball.

So this is what would have happened at hooch training for Alfie. He would have learnt to link the smell of the home-made brew to the high of playing with his beloved ball.

The spaniel returned from doggie school a few weeks later with a distinction – a licence – just in time to ruin Christmas for all those prisoners thinking they could get high on their own supply.

Back in the day when I was an officer on the wings, we always did a hooch run – officers searching everywhere from cells to the showers to the store cupboards – just before

Christmas because that's when the brew-making was most prolific. We had a fair to middling success rate because prisoners were great at hiding things.

Let's see if they could outfox Alfie's nose!

On our very next security meeting in the chapel, I made an announcement to all the staff. 'Listen up, everyone. We now have a fully licensed dog that can sniff out hooch, so if anyone has any suspicions on their wing please contact the dogs section and we'd be more than willing to try him out.'

There probably were a few sniggers and raised eyebrows, but I was confident that Alfie wouldn't show me up. He was our best, our most clever active dog.

Within a few hours Alfie had his first request. I didn't have time to follow him onto C wing but I got a full report back from Tracey when she came charging into the security office brandishing her loot.

Two gallon containers and a two-litre bottle of hooch.

'Bloody hell,' I exclaimed, looking down at Alfie. 'Well done, mate.'

I don't think he could hear me above the racket he was making though. Alfie had hold of his favourite water bottle and was crunching it noisily, his tail wagging with contentment.

'Couldn't put it better myself,' I said with a nod to our master hooch pooch.

Chapter 27

READY-MADE FAMILY

HMP Wormwood Scrubs:
July 2011

It would be fair to say my work–life balance was not in harmony. I didn't have much of a life outside of work because, if you haven't guessed by now, being a governor was all-consuming. I lived and breathed that jail. I was, in want of a better phrase, married to my job.

I haven't spent my entire life alone though. I've been in a long-term relationship for the past ten years but it hasn't been a smooth ride; there have been many breaks-ups and make-ups and the reason I haven't mentioned it up until now is out of respect to my wife. The love of my life. The person who showed me there could be equilibrium, that I didn't have to take the world home on my shoulders every night. I could share the load.

Without further ado, I'll introduce you to Julie, or Ju as I call her.

* * *

THE GOVERNOR

I didn't look up from my desk when she first walked into my office. As usual, I was knee-deep in sorting out a crisis. Often it felt like my office was a revolving door; someone always wanted me for something. The very life was being sucked out of me. A typical day could see the education teacher come charging in, demanding a prisoner be banned from a class for abusive behaviour, closely followed by the imam, who needed extra security in the mosque. The visits officer then asks me to sign off the banned visits list. The reception staff want me to help organise the transport of a prisoner's property when he gets moved on to another jail. The orderly officer tells me he is desperately understaffed for the evening shift and could I allow for such an such officer to be paid overtime to come in and cover. A whole plethora of problems on top of me running intelligence operations and all the rest of what a head of ops does.

Healthcare was just another thorn in my side, particularly with the security changes that had come about with it being taken over by the NHS. Up until this point, prisons had been in charge of recruiting their own doctors and nurses, much like a private hospital.

Julie Harris was a high flyer in healthcare management and she'd won the contract for Central London Health Authority to be the provider for the Scrubs. She was now in charge of contracting the doctors and nurses, supplying the medicines, everything and anything to do with the prisoners' health and wellbeing. It was a demanding and stressful job. We hadn't been properly introduced yet. She cleared her throat.

'I was just wondering when I might be able to have my own set of keys,' she said.

I peeled my gaze from my computer screen and almost did a double-take. First impression, apart from the fact, like me, she was very assertive – she was stunning. Her blonde curly hair bounced around her shoulders. She had on a crisp white tailored shirt and suit trousers and wore subtle make-up. Everything about her was polished and classy.

'Hi,' I said smiling. Charmed from the get-go.

I just assumed she was straight and so not the slightest bit interested in me, so I swatted away any thoughts of fancying her. I suppose that's me to a tee – I'm a practical sort of person who doesn't sit around torturing myself over things that aren't going to happen.

Long story short: I got it wrong. Ju had been married and had a daughter with her ex, but she now preferred women, and of the opinionated type, it turned out. She also loved animals, which was a major plus for me.

When we officially got together it was actually over a chat about how we were never going to be an item. Ju was at the end stages of a somewhat tempestuous destructive relationship. We were sat on a bench in St James's Park. It was a glorious summer's evening, the park was buzzing with people having fun relaxing after work, joggers, sporty types working out, kids playing. Sparks were flying between us but there was no way I was going to do anything about it.

Despite being a bulldog in the prison, making the first move on someone I liked would be something I'd almost run away from. From fear of being rejected, of being hurt – but mostly for fear of letting down that guard I'd built up. It's frightening to allow someone in when you've spent your entire life building up walls. What if it leads to your unravelling? Plus, I was a stickler for rules and I couldn't get involved with someone who was officially with someone else. No grey areas, thank you.

Ju probably knew she was never going to get anywhere with me unless she made the first move, so after agreeing it was the greatest thing to have never happened, Ju leaned in for a kiss.

The rest is history. Just this once I allowed myself to bed the rules and be swept up in the moment. Twenty-four hours and a lot of drama later, Ju had called time on her relationship. Of course I now felt an enormous pressure and responsibility on my shoulders to fill the void that had been left, but at the same time I wanted to be happy and I knew I could be with Ju. I've always wanted to get married and share my life with someone.

Just take a chance, Vanessa, throw caution to the wind. Accept there are some things in life you can't plan in advance. Obviously that was incredibly difficult for me considering my job was all about foreseeing and preparing for the worst possible scenario. But I did it nevertheless. I let down my wall of steel an inch and gave it a shot.

The strange thing is, once I gave into it, I felt an enormous wave of relief. I wasn't alone any more. I could share my battles. I suppose it helped a lot that we worked in the same prison and understood what it took out of you.

When I first got together with Ju I didn't really register she had a daughter, but as things between us took off at a hundred miles an hour I quickly found myself with an instant family. I'll never forget the moment I was introduced to seven-year-old Annie-Mae, the ballsiest little girl I've ever met. People now joke we must have been separated at birth we're so similar.

Ju lived on the other side of London from me, next to Raynes Park in the south, and she told me not to come straight to her house but to meet her in the car park of Waitrose. As I was parking, I spotted Ju with her shopping bags and a young girl beside her. I got out, leaned with my back against the door and waved.

As soon as I did that, the girl took off and came tearing towards me, her mop of short dark hair bouncing. She had a huge grin on her face. She didn't stop there though. She yanked open my car door and hopped into the back seat. Brimming with confidence. I peered in after her.

'So you're Annie-Mae then?'

'Yes, nice to meet you. I'll show you the way home.'

'Oh, okay,' I said, slightly in shock. 'I could be a crazy axe murderer.' I knew a few of those. 'You shouldn't just get into anybody's car,' I warned her.

'Nah.' She fanned my warning away. 'You're alright. You're Mum's girlfriend.'

Ju arrived by my side and I flashed her a look.

'So you've met Annie-Mae then,' she laughed.

From nought to hundred overnight was a bit disorientating and overwhelming at first. Honestly, I never saw myself having a family. I love kids, don't get me wrong, but I didn't think it was for me. Annie-Mae changed all of that. Having a family completely transformed me – making me a much more well-rounded person. I stopped being so fixated on the Scrubs and as a result my work productively increased even more because, I think, I was able to better shrug off the stress. So life became more balanced and harmonious.

We kept our relationship under the radar at work because a prison is a hive of gossip and my reputation as governor meant everything to me. I didn't want anyone thinking I was giving the healthcare department priority or passing favours its way because I was involved with the head of it. In fact, I used to say no to Ju all the time, even when she looked at me sideways with those big eyes of hers. Ju didn't want it getting out either; she'd worked very hard to get to where she was and she didn't want her reputation smeared. I worked on a need-to-know basis and nobody needed to know, for now.

Who was I kidding? It was a jail. Word got out and spread like wildfire and it took no time for Ju and I to become public knowledge, though, as it turned out, everyone was incredibly happy for me. Some even dared to say that being in love suited me.

'Yeah, yeah, get back to work,' I'd say. Secretly glowing inside.

Chapter 28

GOTCHA!

**HMP Wormwood Scrubs:
August 2011**

'Victor Charlie 4-0, our ETA is two minutes, I repeat two minutes.'

The police convoy in front cornered sharply into the street to the left. I grabbed onto the seat to stop myself from flying.

'Five-zero in position on Bravo route,' the copper driving us to the suspected drugs den said into his radio.

Our blues and twos were off. This dealer was going to get the surprise of his life.

It was 5 a.m. and London was still fast asleep. Outside was pitch black and freezing. Condensation had collected inside the car, probably from my nervous breathing. I rubbed the window with my sleeve, clearing a portal on to the council estate. My heart was hammering so loudly in my chest I could hear it. Boom. Boom. Boom.

'Victor Charlie 4-0, we're in position.'

The police van and car ahead suddenly pulled into the curb and we stopped right behind them. The street lamps were bright, lighting the faces of the two officers in the front seats. Dave, our new police liaison officer who'd replaced Justin, was next to me in the back. The copper driving turned to brief us.

'As you know, our intelligence sources and forensic evidence has led us to believe the suspect in the property is in possession of drugs with the intent to supply.'

The door of the van in front ripped open along its rail. Half a dozen officers dressed in black with bulletproof vests and helmets jumped to the ground, their boots thudding on to the concrete pavement.

'The suspect is a known criminal,' he went on. 'He could be armed and we're not taking any risks.' The men in black began approaching the house armed with a ram to batter down the front door.

'Ready?' Dave said.

'Hell yes!' I replied. I'd been waiting for this – that glorious moment when we got to nab the drug dealers on the other side of the prison wall. Finally, I was getting to the source of the problem!

My policing of the outside from the inside of prison was continually growing. Thanks to forensics, *CSI* style, I was able to start tracing where the packages that were being chucked over the wall were actually coming from.

It kicked off with an email from Dave who'd pulled some strings with head office. Forensic work is costly, so I was over the moon when he said we could start sending some of these deliveries off for analysis.

His office was directly below mine. I appeared at his door moments later.

'Have I got this right? We can actually get them finger-printed and tested for DNA?'

I was a huge fan of *CSI*, I'd seen pretty much every episode going, plus the spin-offs. I envisaged this grimy little parcel being sent off to a shiny white lab, ultra-violet lights, microscopes …

'Great news isn't it?' Dave leaned back in his chair, locking his hands behind his head in a rather pleased manner.

This wasn't something that normally happened in the prison service. We were putting the Scrubs on the map yet again, for piloting a crime-busting initiative. I was chuffed to bits; it was a reflection of all the great results we were achieving and the good relationship we'd established with the Old Bill.

I was also happy because, as amazing as the results of the bird netting had been, there were a few small areas of the jail it couldn't quite reach, like behind the workshops and near the garden sheds. It was a daily, hourly battle. We had patrols with dogs and without dogs doing the rounds morning, lunch and dinner but that still wasn't enough. Packages were still getting to the wings, so to find out who the blee-din' heck was sending them was going to be a massive advantage in our war against drugs. As you might imagine, there was no 'return to sender' address stuck to them to give us a clue.

'So we have to make sure all the officers making the patrols wear gloves when handling the packages.'

I nodded. 'Makes perfect sense.'

So that's what we did, cherry-picking several of the largest packages for forensic testing.

As it turned out, *CSI* is a load of make-believe. Fingerprint lifting can't be done in a matter of hours. Try six weeks. Well, that's how long it took to get our results back.

But we didn't just get a fingerprint – we also hit the jackpot.

'We've got a name!' Dave rang me up. He was over at head office on Embankment. They'd manage to extract fingerprints from only one of the parcels, but it had been an immediate match with someone they had on their criminal record system.

Lucas Cavanagh. A petty criminal, involved in gang crime who'd even done some time in the Scrubs. He lived, would you believe, just a stone's throw from the jail, behind A wing to be precise.

Gotcha!

The excitement didn't end there though. Dave asked me to do something I'd always dreamed of doing since I was a young girl: catch the baddies.

'We're going to do a dawn raid on Cavanagh's place. Seeing that you helped make all of this happen, do you want to come along with us?'

Did I ever. 'Oh, yes, of course I would!' I said ecstatically.

Suddenly visions of Hollywood streamed through my mind. I saw myself as one of Charlie's Angels, kicking in this dealer's door with the police rushing in after me.

'Excellent, we're going first thing tomorrow morning.' They didn't mess around.

'Can't wait.' And I couldn't. This felt like a massive breakthrough.

What do you wear to kick someone's door in? I stared into my wardrobe, which consisted almost entirely of collared shirts and, because I don't have much bum or hips, black trousers. I could wear whatever I liked to work now I was a governor, but I hated having to think about what I was going to put on in the mornings. So I stuck to my uniform, simply replacing the white epaulette shirts for M&S striped ones. My casual attire wasn't any more diverse. I settled on a combo of the two, smart-casual. I pulled a blue and white striped shirt from the rail and grabbed a pair of black jeans. Job done.

I was meeting Dave at 4.30 a.m. outside the Scrubs. I had a Barbour coat on to keep me warm but the freezing air tickled my lungs every time I breathed in. I buried my hands deep into my pockets, hunching into myself to keep the heat in. Excited but at the same time nervous would be a good way to describe my disposition. I hadn't done anything like this before; it was totally out of my comfort zone. I liked being challenged though. It's good to be tested; keeps you on your toes.

My eyes were trained to the road, watching every car that passed like a hawk, thinking it would be Dave in his unmarked vehicle.

Instead, I got the cavalry. Du Cane Road was suddenly lit up like a Christmas tree as two police cars and one van tore along in convoy, their lights flashing blue and red.

Bloody hell! A tad overkill?

The last of the three vehicles pulled over and David wound down his window.

'Hop in!' His expression was full of energy.

'Are you expecting trouble?'

'Well, you never know with these kind of things. The address isn't known to us – it might be a drugs den. We don't know much apart from that the suspect is registered to live there.'

An image of a dingy squat filled with drugs *Scarface* style suddenly came to mind.

'It's better to be safe than sorry,' David said.

'Quite right.' I jumped into the back.

It was like stepping on board the *Starship Enterprise*. There were lights going off everywhere. The dashboard was flickering. The radio crackling with instructions from the police station as well as from the cars in front.

'This is Victor Charlie 4-0, radio check.'

'Victor Charlie 5-0, radio check,' our driver joined in.

I'd like to say there was an exciting high-speed drive that tore through the streets of London, but the suspect's place was only three minutes around the back of the Scrubs.

GOTCHA!

We whizzed around a few corners then we were outside Cavanagh's house. Obviously they'd turned the car lights off by this point or it would have been like Blackpool Illuminations outside his house.

We were now in a cul-de-sac on a dodgy estate. There is no delicate way of putting this: the house in question was a shit hole. I'd seen enough from where I was sitting. The garden was overgrown with weeds. It was littered with fag butts and rubbish. The house was originally red-brick semi-detached but now it was more the colour of brown sludge. The porch and window frames had rotted. The paint was peeling off. The ground floor had white net curtains but they looked like they hadn't been cleaned since time began, a dark mustard from dirt and fag fumes no doubt. Although I couldn't wait to catch Cavanagh, I was in no rush to step inside that hole.

The officers climbed out dressed top to toe in jet-black protection gear. Their batons in hand.

'Let the guys go in and stay at the back with me,' Dave instructed. I was absolutely fine with that. I didn't fancy kicking in that grimy door anyway.

They charged up the pathway to the porch, surprisingly light on their feet for the big burly blokes that they were. We were close behind. I watched the windows for any sign of life – curtain twitching, a light turning on – but nothing. Cavanagh was either not at home or fast asleep.

They'd clearly picked the biggest officer to lead the squad: he looked about eight foot tall. He was also armed with the battering ram. He turned back to his team, making eye contact before lining the ram up to the door. One tap, that's all it took, and the door went flying open.

'Go! Go! Go!' They all rushed in like a herd of elephants, their boots smashing against the ground. You'd have been flattened if you'd been stood in the way.

I peered in after them. The hall floor had a patterned carpet but it was as dirty as the front yard, covered in fag papers, fag burns and moth holes. I could see through the hallway to the kitchen where there were stacks and stacks of dirty plates. It reminded me of one of those places you'd see on a hoarder TV show. You'd want to wipe your feet on the way out instead of the way in.

While my nostrils were being overwhelmed with the stench of stale cigarettes and rotting food my ears were hit by the cries of the officers as they rushed upstairs and downstairs.

'Secure!'

They entered another room. 'Secure!'

'Secure. Secure.' And then …

'Get up. Stand up. Put your hands behind your back. Don't move.' Followed by: 'I haven't got any bloody clothes on! Fucking hell, mate.'

A woman's voice shrilled after him: 'I haven't got any clothes on either!'

Boy, was I relieved I wasn't upstairs. Something told me from the way the place was kept it wouldn't have been a pretty sight.

I heard a police officer shout: 'Put a sheet around yer!'

Dave and I exchanged glances.

They were on the move. The sound of stomping down-stairs echoed into the front yard. There was a policeman leading the way, one at the back, and sandwiched between two bedraggled-looking individuals who were handcuffed. They'd managed to put some clothes on, of some descrip-tion. Cavanagh – I assumed it was him – was about five foot ten with dark hair, stubbly, wearing a crumpled T-shirt and boxer shorts. He had a load of tattoos on his arms and legs. His partner was dressed in skin-tight leggings and a formerly white oversized T-shirt that bunched at her bulging stom-ach. They looked unkempt and unwashed.

The officers brought them into the lounge and then out came the warrant. Dave and I gingerly stepped into the hallway to get closer to the action, doing our best not to touch anything. We hovered by the doorway.

'We have the right to search your house,' the tall police officer leading the raid announced.

The warrant was quickly followed by the 'Miranda' rights – the British version of it.

'You do not have to say anything ...'

'Eh? What's going on?' Cavanagh eyes searched around him. 'What you on about?'

'We are arresting you on the suspicion of possession with intent to supply.'

'Oi, what? What d'you mean? I ain't been dealing drugs to no one,' he shouted.

'We will discuss this in due course,' the officer said over his shrieking. 'You will now be taken to the police station where you will be questioned.'

That was our cue to back out of the house.

David and I stood side by side on the street pavement as they escorted the pair to the van. Half the cul-de-sac was now awake, having a nosey out of their windows at the commotion. A couple in their dressing gowns had even gathered in their driveway to watch.

Dawn had broken across London and the sun was streaking through the grey clouds.

Cavanagh looked at me as he passed. Still half asleep and bewildered. The missus wasn't much different. She gurned as they showed her the back of the van.

Now the suspects were out of the way, the coppers got on with the important job of searching the house. I knew from my experience, from seeing the difference between a drug dealer and someone who ran the equivalent of a cartel, that these two were small fry in a much larger operation.

The search confirmed my thoughts. The officers found heroin, cannabis and pills. Nothing to write home about but enough to get them on possession with intent to supply.

From the feedback we later received from the police station, Cavanagh and his partner were, as I suspected, a small part of a much larger operation. The bottom rung in the food chain. They probably knew very little, if anything, about who was actually running the show. The head honcho is always the elusive character slipping unnoticed in the background; they'd probably never met him or her.

At a guess they were doing drugs themselves, getting high off their own supply and all that. It wasn't a huge bust for us, but it was a good starting point. Police could use that intel to chase their way to the top of the food chain.

Small fish, big fish, whatever way you looked at it, it was one up to us. That supply route into the jail was now cut dead.

An hour and a half later I was back at work. I didn't want to outstay my welcome. It was very unusual for the Old Bill to let a civilian, so to speak, be privy to something like that.

Cavanagh was charged and rather fittingly sent to the Scrubs a matter of days later on remand awaiting his trial. I didn't cross paths with him again after that day on his porch but when he was found guilty a month or so later, I made sure he was moved on to another jail. I couldn't have a dealer mixing with the people he'd been supplying. It would only be a matter of time until he was up to his old tricks, smuggling in drugs and phones. He had all the contacts in place to carry on like before, after all.

While I was busy keeping tabs on criminals trying to compromise the prison's security, someone was keeping a close eye on me. They were noting down all the things I'd been achieving, storing them up. Only I didn't know it yet.

Chapter 29

BENT COPPERS

HMP Wormwood Scrubs:
September 2011

Just when everything was going swimmingly with the police, something had to go and bollocks it up.

Sometimes the Old Bill asked if they could take a prisoner out of the jail 'to be produced'. This was when a detective wanted to interview a prisoner in relation to an old or a new crime. There were many different reasons a production order might be made, to take part in an ID parade for example. Often it was to help solve outstanding cases.

I could receive as many as a dozen requests a day from police forces across the country. Occasionally they would ask to keep the prisoner overnight. Only in exceptional circumstances, and I mean *exceptional*, would this be allowed.

An example of why a request might be made could be: Joe Bloggs has been done for burglary and is in the Scrubs awaiting his trial. The police ask to interview him again while he's on remand in connection with another ten burglaries. If he's guilty and admits to them, when it comes to the trial Joe's barrister can plead with the judge that the admission of guilt to the extra ten crimes to be taken into consideration. The result being, Joe Bloggs would more than likely be handed a more lenient sentence. The benefit for the police? They solve ten extra crimes and improve their all-important crime clear-up record.

So everyone wins, except us, who have to fill out a load more paperwork, especially if the detective insists on doing the interviews from the police station. This might be because they want to put the prisoner in a line-up. Whatever the reason, it's a pain in the arse for us. As you know, I'm very reluctant for prisoners to be sent out, especially after what happened with Faulkner.

I didn't have to say yes. As head of operations and security I had the final say – the prisoners were under my care, I had their warrants. However, in order to keep up the good relationship between us and the police, that two-way street I've been going on about, I often felt compelled to say yes unless it was a serious security risk.

So when a production form came through for Joe Monk, the first thing I did was check his file. He was a dealer, on remand for possession with intent to supply a large quantity of class-A heroin and cocaine, so he was looking at a big sentence, between five and ten years. The police wanted to get him for a few more charges of supplying drugs.

He wasn't dangerous as such, but there was a big red flag flying high next to his name. We'd acquired some intelligence an hour earlier that Joe was going to attempt to get drugs and mobile phones into the Scrubs while he was on his production. An officer on the wing had eavesdropped on a conversation. We didn't know how, we didn't know at what point during his production, but apparently he'd found out he might be going out and had plotted something.

We never told the prisoners they were going out on production. That left the question, who did? Joe might have found out via his solicitor who would have been notified of the order. He could have been told by the police themselves. He might even have been the one to contact the Old Bill in the first place, saying he had something to confess.

What pissed me off most about this potential security breach was that it was a counter-attack on my war against drugs. I was not happy.

I called Dave, the liaison officer, up to my office and told him what we'd heard. Staring at the production form in front of me, the pen in my hand. I said: 'I'm reluctant to sign this, David.'

Dave shifted from one foot to the other. 'I promise you, he'll be in police custody the entire time, you don't need to worry.'

If you've watched *Line of Duty*, about unit AC-12, you'll be familiar with police corruption, how the Old Bill can be as bent as some prison staff. I wanted to think the best, but it was my job to be ready for the worst.

My hand hovered over the signature line. It was a tough decision to make because maintaining our working relationship was equally important. Monk wasn't dangerous – he was just a dirty dealer who could, quite possibly, be bragging to his mates on the wing to make himself sound more impressive.

I leaned in. 'If you can reassure me he won't be let out of the police's sight on his production order, I suppose I will sign it.'

'Absolutely. I'll get the police officer in charge to speak to Mark in the intelligence office and give him a full briefing,' Dave promised.

'He will be strip-searched before and after he leaves the prison.' That was a non-negotiable.

'No problem.'

I looked at him warily. 'This better not fuck up.'

'It won't,' he reassured me.

I gave him one more lingering look and then signed the form.

I made sure I was in reception when Monk was handed over to the police. Mostly because I wanted to give them one final warning.

'We have intelligence this prisoner is going to try something on. I do not want him left alone at any stage in this production, or left in a position where he could get hold of drugs. Do I make myself clear?'

Monk was out of earshot, handcuffed to one of the officers with another escort alongside him. He was bald with a week's worth of stubble on his face. Skinny. Sinewy arms. Five foot nine. Pretty nondescript except for the bored look he was wearing on his face. He had on the grey prison-issue tracksuit, with his trousers hanging down his arse and his checked boxer shorts on show.

The officer in charge was annoyingly cocky. His hands were casually shoved in his pockets as he addressed me: 'Yeah, yeah, whatever, we got this covered.' He shrugged.

I gave him the stare-down. 'No, not whatever. Watch him!'

Clearly, all the officer cared about was getting the prisoner out.

I reiterated: 'The only reason I'm signing this production order is that I've been reassured precautions will be taken with this prisoner.' My words were almost hissing as they came out.

'Yeah, all right. You don't need to tell me twice.'

There went that gut feeling again. Niggling. Churning. Telling me something was going to go wrong with the operation. I wasn't confident at all with the guy's reply. In fact all three of them were cocky, fly by night, thought they knew it all and then a bit more.

The officer in charge, who had black curly hair slicked back off his forehead, avoided my gaze and turned to leave.

I followed the three men out and watched them load Monk into the back of the police van. One officer was in the back with him, the other two climbed into the front.

'I want him back by six. On the dot,' I stated.

The officer in charge pretended to doff his hat and then wound up the window.

Mark, my PO of intelligence who'd also come down to see Monk out, gave me a look, summing up my thoughts exactly.

'When Monk gets back, we put him on the BOSS chair. We strip-search him. We put the dog on him and see what happens.'

'Try and stop me, gov.'

I'd told reception to ring me as soon as Joe Monk stepped foot back inside the Scrubs.

'I'm on my way.' I'd already sprung out of my chair before I'd put down the phone. Mark and I legged it down to reception while simultaneously putting a call in to the kennels. Monk was going to get the full welcome committee.

The police officers hadn't stuck around; they'd dropped the prisoner off and left in the van. Two of our staff had hold of Monk, who was looking significantly less bored than when he left. In fact, I'd go as far to say he'd acquired a sparkle in his eye.

I looked him up and down suspiciously.

Monty and his handler Tracey appeared moments later, which immediately wiped the pleased look off Monk's face.

'Let's move him in here.' I indicated to the side room where the thorough examination was to begin.

We all bundled inside and Monk stood as stiff as a board as Monty approached.

'Afraid of dogs are we?' I quipped. Couldn't help myself.

Monty lifted his shiny wet nose into the air, his nostril flaring as he picked up a scent. He calmly padded across the floor towards Monk who recoiled into himself. One more sniff of the prisoner and Monty sat down.

A lump of anger rose in my throat. I tried to swallow it down but it wouldn't budge. I coughed hard and then unleashed. 'I believe you have drugs on you. I'm going to authorise for you to be put on the BOSS chair to confirm my suspicions.'

I braced myself for the usual protests. The 'I don't know what you're on about, gov'.

Instead I got: 'Don't worry, I'll give it to you.'

Huh? That was easy.

'Okay great, hand it over.'

Monk began pulling down his tracksuit bottoms.

Dear God, was he about to pull a load of contraband out of his arse? I didn't have the stomach for this.

'Wait!' I held up my hand and then exited the room sharpish with the dog handler, leaving the two male officers to deal with the extraction.

A matter of minutes later one of the officers emerged from the side room with a quantity of heroin, a quantity of cannabis and two mobile phones.

'Bloody hell!' I exclaimed. The cheeky bugger was going to bring all of that into the prison. My anger swelled again.

It hadn't been stashed where I'd assumed though. Although its location wasn't much cleaner. The contraband had been shoved down his boxers, festering near his tackle. I certainly wasn't going anywhere near that.

Yes, you guessed it, it was down to the Seg for him. Meanwhile, I was seething. Those cocky coppers – I knew they were going to bollocks it up. How many more times had I needed to tell them to watch Monk like a hawk? And how? How the hell had he got his hands on the drugs? None of this added up. I had a nose for bullshit and this smelled to high heaven.

Heads were going to roll!

First on my list was our liaison officer, David. I liked him very much but promises had been broken and questions needed to be answered. I called him on his personal mobile as it was now 7 p.m. He probably had his feet up in front of the telly. This couldn't wait.

'We need to meet first thing in the morning,' I announced. 'I'll see you in my office seven thirty.' It wasn't up for discussion.

'Is there something the matter?'

I tried to keep a lid on it. 'Oh yeah, something's the matter all right and I can assure it's going to blow wide open.'

I must have gone through half a dozen episodes of *CSI* that night to try and calm me down. I was absolutely fuming with the police. I'd given them the intelligence and they'd completely disregarded it. I'd been trying everything under the sun to crack down on drugs smuggling and the very establishment I'd been working with to help me do that had acted like none of it mattered. They'd had zero thought for the damage the drugs could cause inside our prison or for our relationship, in which I felt we'd worked hard to establish trust.

It's a dangerous word to throw around but what happened with Monk had police corruption written all over it. How else did he get his hands on drugs and, more importantly, know he'd be able to get hold of them.

I was tired but wired the next morning and ready for a scrap. I had a cup of tea next to me and the drugs and phones piled on my desk.

David appeared on time. He walked into my office, looked at me and at the drugs, and flinched.

'Please don't tell me it was Joe Monk?'

'It was,' I said, much more calmly. 'I want a full written explanation as to how this happened, because he was searched from top to toe before he left the prison so somehow he got those drugs when he was out with the police.'

'All I can do is offer my apologies.'

I shook my head. 'I'm not being funny, David, but your apology is worth nothing at this precise moment in time – until I know the ins and outs as to what the bloody hell happened yesterday.'

He left with his tail between his legs.

If you think I'd blown my stack, you should have seen the number one governor. 'For fuck's sake. What the bloody hell has gone on?!' Phil Taylor blasted so loudly the blinds almost rattled.

A bit later in the morning I received a phone call from chief superintendent somebody at Hammersmith Police Station saying how sorry he was at what had happened and he didn't know how it came about, how he valued our contributions to their intelligence and blah blah blah. I was too angry to listen to excuses.

'I'm not interested in your verbal apology; this goes far far deeper than that. This is about trust and the effect drugs and mobiles have in prison on safety – on staff safety, on prisoners' safety and visitors' safety.' I didn't stop there. 'As I said to the liaison officer this morning, I want a full written explanation as to what the bloody hell happened.'

I needed to know. There wasn't going to be any cover-up on my watch.

Meanwhile, the number one gov got on to the area manager Nick Pascoe for all the London jails. A Big Shot. He then got on to the director general of the prison service, Michael Spurr. An even bigger shot. Next thing we knew, Phil Taylor received a call from the City of London Police's assistant chief constable inviting him and yours truly to Gold Command HQ in Westminster for an explanation.

It had worked its way up to the top. Which meant only one thing – it was a much more serious matter than a copper being negligent.

Gold Command was where the major incidents were dealt with. Where all the bigwigs had their offices. It was located in a forbidding-looking building on the Thames riverbank next to the Houses of Parliament.

Your neck cricked just looking up at it. It was huge, dating back to what looked like the Victorian era. It had a Fort Knox set-up, with reams of security officers, gates, barriers and cameras surrounding the premises.

The inside was surprisingly modern though.

THE GOVERNOR

The number one and I were led through a rabbit warren of corridors and into a boardroom which was as big as our entire security office.

The meeting had been arranged with the assistant chief constable and the gold commander, but around the oval table sat twenty of the most senior chiefs in the entire Met Police force, all impeccably dressed in their black jackets, white shirts and ties. There were so many silver pips in one enclosed space, it was blinding!

It was also very warm in there, or maybe that was my temperature rising as it suddenly dawned on me how serious a matter this had now become.

We introduced ourselves. Shook hands and took a seat in the plush blue chairs next to the assistant chief constable.

In a nutshell, there was a lot of bowing and scraping – obviously not by us – as the truth was revealed. As we discovered what the three police officers who had taken Monk from us had really done with him that day.

Chapter 30

SURPRISE OF MY LIFE

HMP Wormwood Scrubs:
September 2011

Bloody hell, what is it with KFC? Being a vegetarian the Colonel's recipe had never really appealed to me, but would you choose it to be your last supper, so to speak?

I couldn't believe the story that unravelled around gold command's boardroom table.

The three police officers who'd picked up Monk didn't bring him back to the station. Oh no, instead they took him for a KFC and then chauffeured him to his partner's place for dessert. I'm not sure if it was his wife or girlfriend, but whatever their relationship status, the coppers left Monk out of their sight with her for an entire hour.

They then came back to the house, picked him up, took him to Hammersmith Police Station and got him to admit to a load of further charges.

They essentially bribed him with junk food and sex to come clean. The consequence of their corruption was giving Monk the time alone to shove a load of drugs and mobile phones down his boxer shorts after he was done with his bird.

'I'd warned your men he was going to try and bring in drugs but getting a result was more important to them. All they cared about was improving their crime clear-up record,' I told the boardroom. 'We feel like we can't trust the Met Police any more. That trust we had with you has been completely destroyed.

'What was in it for the officer in charge? Was he angling for a promotion?' I had to ask.

There was more bowing and scraping from gold command.

To be fair to them, at least they hadn't let the matter drop. In fact, they wanted me to come back and give evidence as part of an internal affairs investigation. *Line of Duty* style. I was very pleased to hear the cocky copper had been suspended in the interim.

'Our sincerest apologies,' the assistant chief constable reiterated. 'We're going to be leading a big review into Met productions of prisoners throughout all London jails.'

He was a gently spoken man, but one whose words carried a lot of weight and sting. You could tell from the way he articulated himself that he was immensely experienced. Definitely not someone you would want to get on the wrong side of.

He couldn't promise it would never happen again but he gave his assurance he would do all in his power to make sure it didn't.

Two of the officers involved in Monk's production were given final written warnings and the officer in charge lost his job, which was the result I'd hoped for. I don't like the thought of anyone being fired but you can't have coppers going around behaving like that. What he'd done was dangerous. Monk could have brought a gun back to the prison, for all he knew.

Not long after the internal affairs investigation, I received some highly confidential news of my own in November 2011.

Earlier I mentioned someone, unbeknown to me, had been watching my career trajectory. Being the self-effacing person that I am, I got the shock of my life when the letter arrived on my doormat.

It was white, official looking and didn't have a stamp. *What the hell is this?* My stomach tightened as I panicked, thinking that I'd been caught for speeding or owed some money to someone.

I gingerly sliced the seal open with my forefinger. *This is all I bloody need before Christmas, a fine or debt that was going to fleece me.* The paper was thick and crisp and felt expensive between my fingers. I shook it open. As my eyes settled on the writing my mouth fell open.

I'm rarely shocked or surprised after everything I'd seen and heard over the years, but I think I may have stopped breathing for a moment.

The letter was from the Cabinet Office and it began with the sentence: *'The Prime Minister has asked me to inform you in strict confidence …'*

Bloody hell. I read on, my fingers shaking.

'*He proposes to submit your name to the Queen.*'

The Queen!

'*He is recommending that Her Majesty may be graciously pleased to approve that you be appointed a Member of the Order of the British Empire (MBE) in the 2012 Honours List for your services to the prison service.*'

Come again! How on earth had this happened? I was just doing my job. I stood in the hallway of my flat, my entire body, trembling. I read the letter again. Miss Vanessa Frake. Again. Miss Vanessa Frake. *It's me, it's really me.*

When I finally came to my senses I pulled my mobile out of my pocket. *I need to tell Ju.* Even though she and Annie-Mae were on the train over to see me I couldn't wait another second.

I could hear the sound of the carriage clunking along the track when she picked up the phone. Ju sounded tired and harassed. London commuting will do that to you.

'Are you sitting down?' I asked, preparing her for the news.

'No, standing room only,' she huffed.

Hopefully my news would cheer her up. 'You're never going to believe this,' I said, pausing for effect.

'Oh yeah what?' Ju sighed again.

'I've only gone and been awarded an MBE.'

There was a three-second pause followed by an ear-piercing scream of joy which must have deafened her entire carriage.

While I waited in the car for Ju and Annie-Mae to arrive at the station I gave my mum a call. My fingers trembled again as I clutched the receiver to my ear. All I've ever wanted was to make my mum proud of me, so my emotions were hanging on her reaction to the news. Mum has never been great at expressing how she feels. She loves me dearly but she's guarded with her words. She's changed her initial – somewhat negative – opinion of the prison service after seeing how much I loved my job. After hearing how my career had gone from strength to strength. She'd always congratulated me on my promotions but it would be fair to say she was never gushing about it. I think her biggest gripe was that she never got to see me as I was always so tied up with work.

The phone kept ringing.

'Come on, Mum,' I muttered as the phone rang. I'd built myself up to this now.

'Hello, love.' She finally picked up. 'I didn't know where I'd left my phone, I could hear it ringing but –'

I cut her short. I couldn't hold it in a moment longer.

'Mum, I've been awarded an MBE for my services to the prison.'

Just like Ju, she digested the words with a long pause.

'Sorry, love, say that again?'

'I'm getting an MBE!'

I didn't expect screaming. I thought I'd get a simple 'Well done'. I was taken by surprise for the second time that day.

'I've always known there was something special about you,' she said, her words faltering with the onset of tears.

'You have?' My eyes suddenly filled up, too.

'Of course I have. You've always been different. You've stood out from the crowd. I knew you'd be a success at whatever you put your heart into.'

'You did?' The words snagged in my throat. My windscreen was fogging up with all the emotion.

'I'm so incredibly proud of you.'

Tears were streaming down my face.

'Thanks, Mum.'

I rubbed a circle in the misted-up window to make sure I hadn't missed Ju. There she was, coming out of the station with Annie-Mae, clutching a single red rose which she must have picked up on the way. I don't think I can remember a moment when I felt happier and more loved.

Chapter 31

DON'T MESS UP THE CURTSEY

Buckingham Palace:
16 February 2012

'Absolutely not!' I stared at the ginormous pants Ju dangled in front of me. 'Not a chance I'm wearing those.'

Ju had bought me a pair of tummy-tuck knickers from fancy lingerie shop Rigby & Peller, which ironically was once the Queen's corsetiere. I'd hoped she'd forgotten about the purchase. No such luck.

'Just try them on.' She smiled convincingly

I groaned. 'Okay, I'll *try* them.'

They were to go underneath the tailored black suit I'd bought especially to meet the Queen. I'd fretted for weeks over whether I should wear a dress. I don't think I've ever worn one in my entire life. Frocks weren't me and I had to be *me*. Plus, the idea of having to buy a matching hat, shoes and handbag filled me with dread. Choosing what shirt to wear in the mornings was stressful enough.

283

I reappeared clasping my stomach. 'I think you've bought me a pair three sizes too small,' I gasped.

'That's how they are supposed to be.'

'I literally cannot fucking breathe!'

'Listen' – Ju's voice softened – 'it's for today, today only. It pulls you in in all the right places, it makes you stand up even taller and look the part.'

I don't know how, but Ju managed to persuade me to keep them on. I was too nervous and stressed out to argue. I'd spent most of the night tossing and turning, panicking about the big day at Buckingham Palace. One of my greatest fears is being late for things. I'm always early, for everything, and my governor brain couldn't switch off. I'd been running through every worst-case scenario and a matching contingency plan to go with it.

What if the taxi didn't arrive on time? What if we got stuck in traffic? What if somebody forgot something and we had to go back for it? We had to be at the Palace for 9 a.m. sharp.

I've always had a reactive stomach, shall we say. When I'm anxious it churns, and the feeling was somewhat exacerbated under air-constricting Lycra.

I needed a fag.

I'd significantly cut back on my smoking since I'd been with Ju because I didn't want Annie-Mae breathing in my fumes. Today was an exception. As I puffed away waiting for the cab, I also started pacing. Striding back and forth, up and down the pavement.

'Calm yourself, it will be okay.' Ju emerged from our flat.

She had gone all out for her Royal visit – looking a picture in a fuchsia pink L.K. Bennett dress with the full matching bag and shoes combo. We'd treated Annie-Mae to her first designer dress from the Dolce & Gabbana kids range. It was black-and-white newspaper print on fabric, which suited her edgy style and confident personality. Ju's mum was also there, dressed up to the nines.

'Easier said than done.' I took another deep inhale, sucking the nicotine into my lungs. I continued pacing, accidently brushing into Ju in the process.

'Oh sorry!'

'It's fine, but you've got to calm down.'

I was off again, striding, one hand shoved deep into my pocket.

'Where is this taxi?' I muttered. Just as I said it, there was this ear-piercing scream.

'Mummy, Mummy, you're on fire!'

I turned on my heels to see Annie-Mae shrieking and smoke billowing off Ju's fur wrap – an antique heirloom from her mum. I must have caught her with the end of my fag.

'Oh hell!' I jumped to her side, frantically patting it down. Annie-Mae was also patting it while Ju tried to take it off. It was like a *Carry On* film.

Miraculously, it wasn't damaged, only slightly singed. The smell of burning hair lingered in the air. Ju was not impressed and neither was her mum. However, she hid her distress well as she knew I was beside myself with nerves.

Throwing on a smile, Ju said: 'It's fine. Don't worry about it. It will be fine.' She wrapped the creature back around her shoulders.

We'd had a disagreement that morning about her wearing it. Being an animal lover I hate all things real fur. She argued it had been dead for a hundred years, which made it less bad. With the smell of my blunder still in the air, now wasn't the moment to readdress the issue.

After all my panicking we had twenty minutes to spare, enough time to meet my mum and dad in a café around the corner from the palace.

Ju tried again to get me to eat something but with the combination of my anxiety and the pants, I couldn't. I pushed the cheese croissant back across the table.

By dad, I obviously mean my stepdad, but I've called him 'Dad' ever since I was around fourteen or fifteen. I've realised over the years it's not the sperm that makes a dad, it's the man, and he deserves the title. Him and Mum had really pushed the boat out for my MBE. Dad had bought a new suit, while Mum had a new dress and a hat on. They looked so smart. As we got up to leave, Dad grabbed me for a hug. Catching me with his eyes he said: 'I look at you as my daughter and I'm really proud of you.'

He'd never said anything like that to me before. I had to bite my lip to stop the tears springing up. Thank goodness I never went in for make-up or I'd have had mascara running down my cheeks.

Sadly, I could only take three people in with me, so I had to wave Annie-Mae and Ju's mum goodbye at the gates. We had a treat in store for them afterwards though.

My heart fluttered as I turned and faced Buckingham Palace. I wanted to pinch myself. How did I end up here? *Seriously, Vanessa, how did you do it?* The number one gov and his deputy, David Redhouse, had been the ones to nominate me for the award. What had I done to deserve them sticking their necks out for me? I kept asking myself all these questions as we walked through the big arch into the courtyard, as we swept up the red-carpeted staircase flanked by guards from the Blues and Royals in their full military uniform, holding their swords high, unflinchingly.

As I strode along a gold-gilded portrait-lined corridor, my mind jumped back to those long bleak corridors I'd insisted on walking alone on my first day in the Scrubs. A smirk arose as I remembered how I'd stubbornly said I'd find my own way to D wing. How bitter and fearful I'd been back then. How terrified I was about working in a men's prison. How certain I'd been that it would spell the end of my career. Well, look at me know. I stopped for a moment, drinking it all in. It was otherworldly. I had to fight my mouth dropping open.

A hand landed on my shoulder and I flinched.

'Are you all right, love?' Mum asked.

'Yeah, I'm okay,' was about all I could muster.

There were ninety-eight other people getting honours that day, from knighthoods to CBEs, including actor Ronnie Corbett and golfer Lee Westwood. All I could think as I waited for my name to be called was *Don't fuck up the curtsey.*

I'd been practising with Ju ever since I got the news. In the kitchen. In the living room. Upstairs before bed – just one last rehearsal. I could have done it in my sleep I was that well practised. So why now, as I waited in the green room while my nerves rattled, was fluffing it all I could think about? The distress my oxygen-stealing pants were causing me paled into insignificance.

'Miss Vanessa Frake ...' My name rung across the high-ceilinged room. We'd splintered off into a group of twelve and had been given a crash course on the rules of etiquette while we waited to meet the Queen. The whole thing ran like a very well-oiled machine. I couldn't help thinking the Scrubs could do with some lessons in efficiency from this royal bunch.

Family and friends had been ushered to another room. I kept a part of Ju with me though. My pink shirt and cufflinks engraved with my initials had both been presents from her.

Nervously, I ironed my shirt with the flat of my hand. I straightened and then crossed the room to where I'd been called.

I was up next.

Ma'am as in jam not marm as in farm. I silently sung the rhyme on how I needed to make my address as I stood at the shoulder of the air vice-marshal. He gave me the nod and a million butterflies flapped their wings in my stomach.

The Queen was standing on a stage in a huge ballroom, carpeted in red and gold and ringed in priceless paintings.

DON'T MESS UP THE CURTSEY

Two Gurkha soldiers were poised either side of her, keeping the Queen safe, their famous knives holstered at their waists. She looked impeccable in her purple shift dress and pearls.

Anxiety squeezed my throat as I made my approach.

Don't fuck up the curtsey.

A full orchestra was playing in the gallery but all I could hear was the thud of my heart. It didn't help that I caught Ju's eye in the second row. I could tell she was just as worried for me as I was.

I managed it though. The curtsey.

'Your Majesty,' I said as I rose to face the Queen.

She hooked my MBE medal onto the clip on my lapel. She straightened and smiled.

'Congratulations on your award, very well deserved,' she said with her cut-glass accent. 'I believe you've been in the prison service a long time.'

'Yes, ma'am.'

'I expect you have seen a lot of changes.'

I smiled. 'Yes ma'am, but not as many as you, I expect.'

It got a chuckle out of her. Her eyes sparkled with mischief.

Then she put her hand out for me to shake.

The moment was short and fleeting but magical nonetheless. I was walking on air as I made my way to the other side of the room, my medal glistening under the lights. I could feel my family and Ju smiling at me, cheering me on.

* * *

THE GOVERNOR

The first thing I did when I arrived for celebratory tea and cakes and champagne in one of London's finest hotels, the Savoy, was sling my tummy-tuck pants in the bin of the ladies' toilet.

Thank God, I can breathe again!

I made my way back to our decadent table where there was a group of ten family and friends. My medal was being passed around in its box. Ju caught my eye and read my expression.

'Everything okay?' she asked.

'Uh huh, it is now, since I got rid of those bloody pants.'

Her eyebrow shot up. 'You're not going commando in the Savoy?!'

'Yep,' I said proudly.

Just as I admitted it, a huge cake ablaze with firework sparklers came rolling towards us on one of those fancy silver trolleys. 'Congratulations Vanessa' swirled across the icing. Everyone held their champagne flutes high to toast me and I think it was at that moment the enormity of what I'd achieved finally sunk in. Among my nearest and dearest, when the stress of the big day was over and I could relax and reflect. The tears that I'd been fighting off surged to the surface and ran down my face to meet my beaming smile.

Chapter 32

PLAYING DEAD

HMP Holloway:
1988

'Do you think she's dead?' The officer peered through the hatch into the cell.

'Let me have a look.' I moved into her place.

Narrowing my eyes I squinted through the rectangular hole in the door.

Rebecca Smith was not what you would call house proud. Her cell was a pigsty. Her possessions were strewn across the cubical. Her dirty clothes piled in the corner. The smell of unwashed skin and hair wafted through to me.

She lay motionless on her bed, her sheets pulled up over her face. All that was showing was a black patch of wiry hair from the crown of her head.

I stared intently, trying to see if her chest was rising and falling. It was impossible to tell.

'I don't know.' I turned to face Dee Merry, one of my best friends at Holloway. Dee read my thoughts. Reluctance.

Rebecca was in for murder: she stabbed her boyfriend more than fifty times to death. She was extremely violent and suffered from a personality disorder. She took delight in attacking officers.

Her party trick was to hide under the covers and pretend she was dead. She was like a praying mantis, lying in wait, ready to attack whoever came in to check on her.

The problem was, she had previous for actual attempted suicide. She'd tried to strangle herself on a number of occasions, tying various ligatures around her throat – bed sheets, her knicker elastic. We'd always rescued her in time though.

That meant we were never sure if she was faking it or had really done something to top herself. It was Russian roulette – we were risking our lives to find out.

I couldn't let anyone die on my watch though. It was 8.30 p.m. and I was an officer on C1, the hospital wing.

'We're going to have to go in.'

Dee pressed the alarm bell. We needed staff back-up. We couldn't wait for them to arrive though; we needed to get in there quick just in case Rebecca had tried to kill herself.

We unlocked the door and rushed in. I threw back the covers to reveal a very alive Rebecca Smith.

With one fluid movement, she leapt up from her bed and came at us with the strength of ten men. Her fists flailing, her legs kicking in every direction. A deep guttural growling noise emanated from her throat.

'Ouch!' was the only word I managed to get out as she battered us.

What made the situation even more diabolical was that she'd covered herself in baby oil (which she'd bought from the canteen), so every time we tried to grasp her and pin her arms down she slipped through our grip. It was a well-known trick that many prisoners used.

We fought her some more and then somehow I managed to grab hold of her. As I locked my arms around her torso she dropped her head, opened her mouth and sunk her teeth into my arm.

I screamed. 'Dee, she's got my arm!'

Dee pulled at her. She tried prising her mouth open. It was hopeless, Rebecca was like a dog with a bone and she wasn't letting go.

The pain was excruciating. I could see my blood bubbling up around the whites of her teeth. As I've mentioned, I'm terrible around blood, let alone my own. I wanted to pass out.

In the end the only thing Dee could do to save my arm and get her off me was to punch her in the face. It was a last but necessary resort. Rebecca released her grip but within seconds she was going for us again. Together we shoved her away; it bought us enough time to scramble out of the cell and lock the door. We fell back against the wall, panting to catch our breath.

Poor Dee had injured her back. She could barely straighten. My arm was a mess. There were teeth marks and the skin was broken. Blood was running into my hand.

I panicked. Rebecca wasn't a clean prisoner by any stretch of the imagination. Before she murdered her boyfriend she lived on the streets. My immediate fear was that I might have contracted something nasty. She could have had Hep B, Hep C, HIV.

I went in an ambulance to the Whittington Hospital in north London to have my wounds tended to and have blood tests taken. When I got to the A&E they saw to me straight away. The doctors and nurses were very good with the prison staff – we were regulars.

I was propped up on a bed in a booth with a blue curtain on a rail for privacy. 'This is going to hurt,' the nurse warned me. Before I had time to digest her words she wiped my bite with some hydrochloric acid disinfectant.

Oh. My. God. The pain barometer went off the chart. I had to be scraped off the ceiling.

Eventually, when the stinging eased and I could string a sentence together again, I asked whether I was going to be okay. Back then you had to wait a week for HIV results, and of course it takes three months for the virus to show up in your system, so that was another blood test scheduled and a whole lot of worry in between.

I was frightened and I was also angry at the nurses in the prison for not revealing whether Rebecca had any medical conditions. They said it would be a breach of confidence. I had to suffer months of worry instead; it didn't seem fair.

Adding insult to injury, when the assault charge went to Marylebone Magistrates' Court, the judge presiding over Rebecca's case had an offensive thing or two to say about the matter.

The first I heard that it had reached court was when a

fellow officer handed me the local newspaper. There was a tiny, blink and you'd miss it, article describing how Rebecca had pleaded guilty to assaulting a prison officer and she was fined £60 in costs. What really stood out was the judge's summing up.

'I don't know why I'm dealing with this. This was all part of a prison officer's job.'

My blood boiled. Being assaulted was part of my job description? I don't think so. I wanted to bite a chunk out of the judge's arm. Drag him to the Whittington, splash hydrochloric acid on his arm, make him have an HIV test and another one three months later and see how he liked it.

It's a wonder I carried on after such a violent assault and a filthy insult to my worth. But that was me all over. I didn't give up.

Chapter 33

MY WAY OR THE HIGHWAY

HMP Wormwood Scrubs:
October 2012

Never in the history of Great Britain had a serving prime minister visited a prison. The Scrubs was performing so well in its audits that David Cameron wanted to pay us a little visit.

His security detail came to meet me a few days prior to have a tour of the jail, to get a lay of the land. We'd locked horns over the small matter of guns.

I stood with my hands firmly on my hips at the gatehouse where I was seeing them off. It had all run smoothly up until this point.

'I don't care if he's the Dalai Lama. No firearms allowed in the prison,' I told them, giving the lay of *my* land. 'You can accompany the PM everywhere he goes but you can't carry weapons.'

There were so many things that could go wrong. A prisoner could try to attack the PM and be shot dead by the protection officer. A prisoner manages to grapple the gun out of the close protection officer's hand and shoots Cameron. The prime minister of Great Britain shot dead on my watch – they had to be joking. The prisoner shoots another prisoner or a member of staff – another possible, doesn't bear thinking about, outcome. These were all worst-case scenarios but when I carried out risk assessments, that's what I had to look at. This PR stunt could end up a blood bath if it wasn't dealt with properly. It would certainly mark the end of my career. My security clearance was one step down from the prime minister's. I couldn't access 'Top Secret' files, but I could see 'Secret'. I had every authority to make this call.

Cameron's close protection officers were just as you'd imagine. Something out of *Men in Black*. Broad shouldered, square jawed, suited and booted in black with serious expressions cemented across their faces.

They were from the close protection unit of the Met Police and their only agenda was protecting the PM. Of course I could see where they were coming from.

The taller of the two men, who walked in such a way that suggested he'd once been in the military, retaliated with: 'If we're escorting the subject into the prison we won't be handing our firearms in.'

'We have a sticking point then,' I said.

'Yeah we do I'm afraid because if you won't allow firearms in, we won't be bringing him in,' the big burly one replied.

They were being politically correct not to mention the prime minister's name as the visit was yet to be officially announced. For now, it was *him* and the *subject*.

It would be fair to suggest they were also trying to intimidate me. Giving it the whole 'we're the PM's bodyguards' bravado. We stared each other down. I could puff out my chest with the best of them.

'I suggest you go back to your bosses and have a word because I'm telling you now, we will not let you in with firearms.'

More eyeballing.

'Well, that concludes that then.' I wrapped up the stand-off.

We kind of agreed to disagree on the matter and off they went. I had no idea what would happen next – if they would come around or call the whole thing off. It was fifty-fifty.

The number one gov would be gutted if Downing Street changed their mind. A visit from Cameron would be a huge coup for the Scrubs – putting us even more firmly on the map as one of the leading London jails, thrusting us into the media spotlight. In a positive way for once.

Coup aside though, Phil Taylor one hundred and ten per cent had my back about where I was coming from. The security of the prison came first. Two days later I was summoned to his office. We had an answer.

A smile spread up my face. One–nil to you Vanessa. I'd got my way.

The number one had received an email announcing that David Cameron would be arriving at Wormwood Scrubs in two days' time.

Two days! Minor heart palpitation.

The message went on to clearly state his security officers would not be bringing firearms inside the jail.

'Ha!' A snort of victory.

The plan was they would travel with the PM in his armour-plated Jaguar but remain with the car once it was parked inside the gates. Cameron would have an unarmed officer shadow him on his grand tour.

'What's this all in aid of anyway?' I asked.

'He wants to use the Scrubs as a backdrop to launch his new law and order agenda,' Phil explained.

The agenda was to propose tougher community sentences; e.g. anyone found carrying a knife would face a prison sentence rather than community service. Anyone sentenced to prison would have to serve their time behind bars even if it meant increasing the prison population. A sweetener had been thrown in for firms and charities working with prisoners trying to rehabilitate them – they would receive payment on proof of results.

'Oh yeah.' I rolled my eyes. It sounded great but then they always did on paper. To be honest, all the government initiatives went in one ear and out the other. They were all bollocks. Excuse my French.

These politicians were convinced they'd come up with something ground-breaking and new that nobody'd heard of before, but we'd tried it a hundred times over already. It had just swung around on a big roundabout. It hadn't work the last time but they thought it would work this time and around it went again.

Cameron was calling it his 'tough but intelligent' approach to crime. Sadly, it was doomed to failure unless more funds could be made available. Rehabilitation, incentives, it all takes money. As for sending more convicted prisoners to jail, we were at bursting point as it was. More than 50 per cent of UK jails were overcrowded thanks to the government's decision to close many down – due to underfunding. Anyway, don't get me started. Politics wasn't my detail. Keeping the PM safe while he visited the Scrubs was.

I was excited but stressed. Cameron's visit spelled security logistical nightmare for me, especially since the number one gov had given the green light for a bunch of journalists, a photographer and a cameraman to enter the prison and ask the PM questions. Luckily, I thrived off these kinds of situations – fixing things, finding solutions. Organisation was my bag.

Should we lock up the entire jail or did we allow Cameron to meet a handful of prisoners? If we did let some prisoners out they would have to be individuals who were performing well and on their way to being reformed. Good press and all that. They would have to be risk assessed. They could not pose a threat in any shape or form. Were we to forewarn the prisoners about the PM's arrival or should we keep it under wraps?

There were a lot of niggly details I needed clarified from Downing Street in advance. For example, the names of who would be entering the jail with the PM. Who would be waiting outside in the Jag? What time would

they arrive? What time would they leave? I'm absolutely regimented about time. There could be no room for
error.

The big day arrived. We'd chosen to show the PM around
B wing because it was the nicest – i.e. an induction wing,
less prisoners, less drama. Honestly, I'd never seen it look so
clean. It smelled of fresh paint and detergent. The floors
were sparkling. The landings were shining. We were like
proud homeowners. If you're having someone around for
tea you wouldn't want your place looking like a dump,
would you? Well, neither did we. We'd worked our arses off
to make the Scrubs shine and this was our chance to show
it off.

Forget my 7.30 a.m. starts. I was at the Scrubs for 6.30
a.m. that day to make sure nothing went wrong.
Miraculously, I didn't go through an entire packet of fags in
one sitting, my abstention for the sake of Annie-Mae and
Ju was working. I had drunk a significant amount of caffeine
by the time the famous reinforced black Jag rolled up to our
gates at 10 a.m. though.

There were riders – police on motorbikes – escorting
him, which surprised me. The car went straight through
into the gated compound where the number one and myself
were ready and waiting to greet David Cameron.

In the end we decided to lock the entire prison down to
avoid any potential disaster. We'd also kept the whole thing
top secret. We couldn't trust the prisoners not to kick off if
they heard the PM was on site. They were gobby at the best
of times. He'd be heckled to high heaven.

The close protection officers got out of the car first, their eyes casting in every direction, looking out for potential danger. The one in the front seat was a woman, the one in the back was the tall guy I'd locked horns with. He opened the door for Cameron, who stepped out onto Scrubs soil with a broad politician's smile. He shrugged his shoulders back and buttoned up his black suit jacket. He was wearing a crisp white shirt that emphasised his holiday tan, and a bright blue tie, naturally.

I took a step back. It wasn't for me to meet him first; that was the number one's job.

Pride swelled across Phil Taylor's face. His chest puffed out. *Look at my beautiful prison* his body language screamed. He met Cameron with a handshake.

Meanwhile, the protection officer shook mine.

'You won,' he said.

'I was never not going to.' I grinned back.

The plan was that I would sort out the close protection team with whatever they needed, cup of tea, etc., and then I'd catch up with the number one, Cameron and the press pack on B wing.

Now that the ice had thawed between me and the PM's team, we got down to the all-important task of having a bit of banter. The female officer caught me staring at the Jag. It was hard not to. Armour-plated. Bomb-resistant. Bulletproof. It was a sleek black mean machine.

'Do you want to sit inside?' she asked.

Did I ever. I played it cool though. 'Yeah, why not,' I said, shrugging.

'You'll be surprised by what you see. There's not much room inside.'

She wasn't kidding. I was expecting to step inside a Tardis. It couldn't have been more different. The thick steel plating on the outside left little room on the inside. I had to fold myself up to fit on the back seat. Everything else was Tardis-like though. The dashboard, for example, lit up with lights and buttons and twirling dials. The police car I'd ridden in to go on the drugs raid paled in comparison. Also it wasn't a patch on this upholstery. The Jag gave a new meaning to the word plush. I ran my hand over the soft leather seat and melted back into the luxuriousness of it all.

From Buckingham Palace to the PM's car, I was really going up in the world.

'Having fun,' the officer said, giggling.

'Yeah, I don't want to get out.'

But a promise of a cup of tea is a promise. I brought the two officers to our security office and left them chatting to my team while I headed over to join the party in B wing.

I stayed in the background and thought I'd got away without having to do the pleasantries, until the number one called me over. I was introduced to David Cameron who shook my hand. He was extremely polite.

'I understand you organised the security for today. It's been a pleasure and an eye opener to wander around Wormwood Scrubs. Thank you very much,' he said.

'No problem, sir,' I replied. Then I escorted him across the yard to where the Jag had been turned around and was ready and waiting for his departure.

THE GOVERNOR

For all the prep and drama involved, the whole thing was over in forty minutes, if that. I was happy for the number one that it had all gone to plan without any hiccups. The publicity would give the Scrubs some serious kudos and hopefully some extra funding.

Ha, famous last words.

Chapter 34

THE BEGINNING OF THE END

HMP Wormwood Scrubs:
Autumn 2012

My gaze was fixed on the number one gov's name plaque. My hand, frozen to his door handle. My pulse, racing.

This was the toughest thing I'd had to do in my entire career and conflicting feelings were screaming inside of me.

Come on, Vanessa. You've made up your mind. You need to see this through now.

I took some deep breaths. The chatter of the security office behind me drowned into white noise as I mustered the courage.

You need to think about your future. Your happiness. Your sanity.

In one jerky movement I opened the door and launched myself into the boss's office.

The cross-breeze from the window opposite spritzed my face. It was just the tonic I needed to sharpen my thoughts.

Phil Taylor looked up from his computer.

'Ah, Vanessa, nice to see you.'

'Can I have a word, sir.' I headed for a seat around the huge conference table. We always chatted there. It was our routine. A habit we'd developed over our time working together.

His leather upholstered chair squeaked as he rose to his feet to meet me. He sat down, crossed his legs and locked me in his gaze. His eyes behind his oval-rimmed glasses were full of expression.

'Is something the matter?'

I sighed again, forcing the words out with a gust of air from my lungs.

'Yes, sir. I want to leave my job.'

It wasn't a knee-jerk decision. The thought had been building for months, ever since the government sent in a crack team called Management Services to go through every department in the jail with a fine toothcomb looking for ways to slash costs.

Cameron's visit, his sparkling new initiative, was just a smokescreen for the real problem – prisons were chronically underfunded. Year on year we were made to cut our budget by 3 per cent. This team was sent in to shake things up even more.

They arrived in their stone-washed suits armed with their calculators and they spent three months sifting through our files. They looked at shift patterns. They looked at staffing. They examined what responsibilities each employee had. It doesn't take a rocket scientist to work out the most experienced staff are your biggest expenditure and the quickest way to make savings is to get rid of them. Slash their duties. Cut staff numbers. Put admin grade staff into the roles of prison officers. It was all done with ruthless and immediate effect.

Between the visit centre, reception, the gate, the control room, security and intel, I'd come to be in charge of the largest team in the prison, close to three hundred staff. Almost overnight I was stripped of half my responsibilities. They completely decimated my areas, taking everything from me except security, intel and managing the drug dog handlers.

Areas such as prisoner visits were downgraded in importance and handed to the gov number five to oversee. Staff numbers on duty were sliced from twenty-four officers to ten and a couple of admin posts.

It felt like I'd been violated. That sounds over the top, I know, but I'd been stripped of everything I'd worked so hard to achieve. I was powerless to fight back because of the need to save money.

I understood why they were doing it but couldn't agree with it because putting less experienced staff in charge made the prison more vulnerable. Not enough people knew what they were doing. For example, having half the amount of officers on visits meant more drugs would slip through the net. The cuts went against everything I'd been trying to achieve. Can you imagine what it must have felt like to build up the Emerald City – albeit a slightly more grimy one with a severe rat problem – to see it crumble before your eyes?

Soul destroying. I was being paid to keep the jail safe, but I couldn't. The glory days were well and truly over.

I found myself getting into too many arguments to keep count of. They would leaf through my paperwork telling me I didn't need this, that and the other and I would snap back saying I did. 'That's the reason why the Scrubs is in such good shape,' I'd refute. It fell on deaf ears.

I imagined my name on a whiteboard somewhere in head office, which the bosses were itching to scrub off. I'd been in the service since 1986. One of the few left costing the government 'too much' money. I may have improved the standard of the prison. I may have made it much more secure, but at the end of the day, I was just a number. I could be replaced. There's always someone who can do your job for less. The prison service was a cut-throat world. *Do more for less* was their motto and they certainly lived up to it.

At first I dealt with my emotions, as per usual, by suppressing them. I buried the anger. I swallowed it back, but the bitterness continued to rise. Fury and frustration turned to pain until eventually, one night, I couldn't hold it in any longer.

She could tell I was chomping the bit as I pretended to watch what was on the telly.

'Do you want to talk about it?' Ju asked.

That was the lovely thing about being with Ju. Because we worked together she could understand what I was going through. She too was facing serious stresses seeing her healthcare budget slashed.

I shrugged. 'Why am I bothering?'

It was frightening to feel this way, because never in my career had I questioned why I was putting effort in. I just did because I loved my job.

'What is the point of me? I'm doing my damnedest, and they're just taking it away from me.' My voice cracked. Tears collected in my eyes. I looked away, fighting the surge of feelings off.

'It's okay to be upset.' Ju cupped her hand over mine. Which only served to make me more upset. Why is it always the smallest acts of kindness that tip you over the edge?

I bit my lip and blurted: 'I'm not sure I can do this any more.'

A silence settled over the room as Ju continued to stroke my hand and soothe me. I was just airing my grievances. Getting things off my chest. I wasn't expecting the conversation to go any further and I certainly wasn't expecting Ju to chirp: 'Retire!'

I raised my gaze to meet hers, staring at her with a mixture of shock and bewilderment.

'Come again?'

'Why don't you retire? Annie-Mae is always in childcare and after-school club because we're both always working late. You can be there for her, she'd love that. You can be there for both of us.' She smiled kindly. 'Just leave it.'

'But what would I do?' Panic suddenly gripped me. 'The prison is my life.'

THE GOVERNOR

I was fifty years old, I had five years left until retirement. It was all I'd ever known. Twenty-seven years I'd been inside. It was my home. The staff were as good as family.

I'd left school with barely any qualifications. What was I going to do with the rest of my life? I was one of those people that needed to be busy.

Financially speaking we would be okay. Ju, being such a superstar, had whizzed up the NHS ladder. The idea of relying on someone else didn't sit well though. My whole life I've worked and never taken handouts or been looked after. I was a grafter by nature.

And what if Ju and I split up and I had to rely solely on my pension? What if ... what if ... that's what working in security did to you. Not being in control is something I find most difficult to cope with in life.

Vanessa, that's no way to live worrying about whether you'll break up. I was having an entire conversation with myself as I stared dewy-eyed at a single spot on the rug.

'Just have a think about it.' Ju tore me away from my spiralling thoughts.

The thought ruminated with me. As I walked the wings. As I marched around the perimeter. As I sat quietly with the dogs and my cup of tea in the morning. While driving through rush-hour traffic to work. When someone did something to piss me off. My thoughts churned.

Maybe Ju was right. Maybe I had reached that point in my career.

The thing that made up my mind in the end was the smell of death. Let me tell you, there is nothing quite like it. When someone dies they lose control of all their bodily functions and, as you might imagine, that's not a pleasant sight or odour to be near.

I was called to deal with a suicide on D wing. It was probably one of seven or eight I'd seen throughout my career. I thought I'd become desensitised to death over the years, just as I had to violence and pain. Yet something about seeing that prisoner strangled by his bed sheets got to me. He'd tied them to his radiator and knelt forward, choking himself to death. The tang of urine and excrement filled the room, making me want to gag.

I dealt with the crisis but the smell of death followed me. It didn't matter how many times I washed my hands. How many breaths of fresh air I drove into my lungs. I couldn't shake that acrid stench away.

It was a sign, telling me – enough.

Better to go out on a high when I'm at the top. Better to be remembered for the good that I'd done and not be there to watch it all slide away. Witnessing the demise of something I loved – it would be the end of me.

I also knew, being somewhat outspoken, I wouldn't be able to hold my tongue for much longer. I'd no doubt shoot my mouth off and get into trouble.

After two weeks of soul searching I came home one evening and told Ju that we needed to talk. I must have said it with such intensity that her first reaction was: 'Oh my God, you're going to break up with me!'

'What? No you daft thing! I'm going to leave the Scrubs.'

She laughed and then hugged me. 'I'm proud of you. It's going to be okay.'

I wanted to go quietly. No fuss. Just the way I liked things. I didn't anticipate feeling so overwhelmed with emotion when I told the number one gov the news.

My mouth was bone dry. The words were snagging. I coughed.

'I want to leave my job, sir. I want to apply for this bumping scheme and take early retirement.'

'Bumping' was a new trendy initiative. The official explanation for it was the practice of redeploying a redundant employee into an occupied role and making that second employee redundant instead.

In layman's terms that meant me standing down and someone being bumped into my job – no doubt on a greatly reduced salary and pension contribution to save the prison service money.

I'd use the redundancy money to pay my pension off and start taking that early.

Phil Taylor stared at me, blinking. 'You're joking with me?'

'No, I'm serious.'

'Who am I going to get to do your job?'

'With respect, gov, that's not really my problem'. I felt guilty enough as it was making the decision. I couldn't take that kind of pressure on my shoulders as well.

'I've come to the stage of my life where I feel I've done all I can. I can't go on with the stress and the thought that

I won't be able to continue giving you and the prison my hundred per cent.'

He knew where I was coming from – he'd had to bear the brunt of the changes.

'I've reached saturation point. There's other things I want to do with my life beyond my career here.' The words flew out. I had no idea what those things were, but voicing how I felt suddenly made me aware there was a life beyond those prison walls. Everything was unfolding so quickly I didn't have time to understand them. I just kept going because if I didn't keep up the momentum, I'd crumble.

'Okay, I understand. I respect that it's taken a lot for you to come here and tell me.' He wore an expression that said I'm not happy but I understand.

'Thank you, sir.'

And then as I got up to leave, I started to cry. It was all too much.

'Oh, Vanessa,' he said, kindly.

I wasn't embarrassed to show emotion in front of the gov. He'd seen me at my most frustrated. He once told me I was his Rottweiler who had a heart of gold. I'm not sure being compared to a dog was a compliment, but I liked it nonetheless.

As I turned to leave, as I wiped the tears away and threw on my game face, ready to step back into the main office and greet the team I'd led for so many years, he patted me on the back and said, 'I do understand.'

Chapter 35

CURTAINS

HMP Wormwood Scrubs: 28 February 2013

It was 3 p.m. on Wednesday, 27 February 2013 when I finally got the news. I had no time to prepare. Just twenty-four hours to say my goodbyes. It wasn't how I envisioned leaving the job that had defined my life but then maybe there's never a perfect way to go.

Arranging my severance package should have been easy but it ended up taking HR the best part of half a year to thrash it out. I'd been stuck in limbo for that entire time, not knowing whether I was staying or going. I'm sure many of you know what it feels like to do a job you've already emotionally checked out of. It's like wading through treacle. Everything you do feels like a massive effort and you begin to resent doing it.

I was at my desk, sorting through a pile of intel documents when the call from HR finally came through.

'Vanessa Frake, Head of Security,' I answered.

CURTAINS

'It's Shared Services here. We are confirming that your last day will be tomorrow, 28 February.'

Bam! It was as unceremonious as that.

'Okay, thanks.' I put the receiver down. Shaking, I slowly stood up, made my way to my door, closed it, locked it, and then leaned back against it and sobbed my heart out.

This was it. This was really it. After twenty-seven years in a job I knew inside out, back to front, it was all going to vanish within hours. It's what I wanted but I wasn't given time to digest it.

The first thing I did was slip off to the toilet and splash my face with cold water. I took a deep breath and told myself to pull it together.

The second thing I did was visit the number one gov.

'You've heard haven't you,' he said as I walked into his office.

'I leave tomorrow.'

'I can't say anything other than I'm sorry. I'm sorry to see you go.'

I could feel myself welling up again. 'I can't stay in the office if you're going to be like that,' I said, sniffling. 'There are people I need to see.'

He understood I was teetering on the edge. I turned on my heels and left.

I gathered my team together to make my announcement. Even the dogs were there with their handlers. The news came as a surprise to everyone. I'd done a good job of keeping it under my hat.

There were gasps. 'You're kidding!' 'Please don't go.' 'Why?' 'Who's going to keep us safe now?' And the all-important 'Who's going to take your job?' I didn't have an answer for them.

Then came the condolences. One by one they streamed into my office and broke down in tears. Never in a million years would I have expected such extreme emotions from my staff. I felt like I was at my own funeral and people were leaving their respects. Shouldn't I have been the one crying? I ended up consoling them with a hug and a pat on the back.

I went home that night and barely slept a wink. Panic, that's what I was mostly feeling. Fear of the unknown. An abyss of nothingness ahead. I'd been so desperate to leave and all I wanted now was to crawl back behind those bars, to the safety of what I knew.

Ju didn't say anything; she just held my hand as I lay wide-eyed next to her staring at the ceiling creating worse-case scenarios from the plasterwork above.

Striped shirt, trousers, belt, key chain. It felt like a ceremony dressing myself for my final day at work.

Everything I did that morning carried meaning. Even the sound of the stones crunching under my shoes as I walked from my car to the prison entrance triggered feelings of loss, and I hadn't even left yet.

I showed my tally to the officer on the gate and then said: 'Mind if I keep this?'

Normally I'd exchange the yellow plastic disc for my keys but this was going into the memento box. Number 4 – it was my number. I felt incredibly possessive over it.

'Course not, gov.' He handed me my set of keys.

Time slipped through my hands like sand that day.

After the number one had made a speech I walked those wings one last time, saying my goodbyes to all the familiar faces. The officers I'd known for years or just a short while. The whole time using all my inner strength to hold on to my composure.

People don't want to see weakness in a leader. They want someone strong who's going to keep them safe. That's what I'd been, and that's what I maintained – I remained strong until the very end.

I turned in at the kennels, giving those wonderful dogs a final pet. They were my golden army; without them we couldn't have fought half the drugs wars that we did.

My voice must have wavered dozens of times during those final hours. Especially while I packed away the contents of my desk into a cardboard box. So many memories. My stapler, my hole punch, my trusty pen. I even slipped my name plaque, Governor Vanessa Frake MBE, in there too. The staff had taken it upon themselves to bring me gifts whenever they ventured on holiday to exotic locations. I had a waving gold cat from China. A plastic Loch Ness Monster. The Taj Mahal. A relic from a mosque in Pakistan.

I slotted them neatly together like a Tetris game and then heaved the knick-knacks – or tut as I call it – into my arms.

'This is me then, I'm off,' I announced.

I couldn't look anyone in the eye as they stood up from behind their desks and clapped and cheered me out.

Stay strong, Vanessa, stay strong.

The long gloomy corridors that led to the exit had never looked brighter; it's as if they were lit up by a spotlight, guiding my path out. I think that feeling came from everyone watching me. I was centre stage, not something I was used to or comfortable with.

'Cheerio chaps,' I said in my usual understated way, making one final arcing wave.

The gate clanged shut behind me. The noise of the prison all of a sudden replaced by the street ahead. Car engines revving, horns tooting in rush-hour traffic.

As I stood there clutching my worldly possessions I couldn't help wondering if this is what the prisoners must feel like, especially the ones that had spent a life sentence behind bars. As they stood where I was now, with their plastic black bag of belongings – did they feel as disoriented, as afraid of returning to the real world?

I walked on to my car. I couldn't bring myself to look back at those iconic towers, or all that composure I'd fought to keep up would come crashing down.

Chapter 36

RIOT ACT

HMP Holloway:
1989

'On my three. One. Two. Three.'

We unlocked the door to the wing and charged in. Thirty of us, all women, kitted up in our blue protective suits, shin pads, shields, helmets, visors. Armed with our batons or PR24s as they were officially called. Storming headlong into the fire, chaos and violence of a riot.

Our steel toe-capped boots hammered along the corrugated metal floor as flaming objects rained down on us, streaming tails of red and yellow through the air.

I crossed my arms, angling my shield at the bottle that was hurtling 100 mph at my face.

'Fucking screws.' 'Die bitches!' The women prisoners screamed at us like crazed animals.

'Come and get us! We're ready for you!' they howled over the landings. Banging the doors with their fists, thrashing the railings with anything they could get their hands on.

THE GOVERNOR

The air was suffocating – saturated with smoke and toxic fumes from burning mattresses. The women had smashed out the lights so the place was pitch black. Couple that with the thick black smoke swelling towards us and we could barely see a thing. Still we charged on, showing no weakness. We needed to reclaim the wing and bring the women under control.

'Come on, girls, go go!' the senior officer signalled to us.

My throat stung from the smoke, my lungs burned with every breath.

Only two hours earlier I'd been on the couch with my feet up watching some crime drama. That was until me and fifteen officers from Holloway had been called to a neighbouring prison as back-up to get a rioting wing under control.

HMP Bullwood Hall in Hockley, Essex, was a Cat C women's prison. It closed down in 2013 but back then it was famous for being one of the last jails to make the prisoners 'slop out' – clean out their own toilet bowl. It was also the setting for the documentary *The Real Bad Girls*. Gives you some idea about the types of women locked up there.

All we knew from the brief was that the prisoners were smashing things up. There were sixty of them, a mixture of convicted criminals and those on remand. They'd set fire to their cells and the officers had withdrawn from the wing to protect themselves.

I'd been trained for this moment. It was my first riot, yet I didn't feel a flicker of fear going in because I knew we were a team who had each other's back. We were pumped with adrenaline and ready for anything.

Our objective was to pull the women out kicking and screaming if we had to. Handcuff them, search them and see them securely onto a bus, as they were to be taken to another jail. They could hardly go back into their wing with all the damage they'd caused. It would take weeks of work to patch up.

'Get me out of here.' One of the prisoners ran screaming towards me. 'I don't want no part of this.' She begged me for sanctuary. Who could blame her? Apart from the danger, rioting or inciting to riot carries a maximum sentence of ten years. I pushed her towards the door where officers were waiting on the other side to detain her.

I was spat on. Called every name under the sun. Kicked, punched, had flaming objects chucked at me. I used my baton like a light sabre, boshing flying bottles and cans away. Water from puddles splashed up my legs, or I think it was water. I dread to contemplate what else it might have been.

Up ahead was a barricade made of upturned furniture and mattresses. Designed to stop us getting in and prevent any prisoners who wanted out getting out. This was about control, on all levels.

The riot leaders were right at the back, guarding the fortress. We had several sets of barricades to smash through to get to them. We formed one long line across, like a rugby scrum.

'On my three,' the senior officer screamed. 'One, two, three.'

We charged, kicking the furniture out of the way, slinging, heaving the debris from side to side.

More prisoners emerged from the black smoke begging to be let out. We grabbed them by the scruff of the neck and yanked them in the direction of the exit. We had to be rough – we didn't know if they were pretending to need saving so they could take a swipe at us. They could have been armed with a knife for all we knew.

We reached the second barricade but it was stacked as high as a fortress. There was no chance of getting through it without the help of a jack to blow it out the way.

Slowly we retreated to the entrance, covering each other's backs for any stealth attacks from above or behind.

As soon as I was out I tore off my helmet. My hair was glued to my forehead with sweat. My eyes were bloodshot from the smoke. Speaking hurt my throat – it was scratched raw from yelling. I still managed a wisecrack through.

'Your make-up is running, darling,' I joked with my friend. Humour was a natural way of finding some sort of come-down from the high.

I was running on so much adrenaline I didn't have time to think about the what ifs. Like *what if* I'd been knocked unconscious, stabbed, set on fire. The camaraderie had ignited my soul. We were a team. We'd braved a serious situation and escaped relatively unscathed. The fear had bonded us.

We'd managed to pull twenty prisoners out, which wasn't bad going, but we had two-thirds of a wing left to conquer.

'Ready, girls?' came the order. We had the jack and more back-up: a load of officers from another jail had rocked up. Nothing was going to stop us now.

We buckled up our helmets and raised our batons. Into the fray we went once more.

It was at that moment I could see how the Prison Service would become like a family to me. No two days would ever be the same. I'd enter and leave in a blaze of glory.

Chapter 37

THE PAST ALWAYS CATCHES UP

Saffron Walden, Essex: Summer 2016

I was walking along the high street in one of the most picturesque towns on the commuter belt. Saffron Walden. My new home. My fresh start with my wife, my family.

I couldn't breathe.

The twisty street curled around another corner revealing more wooden-beamed Tudor buildings and historic buildings dating back to 1141 when the town was built around a castle. Coffee shops, trinket shops, independent businesses selling home-made soaps and locally crafted gifts.

I couldn't breathe.

I was surrounded by wholesome-looking individuals, a world apart from the prisoners I used to deal with. Mothers with children, the elderly, ambling to the local shops, and yet I couldn't draw air into my lungs.

Everyone is staring at me.

My chest tightened. It felt like my ribcage was crushing my lungs. The more panicky I grew the tighter the vice grip they had on me. I grew more dizzy. Oxygen starved. *I was going to pass out, make a spectacle of myself.*

I was having a panic attack. One of many I'd suffered since my retirement. Only I didn't know it. I'd been suffering in silence over the years, trying to cope but failing miserably. I never failed at anything.

I wish I could tell you a happy story of how I breezed into my retirement with a skip in my step. The reality was, my world fell apart. I was blighted by a succession of health troubles that began a month after leaving the Scrubs. I went straight into the menopause, which played havoc with my moods. Months after that, in November, I was taken into hospital to have a vertebra removed because of a nerve that had become trapped in my spine and had cut off feeling to my arm. I'd barely recovered from that operation when the doctors had to whip out my gallbladder because it had shrunk to the size of a pea. I needed fifty-two staples to stitch me back up. It was only a matter of months later that I was back in hospital, this time for a fundoplication, an operation to help me swallow. My stomach valves had stopped working and food was regurgitating up into my throat, choking me.

My body had given out. It was as if all that stress I'd been bottling away during my years in the prison service had come to get me with tidal-wave force. Why do you always end up being struck with a cold or the flu when you go on holiday? It's the same sort of physiology. I think your body relaxes and that's when illnesses catch up with you.

On top of being stuck in a cycle of illness, I wasn't coping well mentally with my retirement. I'd lost my purpose in life and on my darkest days I started to think what was the point in going on.

That wasn't me. That wasn't the Vanessa Frake who'd run one of the most infamous prisons in Great Britain. I'd become a shadow of myself.

Poor Ju. Between my moods and Annie-Mae's adolescent tantrums and holding down a stressful job, she had little time for herself.

She'd been trying to get me to go to the doctor for some time but I'd stubbornly resisted. As usual, I thought I could cope, I could fix the problem. I'd convinced myself it would get better if I kept plugging away at it. I was wrong. Finally, I relented and went to see someone at the local surgery.

The GP welcomed me with a big smile and chirped: 'Hello, how can I help you?'

She was a port in a storm. Within seconds of taking a seat, I broke down into one big snotty mess.

The GP immediately reached for the tissue box and placed it under my nose. She didn't need to say anything more; between heaving sobs, I blurted out everything I'd been bottling up. I told her how I felt. How I'd had enough. How the world was closing in on me. How I'd gone through all these ops and I was sick to death of feeling unwell. How I'd retired from a job that was my life.

'I feel frantic and anxious. Frustrated. The slightest thing sets me off, either making me snap or break down in tears. I don't recognise myself.'

She nodded, her eyes full of concern.

'My weight goes up. It goes down. Some days I'm in such a dark place I don't want to get dressed. I don't want to go out. I feel panicky in crowds. It's not that I think I'm special, but I feel like everyone is looking at me.

'I get up at 5.30 a.m. when my wife does. I'm determined to keep busy. I keep my routines – having lunch at the same time each day. Twelve sharp, just as I did in the prison. I hoped the structure would keep me sane but it isn't working.' I barely paused for breath. 'I miss the banter of the jail. My colleagues. Some days I don't talk to anyone. I suppose I still can't believe my career is over. I feel like my life is over. What's the point of the rest of my life? Am I just waiting around to die?'

She pressed her lips together sympathetically and, again, with concern.

'Don't get me wrong, I don't regret my decision. I couldn't go on there. I just don't know how to deal with what's left.'

The more I talked, it all of a sudden dawned on me – my past had caught up with me. You can't go through a lifetime's worth of brutality without it leaving scars. The titanium wall I'd built up to protect me in the prison had served me well then but was hurting me now. I suppose in a strange sort of way, like many of the prisoners who leave after years on the inside, I too had become institutionalised.

My continuation of the routines and rituals were a symptom of that.

The GP didn't say in so many words that I had post-traumatic stress, but I was now more certain than ever that's what I had. From the illnesses, from the stress, from living with death, violence, brutality for twenty-seven years. My body had gone into shock.

Her voice softened as she said: 'I don't know how you feel about this idea, but I think you need to go on antidepressants for a while.'

I flinched at the word. I guess I'm a bit old-fashioned and never really believed in taking pills to help your mental state. I'd always shrugged off my worries. However, I was aware what a desperate state I'd got myself into. I was depressed. I couldn't get out of this black hole alone. So I bit the bullet and accepted her prescription for help.

'The pills will take about six weeks to work.' As I left the doc reassured me not to panic if they didn't work immediately.

She was right. The pills took a while to kick in, but when they did, I quickly felt much better. I was able to think rationally again. The fog of depression lifted. I could see the joy in the small things. I could appreciate the silence and beauty of where we lived in the countryside.

I could breathe.

And it wasn't long after that I experienced the second major shift in my life. I discovered I had a hidden talent. One that couldn't be more different from running covert operations and drug busts.

It all began when Ju gave me a Mary Berry dessert book as a present. After that I became slightly obsessed with watching *The Great British Bake Off* and making cakes. I started off simply with a Victoria sponge but pretty soon I was creating Black Forest gateaux dripping in cherry liquor and sprinkled with dark and white chocolate shavings, and chocolate cake with mint frosting. Seeing Annie-Mae's face light up when she came in from school and saw what I'd whipped up made me glow inside. Ju kept telling me off that I was making her put on weight. I reined it in slightly and then she spotted an advert in the local paper.

'Why don't you apply for this?' She shoved the notice under my nose.'

'Kitchen hand?' I looked at her. 'Really?'

'You'd be brilliant at it. You're talented at baking and it will get you out of the house. It's just around the corner you can walk to work.'

I shrugged. Why not? I doubted I'd even get a look-in. Me, who'd lived off 'ping ping' meals for my entire life. I left out my prison credentials on the application form.

To my amazement, the owner of Angela Reed café just off the main square in the town asked me to come in for a chat a few days later.

I can't tell you how much I panicked over how I'd come across. It was like the MBE all over again. Well, not quite, but almost.

Just as we'd rehearsed the curtsey for the Queen, I practised what I was going to say in the interview. It sounds silly I know; you'd assume I'd be confident after everything I'd achieved. But I was outside my comfort zone. I'd regressed back to level one. I was overqualified and underqualified for a minimum-wage job at the same time.

'What the hell do I say?' I turned to Ju for more coaching.

'Start by telling Angela you really admire what she's doing and you've got an interest in baking and you'd like to develop it.'

'Can we role play it?' I was stressing.

Ju giggled. 'Okay, if you like. You don't need to.'

'*I do* need to.'

Ju humoured me and pretended to be Angela. I acted out coming into the interview, sitting down, answering why I wanted the job, all while Ju tried to keep a straight face.

Deciding what to wear for the interview was just as big a hoo-hah. You've got the gist of how I operate by now. Choosing what to wear was something I did not enjoy doing. The big day arrived and half my wardrobe was strewn across the bed.

'This one?' I held the Marks & Spencer blue-and-white striped long sleeve up to my face.

'Perfect,' Ju replied.

'Hmm.' I threw it down. 'Maybe this one?' I held up the pink checks.

'That one is good too.'

I reached for my suit. 'Maybe I should look more formal?'

Ju stepped in. 'No!' You don't need to wear a full suit to the interview, for goodness' sake.'

In the end I settled for a shirt and indigo jeans.

The walk to the café was three minutes door to door but it felt like an eternity. I'm not exaggerating when I say I spent the entirety of that time rehearsing my lines. Why do I want this job? What is it about Angela Reed's that separates it from everywhere else?

The café is a very special place in the town. The downstairs is an Aladdin's cave. It's a shop selling the most beautiful furniture, hand-crafted locally, with a distressed wood appearance. I could fill my house with the stuff. Upstairs is a cosy café with chunky wooden tables and chairs. It has a whitewashed by-the-seaside feeling to it.

I loved the fact that they used only local fresh produce. That their food was experimental. They had a whole array of gluten-, vegan- and dairy-free cakes on top of the favourite recipes. It posed a challenge and I like challenges.

As it turned out, I had nothing to worry about. My interview consisted of helping out in the kitchen with the lunch prep. I cut, I sliced, I arranged what needed doing, all under the watchful eye of Angela and her daughter Alison.

'Can you make this cake for us?' Alison handed me the gluten-free lemon and almond signature cake.

'No problem,' I replied confidently. Luckily it was simple to follow as it only had four ingredients.

I had no idea if I'd passed the test. I'd revealed that I'd once worked in the prison service but didn't go into details. They didn't seem interested in my past; all they wanted to see was if I had potential.

I felt like a contestant on the *Bake Off* when it came to the ending of my interview. I stood back from my cake, waiting for my performance to be dissected. My mouth had turned as dry as a Rich Tea biscuit. My palms were clammy.

Just put me out of my misery.

Alison smiled. 'Thanks, Vanessa, you've been great.'

Oh no, here it comes. I braced myself.

'Your hours will be Mondays and Wednesdays to start with. Is that okay?'

'Uh huh,' I mumbled in disbelief.

'8 a.m. to 5 p.m. okay with you?'

'Yes.' I cleared the frog in my throat. 'YES!'

Chapter 38

LET SLEEPING DOGS LIE

Saffron Walden, Essex:
Now

I get home from my shift at Angela Reed. Before I have time to slip my shoes under the coat pegs I'm bombarded with wet sloppy kisses from our two labradors, Gertie and Rupert, and our sprightly Jack Russell, Ruby. Our cats, Rigby and Pella, brother and sister double-trouble act, and Oriental, Barry, loiter in the background, waiting for their turn to be petted and fed.

'Okay, okay, I'm coming!'

Barry weaves himself through my legs as I spoon their food out of the packet and into their bowls. I then pour myself a large glass of white wine. There was a slice of pear and almond cake going spare at the café today which I extract from its Tupperware and place on a my finest china plate.

It's a glorious summer's day and only the best will do to celebrate. I have a sacred hour to myself before Annie-Mae gets home from school and I start on the cooking. I make my way from the kitchen to the living room, balancing my wine in one hand, my cake in the other, while dog tails bash excitedly at my calves and the cats run skittishly under my feet.

The sunshine pours through the patio windows onto my face, giving me a taste of what's to come. I open the floor-to-ceiling door, position the heavy stopper to prop it open and step out into the lush green garden. It's an explosion of colour. When I'm not baking I turn into a green fingers, tending to my flowerbeds.

Carefully I place my afternoon indulgences down, flashing Gertie a warning look in the process.

'No!' I waggle my finger at her. 'That's my treat, you've had your tea.'

I grab the sun lounger. It scrapes across the patio stones as I position it to face the sun. Here comes the moment I'd been yearning for all day. I lean back in the chair, pressing my back into the soft cushions, sighing out as the rays wash over me, warming me up like a hot bath. Bees hum. Birds cheep. The smell of warmed grass and pollen wafts my way.

The tangy fruity scent of the grapes hits my nose as I raise the glass to my lips.

'This is the life, girls and boys,' I say to the pets. Gertie and Rupert wag their tails in agreement.

Just as I'm about to take a sip, something interrupts me. A magnetic pulling sensation. I turn my head a fraction and glance back at the terrace door. At the doorstop wedging it open.

It's not any old doorstep though. It's a chunk of concrete and steel from the wall of the Scrubs. When we had new giant extraction fans fitted on the wings to make them safer in the event of a fire, the builders asked if I would like to keep a piece of the rubble from A wing. I didn't know at the time it would come in so handy. I smile and nestle back into position. Comforted in the knowledge that a piece of the past is by my side.

I've moved on. I've found a new kind of fulfilment. I've baked myself back to happiness and I can proudly say my scones have become the talk of the town. I also do volunteer work at the local animal rescue sanctuary Wood Green once a week.

The Scrubs will always be with me though. The good, the bad and the downright ugly, it's all filed away in the archives. I'll carry the memories of my prison career in my heart till the day I die. I wouldn't have it any other way.

'Cheers,' I say, and raise a toast to myself.

ACKNOWLEDGEMENTS

When they said you need to write acknowledgements for your book, I thought, good grief, it'll be longer than the book! I have so many thanks to give. I hope there's enough to go around!

First and foremost, I'd like to thank HarperCollins for publishing my book and in particular Kelly Ellis for putting her faith in my story. I'd also like to thank my agent Susan Smith of MBA Literary Agents. Susan has been incredibly supportive in guiding me through the process of writing a book. My thanks also to Ruth Kelly, my ghost writer, who is uniquely talented and, in her quest to bring my story to life, put up with my many finickety ways along our journey. Ruth is always passionate and creative from start to finish. I wish her well on her journey as an author and can only imagine she will go from strength to strength.

Of course, I have to thank the prison service and the many wonderful, hardworking and dedicated staff that I have had the pleasure to come across over my 27-year career. You are without doubt the forgotten service and do an exceptional job in exceptional circumstances on a daily

...sis. I hope this book will give some insight to the many people who have no idea what really goes on in a prison.

Without the support of my family none of this would be possible. So thanks must go to my wife Ju, without whose love and understanding I could never have dreamed of having a book published. My daughter Annie-Mae who's been so enthusiastic about having a mother as an author and who makes me prouder every day. My mother and father (Maggie and Mike) who gave me the grounding in my early years and taught me to be independent, or perhaps a stubborn individual is a better description.